READING OLD ENGLISH BIBLICAL POETRY

The Book and the Poem in Junius 11

JANET SCHRUNK ERICKSEN

Reading Old English Biblical Poetry

The Book and the Poem in Junius 11

UNIVERSITY OF TORONTO PRESS
Toronto Buffalo London

© University of Toronto Press 2021
Toronto Buffalo London
utorontopress.com

ISBN 978-1-4875-0746-6 (cloth)
ISBN 978-1-4875-3630-5 (EPUB)
ISBN 978-1-4875-3629-9 (PDF)

Toronto Anglo-Saxon Series

Library and Archives Canada Cataloguing in Publication

Title: Reading Old English biblical poetry : the book and the poem in Junius 11 / Janet Schrunk Ericksen.
Names: Ericksen, Janet Schrunk, 1964–, author.
Series: Toronto Anglo-Saxon series ; 31.
Description: Series statement: Toronto Anglo-Saxon series ; 31 | Includes bibliographical references and index.
Identifiers: Canadiana (print) 20200209205 | Canadiana (ebook) 20200209256 | ISBN 9781487507466 (hardcover) | ISBN 9781487536305 (EPUB) | ISBN 9781487536299 (PDF)
Subjects: LCSH: Caedmon manuscript. | LCSH: Reader-response criticism. | LCSH: English poetry – Old English, ca. 450–1100 – History and criticism. | LCSH: Christian poetry, English (Old) – History and criticism. | LCSH: Manuscripts, Medieval – England. | LCSH: Manuscripts, English (Old)
Classification: LCC PR1624 .E75 2021 | DDC 829/.2 – dc23

University of Toronto Press acknowledges the financial assistance to its publishing program of the Canada Council for the Arts and the Ontario Arts Council, an agency of the Government of Ontario.

Canada Council for the Arts　Conseil des Arts du Canada

Funded by the Government of Canada　Financé par le gouvernement du Canada　Canada

Contents

Acknowledgments

The research and writing of this book spanned many years of intermittent work, and the support along the way has been both broad and deep. Generous funding from the National Endowment for the Humanities (NEH) allowed me both time and travel to work in libraries with more extensive holdings than my own as well as access to manuscripts, including Oxford, Bodleian Library Manuscript Junius 11. NEH support extends to a long-ago NEH summer seminar at the University of Cambridge, which provided foundational guidance and experience in manuscript research. A subsequent visiting fellowship at Clare Hall at the University of Cambridge helped me begin the book-writing as a coherent project. Formal support for this project also goes back to that provided by the Vanderbilt University Research Council – for chapter 2, in particular. Since then, the University of Minnesota as well as, specifically, the University of Minnesota Morris have reliably and generously supported my research requests.

My thanks to Martin Kauffmann of the Bodleian Library, Oxford for allowing me repeated access to MS Junius 11 and to Timothy Graham for helpful suggestions regarding Junius 11 and many other manuscripts. Feedback from colleagues has been important throughout. The careful attention and guidance from the anonymous readers at the University of Toronto Press (UTP) were extremely useful in improving the book, and I am grateful that those readers were willing to invest their time and energy to provide such valuable work. My thanks, too, to Suzanne Rancourt at UTP for her patience and guidance and to the careful and very helpful copy-editing of Stephanie Stone. An earlier version of chapter 4 appeared as "The Wisdom Poem at the End of Junius 11," in *The Poems of MS Junius 11: Basic Readings*, edited by R.M. Liuzza (New York: Routledge, 2002), 302–26, and versions of both it and other chapters have been given as conference papers at Leeds, Kalamazoo, and elsewhere.

Among the many scholars and friends who assisted with this book are Charlie Wright, whose intellectual guidance and extraordinary mentorship laid the best foundation for my career, and Tom Bredehoft, whose thoughtful readings were fantastically generous and useful in helping me shape the book. Jim Hall, David Johnson, Roy Liuzza, Tom Hill, Dabney Bankert, and Lisa Bevevino also read, discussed, and responded to various sections, and I am deeply grateful for the suggestions, comments, and support that came from all these people. Sheri, Sarah, and Heather provided much needed encouragement as I worked toward finishing the book while adapting to life as a full-time university administrator. My colleagues, in the broadest sense, have been so generous for so long that I am sure to have neglected to acknowledge some of them here, for which I apologize, as I do also for the errors that undoubtedly persist in the pages that follow and are, of course, entirely my own.

Indirectly, the many students to whom I have taught Old English over many years have also supported this project, not least by providing me with regular evidence of why I love Old English literature. To them I owe thanks for their sustaining enthusiasm and for demonstrating a diversity of approaches to Old English texts. My children, Owen and Peter, have endured much on the way to the completion of this book, not least repeatedly adjusting to playgrounds and schools in England while I spent long days in libraries. Their adaptability, their curiosity, and their love of reading continue to please and awe me. My own love of reading was fostered by my parents – my mom, who let me get away with reading even when I was supposed to be doing other things, and my dad, whose idea of a pleasant evening included visiting a library or bookstore with me. The greatest debt and greatest thanks I owe, however, are to my patient reader, incisive critic, excellent editor, and constant supporter, David Elliott Ericksen, without whom I may never have even finished graduate school, let alone completed this and so many other projects.

Abbreviations

ACMRS	Arizona Center for Medieval and Renaissance Studies
ASE	*Anglo-Saxon England*
ASMMF	Anglo-Saxon Manuscripts in Microfiche Facsimile
ASPR	Anglo-Saxon Poetic Records
BL	British Library
BNF	Bibliothèque Nationale de France
CC	Christ Church, Canterbury
CCCC	Cambridge, Corpus Christi College
CCSL	Corpus Christianorum, Series Latina
CEMERS	Center for Medieval and Renaissance Studies
CMCAS	N.R. Ker, *Catalogue of Manuscripts Containing Anglo-Saxon*
CPL	*Clavis Patrum Latinorum*
CSASE	Cambridge Studies in Anglo-Saxon England
CSEL	Corpus Scriptorum Ecclesiasticorum Latinorum
CUL	Cambridge, University Library
EETS	Early English Text Society
EH	Bede, *Ecclesiastical History*
ELN	*English Language Notes*
GenA	*Genesis A*
GenB	*Genesis B*
Handlist	Helmut Gneuss and Michael Lapidge, *Anglo-Saxon Manuscripts: A Bibliographical Handlist of Manuscripts and Manuscript Fragments Written or Owned in England up to 1100*
HBS	Henry Bradshaw Society
JEGP	*Journal of English and Germanic Philology*
MLN	*Modern Language Notes*
NM	*Neuphilologische Mitteilungen*
NM	New Minster, Winchester

n.s.	new series
OE	Old English
OEN	Old English Newsletter
o.s.	old series
PG	*Patrologiae cursus completus*, Series Graeca
PMLA	*Proceedings of the Modern Language Association*
RES	*Review of English Studies*
SK	Dieter Schaller and Ewald Könsgen, with John Tagliabue, *Initia Carminum Latinorum saeculo undecimo Antiquiorum*
SR	*Saltair na Rann*
SS	*Solomon and Saturn*
s.s.	supplementary series
StA	Saint Augustine's (Canterbury)

READING OLD ENGLISH BIBLICAL POETRY

The Book and the Poem in Junius 11

Reading Junius 11

i mycel englisc boc be gehwilcum þingum on leoðwisan geworht[1]

Like other surviving English books from about the year 1000, Oxford, Bodleian Library Manuscript Junius 11 is, in some ways, highly similar to the much more recently produced books that fill our shelves: black text on a pale page, left-to-right sequentiality on the page and in narrative sections, guiding headings and section numbers, and a sturdy covering at front, back, and spine. The page numbers now visible in the Junius 11 manuscript are, though, not medieval, and Junius 11 as material object is distinctly not identical to any other surviving early medieval book, nor does it have much in common with, for instance, a hardback edition of Philip Pullman's *The Golden Compass* (1995), although both include an account of Adam and Eve's Fall and both are, indeed, books in English. To those of us accustomed to mass-market books, the medieval (but not original) wood-and-leather binding of the Junius 11 manuscript is substantially different from our own hardbacks

1 "One large book in English about various things composed in verse" is an item in Bishop Leofric's donation list for Exeter Cathedral. While the reference may be to the Exeter Book, the description is so general that it might instead refer to a now lost collection. Richard Gameson points out the separation of this entry and the Boethius book right before it from the group of *raedingbec* (reading books) earlier in the list: "Whether their position here reflects a status distinct from that of a reading book, or merely the fact that they were written in the vernacular is an open question"; see "The Origin of the Exeter Book of Old English Poetry," *ASE* 25 (1996): 141, 143. See also Olga Timofeeva, "*Of ledenum bocum to engliscum gereorde:* Bilingual Communities of Practice in Anglo-Saxon England," in *Communities of Practice in the History of English*, ed. Joanna Kopaczyk and Andreas H. Jucker (Philadelphia, PA: John Benjamins, 2013), 214.

and paperbacks – more durable, less delicate, and more distinct from the pages it encloses. The manuscript pages have greater visual and tactile variety than the pages of even a well-worn, well-annotated, late twentieth-century book, in part because different hands put the poems on the pages and because the original plan for the book's illustrations was never completed.

Other surviving early medieval books, however, make clear that such variety is more remarkable to us than it would have been to the book's first generations of readers. The variations in page layouts, scribal hands, illustration, and texts themselves within a single medieval book imply both that early readers were comfortable with inconsistency – visual and textual – and that they likely employed multiple ways of building meaning from texts and did not rely on or rigidly privilege consecutive structure. Indeed, while Junius 11's frontispiece illustration of God in majesty, the biblical chronology evident in its poems on *Genesis, Exodus, Daniel,* and *Christ and Satan,* and even its section numbers meet our expectations for reading that begins at page 1 and continues through to page 229, such reading should not comfortably be assumed to have been the automatic or even most frequent approach to this, or to any, book in tenth- or eleventh-century England.

Reading as an act is both familiar and complicated, a shared practice and yet not a fixed and single process. Maryanne Wolf, in her memorably titled book on the history and science of reading, *Proust and the Squid,* explains that distinctions in reading are "biological and cognitive" as well as "cultural–historical":

> The alphabet-reading brain [for example] differs substantively from that of the earlier logosyllabary reader in the decreased amount of cortical space it needs in some areas. Specifically, the alphabet reader learns to rely more on the posterior of the left hemisphere, specialized regions with less bihemisphere activation in these visual regions. By contrast, the Chinese (and Sumerians) achieve efficiency by recruiting many areas for specialized, automatic processing across both hemispheres. … Reading in any language rearranges the length and breadth of the brain; and … there are multiple pathways to fluent comprehension.[2]

Wolf uses cognitive neuroscience, combined with the study of human evolution and cultural differences, to explore "the complex beauty of the

2 Maryanne Wolf, *Proust and the Squid: The Story and Science of the Reading Brain* (New York: Harper Collins, 2007), 17, 61, 64.

reading process" in broad terms.[3] She lays out evidence for the fact that reading is not and never has been a uniform human practice at any level, physical or intellectual. Wolf's emphasis is developmental and neurological, but her historical and cultural connections underscore the idea that, at every level and in every period, reading is a multidimensional act. This is true even when books and reading in English were relatively new, and my interest in the following pages is how one tenth-century book speaks to the multidimensionality of reading in early medieval England. My focus lies, then, not on the biological but the intellectual evidence.

As a hand production, every book could be shaped for one particular reader, and no book exactly duplicates another. At the same time, early medieval readers negotiated books that were not created specifically for them, and they brought to the work of reading a variety of skill and experience. How an early medieval reader approached and read pages bound together – a book, a manuscript, a volume, a collection – must have varied at least as much as the available books did, and, although in biological terms early medieval readers probably used the same parts of the brain as we do, expectations of and interactions with books – the cultural place of reading – have changed at least as much as have books themselves.

Wolf's interest lies primarily in what cognitive neuroscience reveals about both past and present varieties of reading. The following chapters of this study work from the opposite direction and focus on the past, approaching the act of reading by way of something that has been read – in this case, one of the major surviving collections of Old English poetry and the only one with illustrations. As both a material object and a container of ideas, the book of Old English biblical poetry that is now known as Oxford Bodleian Library Manuscript Junius 11 attests to community and multiplicity among its early readers. It possesses coherence, and yet it is not consistent in its contents, either in text or in presentation. The poems build meaning sequentially, but, at the same time, as the following chapters demonstrate, they do not necessitate sequential reading and, indeed, encourage other ways of approaching and understanding the book's contents. Overall, and even as they speak to differences, the texts in Junius 11 reflect a self-consciousness about reading that makes the volume a particularly attractive case study in the exploration of evidence for early medieval reading and "multiple pathways to fluent comprehension."[4]

---

3 Ibid., ix.

4 Ibid., 64.

Foundational to that variety is a shared acceptance of the importance of Christian history presented in the vernacular – that is, a reason for reading the kind of book that Junius 11 is. Just inside its front cover, Junius 11 declares that premise: the book opens with a full-page, colour illustration of Christ in majesty, facing text that positions the reader as part of a community that honours Christ. The first lines of text boldly proclaim, with an animal-interlace first letter and then a line of all capitals in bold ink, "US IS RIHT MICEL ÐÆT we rodera weard wereda wuldorcining wordum herigen" (for us it is very right that we should praise with words the heavens' guardian, the glory-king of hosts). Readers should read, in other words, the kinds of texts contained in the pages that follow in this manuscript. Those pages include at least four units – consisting of perhaps as many as seven separately authored poems – that attest further to Christ's majesty and do so both independently and with thematic as well as chronological connections, not least in the fact that the book begins with Creation and ends with Christ.

Such features have encouraged readers since at least the nineteenth century to read the Junius 11 manuscript, more so than the other surviving books with extensive Old English poetry, following first-to-last page continuity and coherence. This front-door approach to reading has yielded persuasive arguments about the manuscript compiler's intentions and about the possible audience at whom that compiler aimed. Scholarship has considered less fully the range of additional approaches that actual early medieval readers might have brought to the book. The page 1 image of divine authority, impressive as it is, anchors the book's contents, but opening the book's front door may also have been a leaping-off point for non-sequential reading, a way to identify which book this was before moving on to a particular part or parts. If we try to enter – and re-enter and re-enter – Junius 11 through the back alley, the side door, or the cellar stairs, or just wander up the back stairs, the book starts to reveal an array of interests, connections, and approaches to understanding that were available to its early readers and perhaps sought after by them even more frequently than was sequential unity.

Reading in England before 1100

Without venturing into the kinds of scientific questions Wolf explores, such as which parts of an early English reader's brain were involved in reading, scholars have made significant discoveries about the history of reading. In particular, Nicholas Howe's and M.B. Parkes's studies related to the word *rædan* and its valences have helped illuminate reading practices in early medieval England. The emphasis of Howe's study is on the act of reading, while Parkes focuses on the training for reading, and both essays identify clear distinctions between our own reading habits and those of tenth- or eleventh-century readers in what we now think of as England. Howe's examination of the evidence for communal aspects of reading points to one of the most distinctive aspects of difference, the idea that a book might be read silently and separately but that it was likely also discussed and that its reader was part "of a community bound together by common texts."[5]

A single person might bring various ways of reading to a book – even a book explicitly designed for that reader – and a single book might have had readers who listened to its words as well as those who saw and processed, alone or in a community, the words on the page. If King Alfred managed "to place reading in all of its various senses – the understanding of written texts but also the giving of counsel and the understanding of obscure matters – at the heart of public life," as Howe claims, then early readers of Junius 11 would presumably have developed their reading with discussion and connection. They may have read texts or sections of texts in isolation, in juxtaposition, or in sequence, and for guidance on such things as interpreting text, or understanding a popular philosophical topic, or considering the extent of God's knowledge.[6]

The multiplicity of approaches that such readers are likely to have brought to a single text and a single book is further supported by the evidence Parkes identifies for trained reading, a basis for expert rather than novice reading practice. Derived from practices in antiquity and emphasizing transmission and interpretation, trained reading consisted of four aspects. *Lectio* was reading focused on identifying and understanding details of construction and pronunciation that would assist in reading aloud, and *emendatio* focused on correction. *Enarratio* "focused on what was necessary to clarify a text in order to understand it," whether original to the reader or copied from another source, such as, in Parkes's example, Ælfric's use of Augustine in his *Preface to Genesis*.[7] The most deeply engaged reading is *iudicium*, a meditative approach focused on "assessing the moral, philosophical or spiritual

5 Nicholas Howe, "The Cultural Construction of Reading in Anglo-Saxon England," in *The Ethnography of Reading*, ed. Jonathan Boyarin (Berkeley: University of California Press, 1993), 71.

6 Ibid., 73.

7 M.B. Parkes, "*Rædan, areccan, smeagan*: How the Anglo-Saxons Read," *ASE* 26 (1997): 13.

values to be found in the text" and a mode especially encouraged by monastic training.[8]

Not every early medieval reader would, of course, have been trained in or familiar with such reading, but the apparent presence of these four reading practices, again, marks both a richness of reading practices and a difference from our own general familiarity with reading. An early medieval reader of a book such as Junius 11 might be a highly educated monastic or secular reader, or a novice using the book to become a better reader. The reading might have been as a thematically unified whole; or as something of a reference text, focusing on just the parts that served some particular purpose; or, indeed, entirely guided by purposes that are now obscured.

Renée Trilling's readings of the Old English poems *The Ruin* and *Deor* stress the changeability of interpretation over time and our own inability to access these and other poems in the same ways in which their early medieval audiences did. The limitations in the number, condition, and contextual information of surviving manuscripts mean that any attempt to understand Old English texts and the cultures in which they operated "demands the same work of imaginative reconstruction that the ruin asks of its observer," without losing sight of the fact that the texts are a "remnant of human activity – culture – impressed upon the materiality of objects."[9] Like the poems that Trilling examines, Junius 11 is both in some ways a coherent whole and in multiple ways a fragmented text, even before we consider missing pages: as a book made from poems independently composed and separated from their compositional context, as a collection of poems excerpted and recombined, as an unfinished illustrated book, and as a series of poems with Old Testament subjects to which was added a unit involving Jesus.

Trying to figure out how and why the book was put together in tenth- or eleventh-century England and how its parts might have functioned together has yielded much excellent scholarship, but Junius 11 has still more to tell us about the ways that early readers might have made sense of its contents – and, in turn, the ways that we have done so. Trilling manages both to mark difference and to make difference a point of connection between early medieval and subsequent readers. She does so by way of Walter Benjamin's figure of the constellation, and the tensions between trying to construct a past reading and undertaking our own reading of Junius 11 as we have it suggest here as well "that within

8 Ibid., 15.

9 Renée R. Trilling, "Ruins in the Realm of Thoughts: Reading as Constellation in Anglo-Saxon Poetry," *JEGP* 108 (2009): 165–6.

medieval poetry itself, the heterogeneous, the antiteleological, and the fragmentary found space to speak to readers, then and now."[10]

In the case of Junius 11, our desire to understand the audience or patron for whom the collection was begun reveals only part of the story that the manuscript can tell. Other early medieval readers, in private or in community, may have considered the book that they actually read – which varied even in its early history since it was produced in at least two stages and suffered excisions at some point – a collection to be approached for a single section or idea or for meanings that could be found in reading its pieces rather than, and perhaps in addition to, its whole. The Junius 11 poems are diverse in style, and its pages are visually inconsistent. The manuscript is both a continuous whole and a collection with ruptures, discontinuities, and functionally independent pieces.

The individualized nature of early medieval books alone should steer us away from privileging our own expectations of books when we read Junius 11. Any collection of material in a medieval book might have been governed by a coherent plan, or it might just as well have been the product of text availability or now obscure aims, including very personal ones. Such factors play into the case of a certain Æthelweard *dux*, for instance, who wanted his volume of Ælfrician homilies to include forty-four rather than the exemplar's forty. Presumably, as Mary Clayton explains, Æthelweard wanted the book for his own private reading, and so he could shape its contents to suit himself, an action that other manuscripts indicate was commonplace. The same manuscript note that refers to Æthelweard's directions firmly dismisses the usefulness of something like a table of contents and suggests little concern for less immediate readers of this particular book: "Quid necesse est in hoc codice capitula ordinare, cum prediximus quod xl. sententias in se contineat?" (What is the need in this book for a list of headings, when we said it had 40 *sententia* in it?)[11]

Because there were relatively few books, readers in England before 1100 must often have known in advance, sometimes quite well, the contents of a book; they might have first acquired familiarity with texts either from listening to them or even from reading them in part or full in other books. Such a reader seems unlikely to have approached

10 Ibid., 144.

11 Mary Clayton, "Homiliaries and Preaching in Anglo-Saxon England," in *Old English Prose: Basic Readings*, ed. Paul Szarmach (Garland: New York, 2000), 177. For the full text, see Ælfric, *Ælfric's Catholic Homilies: The First Series; Text*, ed. Peter Clemoes, EETS, s.s. 17 (London: Oxford University Press, 1997), 8.

reading the pages within a set of boards in the same way that a reader trained by mass-produced fiction would approach a newly acquired book. Perhaps early medieval readers approached unfamiliar books by reading sequentially and books with familiar contents more selectively, but that implies a high particularization of practice within the scope of the relatively small number of books that most of these readers are likely to have encountered.

The person for whom a book was begun may have requested a particular subject matter in its contents, or a particular thematic concern, or a specific set of texts. The Junius 11 poems' emphasis on power might have been the compilation driver for a single anticipated or actual reader, perhaps "for a politically powerful lay reader who moved in royal circles" as a book of "biblical history organized and presented for the lay reader practising political power in this world," as Daniel Anlezark has argued.[12] Such a reader and subsequent readers, however, may have come or returned to the book for quite different circumstantial reasons, and even a reader who had not read the book before may well have had prior knowledge of its contents – what kinds of things were among the "gehwilcum þingum" (various things) in it, to quote the Bishop Leofric booklist again – and so could approach the book as a resource for other purposes than that which guided the compilation.

Michael Lapidge suggests that the largest library in early medieval England might have been that at Monkwearmouth-Jarrow, with perhaps more than two hundred volumes, and that most libraries were far smaller, with fewer than fifty books, or only as many books as would fit in a single chest.[13] In such a library, readers might swiftly gain a sense of the books' content, whether by reading them all or by hearing others' summaries of them. Despite single-reader directives such as the one that Æthelweard *dux* gave for his homily book, the pages of most surviving early medieval books make clear that multiple readers interacted with them. The same labour that individualized a book also heightened its value, making it unlikely that any book would have had just one reader, even if it was commissioned by a single patron, and these readers would have brought to a book their own interests, abilities, and interpretations. A reader who spent a year with a single book,

12 Daniel Anlezark, "Lay Reading, Patronage, and Power in Bodleian Library, Junius 11," in *Ambition and Anxiety: Courts and Courtly Discourse c. 700–1600*, ed. Giles E.M. Gasper and John McKinnell, Durham Medieval and Renaissance Monographs and Essays 3 (Toronto: Pontifical Institute of Medieval Studies, 2014), 76, 87.

13 Michael Lapidge, *The Anglo-Saxon Library* (Oxford: Oxford University Press, 2006), 127, 61–2.

as directed, for instance, by the monastic ritual described in a manuscript from Fleury, would presumably develop a relationship with its contents that included revisiting passages and pages and intellectually connecting pieces within the book to things across and outside the book.[14]

The Tangible Book

Even as the single material unit of a collection of pages bound together between boards, Junius 11 offers signs of both unity and disunity, on its pages themselves as well as in the scholarly perception of them. The earliest post-medieval references to the Junius 11 manuscript come in the mid-seventeenth century, from scholars whose interest in the book had little to do with its narratives, its place in early medieval literary culture, or its physical appearance. Instead, reflecting the antiquarian interests of their time, these readers attended primarily to the linguistic significance of the words on the book's pages. The first known direct reference to Junius 11 in these terms is in a 1655 glossary, with the publication of the text of an eleventh-century paraphrase of the Song of Songs by Williram, abbot of Ebersberg in Bavaria. *Observationes in Willerami Abbatis Francicam Paraphrasin Cantici canticorum*, published by Franciscus Junius in Amsterdam, includes, as Peter Lucas describes it, "an annotated directory of Germanic and Welsh monosyllabic words," and "[u]nder the entry for *ord* on p. 248 [Junius] notes that he had received what is now MS Junius 11 from Ussher, the entry being referred to in Junius's preliminary remarks *Ad Lectorem* in the *Cædmon*."[15]

While recent research has helped define James Ussher's sphere of manuscript collecting in the early seventeenth century, from whom or exactly when Ussher, who was archbishop of Armagh from 1625 to 1656, acquired the book remains unknown. Joannes de Laet appears to have used Junius 11 in about 1637, while working to create an Old English dictionary, and his access probably came in England. B.J. Timmer's review of the evidence concluded that Junius 11 was likely to have "at one time belonged to Sir Symonds D'Ewes," as is confirmed by a note from William Somner in his transcription of the text. "When de Laet was in England, he probably used the MS. in Sir Symonds's

14 Anselme Davril, ed. *Consuetudines Floriacenses Saeculi Tertii Decimi*, Corpus Consuetudinum Monasticarum 9 (Siegburg, Germany: Franz Schmitt, 1976), 52.

15 Peter J. Lucas, ed., *Franciscus Junius: Caedmonis monachi paraphrasis poetica Genesios ac praecipuarum sacrae paginate historiarum, etc.*, Early Studies in Germanic Philology (Atlanta, GA: Rodopi, 2000), xiv–xv. See also B.J. Timmer, *The Later Genesis* (Oxford: Scrivener, 1948), 4–5.

library or borrowed it from him. D'Ewes was, however, not very much interested in its contents and probably gave it to Ussher, who passed it on to Junius."[16] Junius, however, did read with more than linguistic interest. He "evidently appreciated the importance of the manuscript ... and his training in Christian doctrine led him to be sympathetic to its contents. And so he produced from it the first edition ever of a volume of Old English poetry."[17]

Junius's publication of the book's text used a distinctive typeface and followed the manuscript's prose layout of the poetry, an indication that he was interested in both its material and its literary content. It did not, however, include such material reference points as a reproduction of the manuscript's illustrations, section numbers, or decorative capitals, although Junius did follow the manuscript in referring to *Christ and Satan* as "librum Secundum." On the whole, Junius's edition "reinforce[es] the sense of textual continuity even against MS evidence,"[18] and, in doing so, it marks the beginning of the long dominant, scholarly discussion of the book in terms primarily and often exclusively of its poems without much sense of their manuscript context.

Although not as evidently influential on literary criticism as it might have been, Israel Gollancz's facsimile of Junius 11, published in 1927, first made the pages of Junius 11 in its entirety more widely available, and his prefatory matter offers what remains one of the most thorough descriptions of the manuscript. For much of the twentieth century, Gollancz's black-and-white images provided many scholars with their only view of the text on the manuscript page, as opposed to edited versions of its texts, as in George Philip Krapp's still used Anglo-Saxon Poetic Records edition from 1931. Gollancz's images, despite their limitations, readily convey the layout of the text and space on the page and the illustrations (and illustration blanks), and they convey a sense of the texts as part of a physical book, something that can be more difficult to grasp from the much higher-resolution, colour digital images now easily accessible.[19]

16 Timmer, *Later Genesis*, 9–10. My thanks to Rebecca Brackmann for the information on Somner's note.

17 Lucas, *Franciscus Junius*, v.

18 Ibid., xix.

19 Israel Gollancz, ed., *The Cædmon MS of Anglo-Saxon Biblical Poetry: Junius XI; In the Bodleian Library* (London: Oxford University Press, 1927). Bernard J. Muir published a high-resolution version in 2004 – *A Digital Facsimile of Oxford, Bodleian Library, MS. Junius 11*, CD-ROM, software by Nick Kennedy (Oxford: Bodleian Library, University of Oxford) – and the full manuscript is now also available online through the *Early Manuscripts at Oxford University* project.

Material aspects of the Junius 11 manuscript have been described in detail several times since Gollancz's facsimile, and they are particularly helpful in assessing the work of compilation. A.N. Doane's revised edition of *Genesis A*, published in 2013, for instance, begins with precise page information: "The manuscript consists of 116 parchment leaves, trimmed to 324 mm. × 180 mm., writing area 224 mm. × ca. 130 mm., paginated [by Franciscus Junius] i–ii, 1–229 (+1)." The pages are in seventeen gatherings, constructed "in quires of 8, that is, four full sheets, folded to make eight leaves or sixteen pages, with the membrane sheets arranged so that the flesh faces flesh and hair faces hair," a presentation that "was becoming standard in England by the end of the tenth century."[20]

The *Genesis, Exodus,* and *Daniel* poems were put on the pages of Junius 11 by a single, practised hand in Anglo-Saxon minuscule, with mostly twenty-six lines per page, although a few are ruled for twenty-five. Doane characterizes this scribe's work as careful, with "frequent erasures and corrections from his exemplar as he proceeds," and most of the small, subsequent, non-scribal corrections are also in a single hand.[21] The fourth section, *Christ and Satan,* was written by probably three hands on pages ruled for twenty-seven lines. The shift at *Christ and Satan* to other hands, as well as an increase in corrections and the addition of one more line of text per page, yields a distinctly different appearance of the page, as does the visible fold line in this section of the manuscript. Forty-eight illustrations – half- and full-page, by two artists – now accompany much of *Genesis,* beginning with the frontispiece and continuing to page 88's depiction of Abraham and Sarah outside the walls of Egypt.

Blank spaces, presumably for additional illustrations, continue to the end of *Genesis* and through both *Exodus* and *Daniel.* Despite arguments that even the final poem, *Christ and Satan,* might once also have had illustrations, no firm evidence of this survives, and the existing illustration blanks in the first part of the manuscript mean that even in late tenth- or early eleventh-century England, the book would have appeared unfinished to readers.[22]

---

20 A.N. Doane, ed., *Genesis A: A New Edition, Revised,* Medieval and Renaissance Texts and Studies 435 (Tempe, AZ: ACMRS, 2013), 2. See also Catherine Karkov's list of the make-up of each gathering, in *Text and Picture in Anglo-Saxon England: Narrative Strategies in the Junius 11 Manuscript* (Cambridge: Cambridge University Press, 2001), 19–22.

21 Doane, *Genesis A,* 22–3.

22 The appendix to Karkov's *Text and Picture* lists proposed images for the blanks and possible missing pages in *Christ and Satan.*

Even with the incomplete illustrations, the chronological and theological logic of the book's contents has supported strong arguments in favour of reading Junius 11 as a sequentially unified whole.[23] In terms of the physical book, the continuous section numbering of the contents reinforces such arguments, although not entirely smoothly. Paul Remley lays out some of the "many irregularities" in the numbering, including the fact that the last section number is fifty-five, on page 209 of the manuscript, but the book includes fifty-six sections up to that point. "Fully thirty-six out of the hypothetical maximum of fifty-six section-numbers," too, "fail to appear in Junius 11" at all.[24] Even in their incomplete state, the section numbers may serve selective reading as much as or more than they reinforce sequential structure; they lift the work of locating a particular passage away from the narrative.

Tension between unified presentation and variation also occurs in the manuscript's distribution of small capitals, a situation neatly summed up by Catherine Karkov: "Their distribution throughout the manuscript and within the individual poems is extremely uneven, and there are long sections, particularly in *Exodus*, where there is no capitalization whatsoever."[25] Zoomorphic capitals appear at least once every six pages up until page 79, marking the start of section 25 in *Genesis A*, and then not again until page 143, marking the start of *Exodus*. No other decorated capitals occur in *Exodus*, although blank spaces on three subsequent pages (146, 148, 149) indicate an intention to add them; "after this someone, possibly the scribe," writes Edward Irving in his edition of *Exodus*, "proceeded to furnish rather simple capitals of his own for the rest of the poem."[26] Only one more decorated initial appears in the manuscript, on page 226, near the end of *Christ and Satan*, in a hand different from the one that produced all the preceding initials.[27]

The punctuation in the manuscript offers a stronger argument for the desirability of consistency. Accents and pointing occur with some

---

23 J.R. Hall's are among the most persuasive on this front, in "The Old English Epic of Redemption: The Theological Unity of MS Junius 11," *Traditio* 32 (1976): 185–208; and "On the Bibliographic Unity of Bodleian MS Junius 11," *American Notes and Queries* 24 (1986): 104–7. But see also Karkov, *Text and Picture*; and Barbara Raw, "The Construction of Oxford, Bodleian Library, Junius 11," *ASE* 13 (1984): 187–207.

24 Paul G. Remley, *Old English Biblical Verse: Studies in Genesis, Exodus and Daniel*, CSASE 16 (Cambridge: Cambridge University Press, 1996), 24–9.

25 Karkov, *Text and Picture*, 30.

26 Edward Burroughs Irving, ed. *The Old English Exodus* (New Haven, CT: Yale University Press, 1953), 2.

27 Karkov, *Text and Picture*, 31.

regularity throughout the manuscript, although, and despite efforts to the contrary, less consistently in *Christ and Satan* than in the preceding poems. Karkov describes some of the *Christ and Satan* punctuation as "a later corrector's attempts to regularize orthography and punctuation with those of the scribe of the first three poems. Thus, while the three scribes of Liber II produced a text that was visually less ordered than that produced by the scribe of Liber I, an attempt was made to suggest a unified structure to the reader."[28]

What the Junius 11 manuscript looked like as a physical whole in its first semi-completed form – roughly the form in which it now exists – still remains difficult to know with certainty, including at what point, if any, its creator or creators pronounced the book finished and at what stage en route to its current condition the first readers of Junius 11 encountered it. Its current binding is not original but is medieval, although its date is debated.[29] At least six pages were cut out sometime after the texts were written and bound, although without much apparent loss of text. Perhaps, as Doane surmises, these pages were entirely or mostly blank, perhaps left for illustration, and as soon as the illustration cycle was abandoned, the pages may have been cut out so that the parchment could be used elsewhere.[30]

Christ and Satan may or may not have been part of the book when it was first encountered by readers. Marked at the end as "Finit Liber II" by one of the poem's scribes, possibly indicating awareness of the shift from Old Testament material to Gospels-based material, *Christ and Satan* differs enough from the preceding sections of Junius 11 to indicate that it may not have been part of the book's initial plan, and no corresponding "Liber I" now appears in the manuscript (see chapter 4 for more discussion of the distinctions). Even if concluding with *Christ and Satan* reflects a chronologically, theologically, and thematically unifying decision on the compiler's part, a reader's perspective includes the visual disruptions in the unfinished illustrations and in the capitals as well as the layout distinctions in *Christ and Satan*. As Remley describes it, "The physical disposition of the copy of *Christ and Satan* in Junius 11 appears to owe little if anything to the ruling of leaves in the earlier quires of the manuscript, or to the apportionment of space there for

28 Ibid., 27.

29 Raw, "Construction," dates the current binding to about 1230, but Peter J. Lucas, "MS Junius 11 and Malmesbury," *Scriptorium* 34 (1980): 197–220 and *Scriptorium* 35 (1981): 3–22, offers a detailed argument for an earlier eleventh-century date.

30 Doane, *Genesis A*, 5.

illustrations, or, for that matter, to the manner of execution of the only partially completed series of illustrations in the first eight quires."[31]

Remley's hypothesized outline of four phases of the book's development bears repeating, in part for the attention it calls to what we do not know about the background of Junius 11:

> First, a compositional stage, in the course of which some or all of the poems, arising under separate circumstances, may have been divided into sections. Then followed a stage of transmission involving the circulation of the poems as separate items. This stage possibly involved the introduction of new sectional divisions or the alteration of existing ones. Next came the stage (possibly a two-part process) at which the texts now witnessed by *Genesis, Exodus*, and *Daniel* were brought together in a single exemplar and supplied with a comprehensive series of section numbers, possibly also involving the introduction of alteration of sectional divisions. The final stage is represented by the sole surviving witness to the whole transmissional sequence – the received text preserved in Junius 11.[32]

Whatever its compositional history, the codicological presence of Junius 11 is not accurately captured in any of the existing reproductions. The book's size and heft, two features distinctly not well conveyed in these reproductions, inevitably factor into a reader's perception. Compared with volumes such as the Old English Hexateuch in London, British Library (BL), Cotton Claudius B.iv or the large-format Gospels of the "Royal Bible," BL, Royal MS 1 E.vi, Junius 11 feels quite modest in its physical weight and dimensions. Claudius B.iv, though not much larger than Junius 11, is characterized by Benjamin Withers as "a substantial manuscript. Though a reader might hold it on his or her lap, resting it on a table makes for more comfortable reading, with folios presenting an average height and width of 330 × 220 mm." for its 156 folios.[33]

More likely still to need a table of some kind for support, the Royal Bible, though now just 77 folios, measures 470 × 340 mm. Junius 11, at 324 × 180 mm and 116 folios (in its modern state), is both much more easily carried and more usable without the support of a table. Indeed, for a modern reader who first encountered the material form of Junius 11 by way of Gollancz's facsimile, which itself measures 420 × 300 mm,

---

31 Remley, *Old English Biblical Verse*, 23.

32 Ibid., 28–9.

33 Benjamin C. Withers, *The Illustrated Old English Hexateuch, Cotton Claudius B.iv: The Frontier of Reading and Seeing* (Toronto: University of Toronto Press, 2007), 18.

the actual Junius 11 manuscript seems strikingly portable. Whether or not its first readers ever carried it around for private reading, the physical dimensions of Junius 11 encourage that possibility, if not quite as conveniently as with a pocket-sized book such as the Irish "Pocket Gospel-Book" (BL, Add. 40618), at 130 × 105 mm, or even "St. Dunstan's Classbook" (Oxford, Bodleian Library, Auct. F. 4. 32), at 243 × 170 mm.

No material evidence reveals whether or not the original binding of Junius 11 was sumptuous. Its current binding seems to be somewhat later than its pages but still medieval, oak boards with whittawed leather over them, perhaps dating to as early as the eleventh century or, as Barbara Raw argues, from the early thirteenth. The binding is not distinctive and is without trace of ornament. It does show evidence of having had three straps to hold the book closed, and Raw points out that the "pin which projects from the back cover suggests that the manuscript was stored flat, resting on its front cover, a point which is confirmed by the absence of tabs (designed for pulling books out of chests) and by the position of the chain-mark. Books chained at the top of the cover were kept on lecterns, usually with a bar running across the top, whereas books chained in presses like those at Hereford or in the Bodleian Library had the chain fixed to the front edge of the cover."[34]

In the first few centuries after the Norman Conquest, then, it seems likely that Junius 11 was stored closed, perhaps on a shelf or in a book chest, and not on a lectern, as were – for some time in their early history – larger and more lavish volumes of biblical material, including Claudius B.iv, which were produced at roughly the time of Junius 11's construction. If its illustrations suggest that display was anticipated, the size of Junius 11 simultaneously suggests different, reader-oriented access, and the visual inconsistencies that date from the time of production unquestionably reflect some changes to the book's status during the production process. The degree to which such material factors affected initial readers of the book cannot be determined, but the surviving evidence for what early readers of Old English might generally have anticipated from the word *boc* – particularly a book written in their first language rather than one written in Latin – suggests that our assumptions and expectations as readers differ from theirs in terms not just of context and access but also of content and construction, including such things as coherence, sequence, and repetition as well as divisions and connections among the texts and across the actual pages.

34 Raw, "Construction," 198–9.

The Intangible Book

Particularly given the questions of completion and post-production changes, the manuscript pages themselves cannot tell us precisely what their first readers found between the boards of Junius 11, or how they understood whatever they read there, or whether they more frequently read the book as a sequential whole from page 1 to page 229 or as an anthology from which to select pieces. While the manuscript's texts do not form a functional, continuous, single narrative unit, and its contents are clearly the work of multiple poets probably across several centuries, the manuscript does seem to have been conceived as a unified whole, one that clearly can be and has been read as having thematic coherence and development, from the opening of *Genesis A* through to the end of *Christ and Satan*.[35]

For some early medieval readers, the book may well have been that neat: a single, coherent narrative in support of that opening image of Christ in majesty, even if the particulars of its coherence are not entirely agreed upon now – and these may not have mattered much to its early readers. The collection might, as Barbara Raw and Paul Remley have argued, reflect Lent and Easter lections, or it might have been constructed as an erudite overview of Christian history from Creation to Last Judgment, as J.R. Hall has argued.[36] Junius 11 undoubtedly possesses continuities and coherence across its contents. It just as clearly possesses discontinuities and challenges to sequential coherence.

Junius 11 includes non-sequential connections across its contents and striking distinctions among them that any sequential reader of this book would have to navigate. The dialogue-rich *Genesis B* section interrupts the surrounding *Genesis A* narrative, for example, and more disruptive is a reader's arrival at *Exodus* from *Genesis A*. If Junius 11 were intended for devotional reading that "was regarded as elementary because in the vernacular, the inclusion of *Exodus* in the manuscript was ill-considered," as Lucas puts it.[37] *Exodus* might best suit an audience accustomed to reading with a particularly Latin-associated attention to the construction of poetry, something far less essential to reading the *Genesis* or *Daniel* poems on either side of *Exodus*. In several ways

35 See, e.g., Phyllis Portnoy, *The Remnant: Essays on a Theme in Old English Verse* (London: Runetree, 2005); and Karkov, *Text and Picture*.

36 Barbara Raw, *The Art and Background of Old English Poetry* (London: Edward Arnold, 1978), 187–207; Remley, *Old English Biblical Verse*, 78–87; Hall, "Old English Epic of Redemption."

37 Peter J. Lucas, ed., *Exodus* (Exeter: University of Exeter Press, 1994), 29.

even more distinct is the *Christ and Satan* portion of the manuscript, not least because it was delineated by the scribe who labelled it "Liber II" but also because of its focus on Christ rather than on the Old Testament and its episodic rather than more linear narrative structure. Certainly the compiler of Junius 11 may, as Karkov argues, have "understood that *Christ and Satan* was an integral part of the manuscript's narrative" in what was "envisaged as a unified book,"[38] but for a reader to make such connections would require an emphasis on thematic concerns above, or in negotiation with, such distinctions as the poetry of *Exodus* demands.

A tenth- or eleventh-century reader's experience with texts and books may well have meant that the reader did not give priority to, or perhaps did not even perceive, whatever unity the compiler envisioned. Indeed, the common practice of reuse and recombination of texts from book to book implies that early medieval readers might have valued non-sequential connections or textual conversations in a book more than they did linear sequentiality. Such flexibility is perhaps best exemplified by homily collections and by the inclusion of homilies in other contexts.[39] The Vercelli Book includes twenty-three homilies, several of which are also found in homiliaries, but it is itself not a homiliary. As Clayton explains, "The source collection behind homilies XV–XVII," for instance, appears "to have been a liturgically-arranged homiliary" – that is, one with a purposeful sequence – but the content of the Vercelli Book on the whole "seems to reflect the personal interests of the compiler in its emphasis on 'penitential and eschatological themes,' texts being chosen as a result of the compiler's interest in their subject matter rather than a need to cover particular feast days."[40]

These book producers and readers, moreover, did not just recombine texts; they re-conceptualized them in part and whole, as attested in the network of overlapping pieces related to the Old English poem known as the *Dream of the Rood*. Whatever the relationships among the Vercelli Book, the *Dream of the Rood*, the Roman alphabet Old English text on the Brussels cross, and the runic-alphabet Old English text on the monumental Ruthwell cross, each presentation of shared text also

38 Karkov, *Text and Picture*, 3.

39 Clayton makes the important point that at least "three types of homiliary existed" in early medieval England, "a fact that is obscured in the analysis of both McKitterick and Gatch," and she notes that the "distinctions between these three different types of homiliaries were clearly not rigid, however, and the texts could be used for purposes other than those for which they were originally written. The boundaries between genres must have been quite fluid" ("Homiliaries and Preaching," 160–1).

40 Ibid., 174, 172.

functions independently and employs its own medium, whether page or silver reliquary or stone cross, to build meaning.[41] The expectations that an early medieval reader brought to any *boc* – perhaps especially one of predominantly Old English verse rather than of Latin text – remain elusive, but undoubtedly for such readers, just as for us, those expectations affected their reception of a book and the texts within it. If we begin reading with a perception that the book is somehow distinctively valuable, then we might respond more harshly to perceived deficits such as unfinished work (as in the illustrations in Junius 11) or more kindly to perceived successes such as striking intellectual connections, intentional or accidental, across the contents. Early medieval readers' material and textual expectations of books in English presumably derived in part from comparison to Latin books or simply from prior experience with English ones, and to judge from surviving examples, expectations of sequential unity or coherence, in particular, may have varied between Latin and vernacular books.

By the time that Junius 11 was produced in the second half of the tenth century, if we accept Leslie Lockett's persuasive arguments on dating the manuscript, books containing predominantly or exclusively Old English appear to have been generally on the rise for some time (despite the probable slowdown at the height of the Benedictine Reform).[42] William Schipper defines an Anglo-Saxon vernacular style of page layout for such books that is most visibly characterized by long-line layout of the text as opposed to the columns familiar in Latin texts, but signs of actual reading practices distinctive to Old English books have not been extensively identified.[43]

Whether with eyes on the page or with ears, readers before 1100 clearly had some different expectations of English versus Latin books, not least in their concerns for reader comprehension. Ælfric, in his *Preface to Genesis* as well as in a letter to Sigeweard, draws attention to the distinct status of books written in English: "Đis man mæg rædan, se þe his recð to gehirenne, on þære Engliscan bec, þe ic awende be þisum" (This a person may read, one who cares to hear of it, in that English

41 Seeta Chaganti, "Vestigial Signs: Inscription, Performance, and *The Dream of the Rood*," *PMLA* 125 (2010): 48–72, particularly in reference to performance and reception, explores "these stone, metal, and manuscript manifestations as a multimedia occasion of devotional tradition and expression" (51).

42 Leslie Lockett, "An Integrated Re-examination of the Dating of Oxford, Bodleian Library, Junius 11," *ASE* 31 (2002): 141–73.

43 William Schipper, "Style and Layout of Anglo-Saxon Manuscripts," in *Anglo-Saxon Styles*, ed. Catherine E. Karkov and George Hardin Brown (Albany: State University of New York Press, 2003), 151–68.

book, which I translated concerning this) and, more negatively, "ic geseah [ond] gehyrde mycel gedwyld on manegum engliscum bocum" (I have seen and heard of much error in many English books).[44] Olga Timofeeva's analysis of *boc* words and the evidence for Latin-English bilingualism in England between the seventh and eleventh centuries supports "the conceptual proximity of 'Latin' and written culture" evident in such compounds as *læden-boc* and *boc-læden*: "A Latin-book is a higher authority legitimizing the utterance that makes reference to it," while "the collocation 'English book,'" other than in book-lists, is "very rare to find" and "for [Ælfric] at least, the authority of English writings is not on par with that of Latin."[45]

The total number of surviving books containing primarily or exclusively Old English texts does not, however, offer an abundant comparison set by which we can gauge the extent of any distinctiveness at the level of the complete book. Neil Ker, in the *Catalogue of Manuscripts Containing Anglo-Saxon*, calculated some time ago that "extant literary manuscripts written entirely or mainly in OE before *c.* 1200 number less than 150, including fragments. If we add to that number the Latin-OE glossaries, the Latin texts that are furnished with a complete OE translation, in the form either of a continuous gloss or of a separate version, and the mainly Latin manuscripts which contain a substantial amount of OE, … the total is still short of 200. In fact more than half the manuscripts containing OE are Latin manuscripts in which the OE takes the form of brief records or notes or of more or less numerous interlinear glosses."[46] As the ensuing overview shows, continuity or other forms of coherence can be identified in many of these books, as with Junius 11, but little about many of them indicates clearly whether they were constructed as physical units explicitly designed to be read sequentially from board to board and whether readers, regardless of a book's construction intentions, treated its contents as a continuous whole, a unified whole, or with some other connective structures – or without any.

The largest group of surviving manuscripts that contain exclusively or primarily Old English texts are ones we generally categorize as anthologies and miscellanies, with the distinction lying in the strength

44 Ælfric, *The Old English Version of the Heptateuch: Ælfric's Treatise on the Old and New Testament and His Preface to Genesis*, ed. S.J. Crawford, EETS, o.s. 160 (London: Oxford University Press, 1922), 33–4; Ælfric, *Catholic Homilies* 1, 50–1.

45 Timofeeva, "*Of ledenum bocum,*" 214–15.

46 N.R. Ker, *Catalogue of Manuscripts Containing Anglo-Saxon* (Oxford: Clarendon Press, 1957; reissued 1990), xiv (hereafter cited as *CMCAS*). Citations refer to the 1990 edition.

of apparent connection among a book's contents. In terms of textual content, homilies and homiletic material are probably the most numerous among surviving Old English texts, followed by glossed psalters, both of which in book form frequently include other material and by their nature need not be understood in relation to cover-to-cover, sequential reading. Relatively numerous copies of Ælfric's *Grammar* – fourteen manuscripts – also survive; indeed, as Kenneth Sisam noted, "No other book in Anglo-Saxon approaches it in the number of copies that survive."[47] But of those fourteen manuscripts, only four survive as stand-alone books; the other ten are now either fragments, in composite manuscripts, or more clearly part of collected texts within a book. Still, it seems reasonable to suppose that early medieval readers considered the *Grammar* and *Glossary* as a standard sort of unit, one that may well have been a familiar single book that was initially read sequentially, then used largely for non-sequential reference.

Other kinds of Old English texts with multiple surviving book presentations include martyrologies, saints' lives, laws, chronicles, and Junius 11's usual companions in modern perception, the collections with significant quantities of Old English verse: the Vercelli Book; Exeter Book; and London, BL, Cotton Vitellius A.xv (the *Beowulf* manuscript). Both the Vercelli Book and Cotton Vitellius A.xv present a mixture of prose and poetic texts; only the Exeter Book and Junius 11 offer entirely poetry, although the boundaries between what is and is not poetry are not perfectly well defined in Old English texts. Of these four, Cotton Vitellius A.xv has the most complicated presentation history; it consists of at least two codices, probably not bound together until well after its period of initial readership.[48] Its collection of texts, both prose and poetic, can be understood in terms of thematic unity, as focused on monsters and the monstrous, and those texts may have a meaningful sequence, if not necessarily one purposefully created. Kathryn Powell has argued that the *Passion of Saint Christopher* and *Judith* were additions that provided a politically relevant beginning and ending frame, one "that shift[s] the collection's focus away from the struggles of heroes and monsters towards the related struggles of rulers and threatening foreigners."[49]

---

47 Kenneth Sisam, "The Order of Ælfric's Early Books," in *Studies in the History of English Literature* (Oxford: Clarendon Press, 1953), 301.

48 For an overview of the manuscript's history, as well as an argument for three rather than two codices, see Kevin Kiernan, *Beowulf and the Beowulf Manuscript*, rev. ed. (Ann Arbor: University of Michigan Press, 1996), 120–69.

49 Kathryn Powell, "Meditating on Men and Monsters: A Reconsideration of the Thematic Unity of the 'Beowulf' Manuscript," *RES*, n.s. 57 (2006): 15.

The Vercelli Book provides easier ground on which to look for sequential coherence since this collection was written entirely by a single scribe (although one whose care in copying has not been admired). Interestingly, its physical size is also close to that of Junius 11. Yet the current sequence of twenty-nine texts, six of which are poems, may not be original, and the compilation strategy, if one existed, remains less widely agreed upon than what has been proposed for the *Beowulf* manuscript. Scragg long ago identified some modest continuities in the Vercelli collection: "Some of the items have a deliberate relationship (e.g. the three Rogation homilies XI–XIII, and homilies VIII and IX for the first and second Sundays after Epiphany), and there is evidence that the compiler drew upon at least one existing sequence of homilies in that homilies VII–X are numbered *ii–v*."[50] It might have been a book compiled for a specifically female readership or as an exploration of soul and body, or for another devotional or even non-devotional purpose.[51]

The Exeter Book has been seen even less often as a sequential whole. It was ordered by someone "at least in part," according to Scragg, but the collection is large and widely varied, so much so that Patrick Conner proposed that the volume began as three smaller booklets.[52] Compilation debates aside, coherence across so many poems – some forty, depending on how *The Partridge* is counted, and aside from counting the ninety-plus riddles individually, although each is actually a separate poem – seems highly unlikely, and consecutive reading from *Christ I*, which opens the volume, to *Riddle 95*, which closes it more than 120 folios later, contributes to no well-defined goal. On the whole, we have little to guide us in determining how early medieval readers would have approached the Exeter Book, but selective reading of it as well as of Vercelli and Cotton Vitellius A.xv seems more than plausible.

All these books make sense either read from cover to cover in sequence or read selectively and out of sequence. That *we* can find consecutive connections, thematic or narrative, in some of these collections of texts provides evidence that their earliest readers could have done

50 Donald G. Scragg, "The Compilation of the Vercelli Book," *ASE* 2 (1973): 190.

51 See Mary Dockray-Miller, "Female Devotion and the Vercelli Book," *Philological Quarterly* 83, no. 4 (2004): 337–54; Amity Reading, *Reading the Anglo-Saxon Self through the Vercelli Book* (New York: Peter Lang, 2018); and Elaine Treharne, "The Form and Function of the Vercelli Book," in *Studies in Anglo-Saxon Literature and Its Insular Context in Honour of Éamonn Ó Carragáin*, ed. Alastair Minnis and Jane Roberts (Turnhout, Belgium: Brepols, 2007), especially 257.

52 Donald G. Scragg, "Homilies," in the *Blackwell Encyclopedia of Anglo-Saxon England*, ed. Michael Lapidge et al. (Malden, MA: Blackwell, 2001), 241–2. See also Patrick W. Conner, "The Structure of the Exeter Book Codex (Exeter, Cathedral Library, MS 3501)," *Scriptorium* 40, no. 2 (1986): 233–42.

the same, but a substantial body of other evidence suggests that materially defined sequential reading (reading in sequence because the pages are bound together and in roughly the same layout throughout) might have been no more common than selective reading guided by varying goals. As a group, surviving Old English books imply that the extent of congruence between a set of connectable narratives and a book as a whole was considerably less than it is among twentieth- or twenty-first-century books, whether paper or electronic.

Yet book and text unity and sequentiality of the kind familiar to twenty-first-century readers clearly did exist to some extent among books written substantially or entirely in Old English, although more evidently with single-authored texts than with the kind of compilation found in Junius 11. One of the clearest examples occurs with the Old English translation of Bede's *Historia ecclesiastica*. The work has intentional – in this case, authorial – sequence still evident, and four of the five of the extant versions appear to have been presented in books initially designed to consist only of this text. Cambridge, University Library (CUL), Kk.3.18 (s. xi²) and Cambridge, Corpus Christi College (CCCC), 41 (s. xi¹) are perhaps the neatest examples of that initial plan, although the latter did not apparently last long as an independent text and includes extensive marginalia.[53]

Single-book presentation of the *Historia ecclesiastica* in Old English, particularly if all five of these versions were originally the sole text of a book, might be the result of a standard presentation of the text's Latin counterpart more than a foundational expectation for Old English books. The twenty-one Anglo-Saxon copies of the *Historia ecclesiastica* in Latin, however, do not yield a clear picture of any such standard: nine of the copies exist as the sole content of a book, two present the

53 London, British Library, Cotton Domitian ix may once have been connected to the CUL *EH*; see item 22 in the *Handlist*. Cotton Domitian ix contains "three tiny excerpts of the OE Bede," all "on a single page"; see Raymond S. Grant's *The B Text of the Old English Bede* (Atlanta, GA: Rodopi, 1989), 3–5. Oxford, Bodleian Library, Tanner 10 is now an incomplete version, as is Oxford, Corpus Christi College, 279 part ii, and for neither do we have conclusive evidence of initial completeness or of when they reached their current form. A fifth and fragmentary survival in London, British Library, Cotton Otho B.xi may also have been an independent book when it was written in the mid-tenth century, but it is now accompanied by early eleventh-century additions, including laws and fragments of the *Anglo-Saxon Chronicle*. Information on all these manuscripts is from Helmut Gneuss and Michael Lapidge's *Anglo-Saxon Manuscripts: A Bibliographic Handlist of Manuscripts and Manuscript Fragments Written or Owned in England up to 1100* (Toronto: University of Toronto Press, 2014); as well as Sharon Rowley, *The Old English Version of Bede's Historiae Ecclesiastica* (Cambridge: D.S. Brewer, 2012), 16–25.

Historia alongside other texts, seven offer only excerpts of the *Historia*, and three are fragments. If anything, the fifty-fifty breakdown in presentations of the Latin *Historia* indicates the difficulty in trying to determine a standard book form, and the majority of Old English books that we have are not matched by versions in Latin.

Another book of continuous-text Old English translated from Latin is the sole surviving pre-1100 copy of Alfred's translation of *The Consolation of Philosophy*, although the manuscript – BL, Cotton Otho A.vi, fols. 1–129 – was severely damaged by the Cotton Library fire in 1731. An entirely prose version in an early twelfth-century copy (Oxford, Bodleian Library, Bodley 180) seems likely to have derived from a similar text-as-book – it runs to ninety-four folios – but the only other direct attestation to the work in early medieval England is an endleaf.[54] Still, enough evidence survives to show that vernacular, sequential texts-as-books were available to readers whose vernacular was Old English. The surviving examples, however, do not reveal the degree of these works' accessibility and influence in this form, and more plentiful survivals come in less sequentially continuous books as well as books with content that straddles a line between sequential and non-sequential.

One step away from the sequential and authorial-book coherence of the Boethius and Bede manuscripts, and in some ways more similar to the Junius 11 manuscript, are texts with more distinctly separable sections that are materially presented as a single, consecutively ordered unit, in some instances also defined with a single author, as in the case of the Alfredian translation of Gregory the Great's *Regula pastoralis* and the Old English translations of Gregory's *Dialogues*. Alfred's prefatory letter to his translation of the *Regula pastoralis* seems to equate complete text and book, referring as he does to his efforts "ða boc wendan on Englisc ðe is genemned on Læden Pastoralis, & on Englisc Hierdeboc, hwilum word be worde, hwilum andgit of angi[e]te" (to translate into English the book that is called in Latin *Pastoralis*, and in English "shepherd-book," sometimes word for word, and sometimes sense for sense).[55]

54 See Andrew Prescott's article on Cotton's library, "'Their Present Miserable State of Cremation'": The Restoration of the Cotton Library," in *Sir Robert Cotton as Collector: Essays on an Early Stuart Courtier and His Legacy*, ed. C.J. Wright (London: British Library, 1997), 391–454; and Greg Waite, *Old English Prose Translations of King Alfred's Reign* (Cambridge: D.S. Brewer, 2000), 28–9.

55 Gregory, *King Alfred's West-Saxon Version of Gregory's Pastoral Care*, ed. Henry Sweet, EETS, o.s. 45, 50 (London, 1871–2; repr. with corrections by N.R. Ker, London: Oxford University Press, 1958), 7–9.

At the same time, Alfred's directions do not exclude re-contextualizing the *Pastoral Care* by copying it into a book with other materials, and his hope for wide readership of the text does not preclude different approaches to that reading, as apparently happened with the adaptation of Augustine's *Soliloquies*: "a composite work based on Augustine's *Soliloquia* and *De uidendo Deo*, but deriving material and ideas also from Gregory and Jerome."[56] A variety of approach is also implied by the fact that the four-part *Pastoral Care* in Old English translation was produced in single-book form across a fairly wide span of time, as in CUL Ii.2.4 (s. xi$^{3/4}$); CCCC 12 (s. xi?); and Oxford, Bodleian Library, Hatton 20 (ca. 890–7).[57] Although the *Pastoral Care* does not have a chronology or narrative that requires sequential reading, the four sections do proceed in defined and purposeful order. At the same time, the text itself as well as the page layouts in the manuscripts facilitate selective, sectional reading. In CCCC 12, for instance, sections are clearly marked, even though the headers were never fully completed (after the opening red capital of the first section, a "small blank (of 3 or 4 lines) is left at the beginnings of the subsequent chapters, for titles and initials which were no doubt meant [also] to be inserted in red").[58]

Old English translations of Gregory's *Dialogues* are presented similarly, at least in the one version that can be clearly identified now as having been – and still being – a book in itself, CCCC 322 (the other three survivals are a fragment and two composite manuscripts), with clearly rubricated sections, which would have helped a reader navigate the text either in sequence or in selective reading.[59] Presentation facilitating both sequential and selective reading likewise appears in the Paris Psalter, and indeed the compiler of that collection seems to

56 Janet Bately, "Those Books That Are Most Necessary for All Men to Know: The Classic and Late Ninth-Century England; A Reappraisal," in *The Classics in the Middle Ages: Papers of the Twentieth Conference of the Center for Medieval and Early Renaissance Studies*, ed. Aldo S. Bernardo and Saul Levin (Binghamton, NY: CEMERS, 1990), 45.

57 All dates follow Gneuss and Lapidge's *Handlist*.

58 Page images can be viewed at the Parker Library On the Web, https://parker.stanford.edu/parker/.

59 For a discussion of the text's "episodic similitude," see David F. Johnson, "Divine Justice in Gregory the Great's *Dialogues*," in *Early Medieval Studies in Memory of Patrick Wormald*, ed. Stephen David Baxter et al. (Burlington, VT: Ashgate 2009), 115. The other three surviving manuscripts of Gregory's *Dialogues* in Old English sit outside this discussion as one (a Canterbury ms.) is a fragment and two (British Library Cotton Otho c.i and Bodleian Library Hatton 76) are within composite manuscripts, and, even within a particular section, the text seems to have had companion texts.

have paid particular attention to providing headings that would help readers navigate individual psalms.[60]

The *Anglo-Saxon Chronicle*, which like the Paris Psalter includes both poetry and prose in the vernacular, demonstrates even more clearly how a book can be both sequential and not. The *Chronicle* poems, in particular, as Thomas Bredehoft has shown, share a consistency of interest despite being the work of writers across well over a hundred years. At the same time, and although chronology fundamentally guides the text as a whole, we could easily read the *Chronicle* as a series of largely discrete entries, dictated by events and localized interests rather than by coherent purpose. Bredehoft, however, lays out evidence for coherence, which leads him to conclude that "clearly, the *Chronicle* was, during this period, something far more than a haphazard collection of variously composed annals: the *Chronicle* and its verse had a rhetorical and political effect that the chroniclers were able to recognize, contribute to, and even turn to their own ends." If we attempt to understand the *Dialogues* or the *Chronicle* in terms of what Bredehoft calls "a 'historicized literacy': [that is,] a scholarly understanding of Anglo-Saxon literate practice as it originally functioned," then we have to allow multiple kinds of coherence as well as flexibility in and around continuity.[61]

In biblical material, the Old English versions of the Gospels likewise offer evidence of clearly unified and just as clearly sectional and not necessarily sequential books. Survivals now consist of "four more or less complete manuscripts and two fragments from the eleventh century, and two complete twelfth-century manuscripts."[62] R.M. Liuzza notes that "all the manuscripts in their original states appear to have contained all four Gospels," a coherence that implies a perception of the Old English Gospels as a single book, at least to some extent, since half – three of the surviving six – of the mostly complete manuscripts exist now as independent books. Liuzza also points out, however, that we have not only "no explicit testimony regarding either the intention of the author or the reception of the Old English Gospels" but also

60 On the headings and their directives to the reader, see Emily Butler, "The Role of Compiler in the Paris Psalter," *English Studies* 98 (2017): 26–34.

61 Thomas A. Bredehoft, *Textual Histories: Readings in the Anglo-Saxon Chronicle* (Toronto: Toronto University Press, 2001), 118, 9.

62 The number is, as R.M. Liuzza notes, "not so many as Ælfric's *Homilies* or the glossed psalters, but more than the various pieces of the Old English Old Testament" (5); see "Who Read the Gospels in Old English?," in *Words and Works: Studies in Medieval English Language and Literature in Honour of Fred C. Robinson*, ed. Peter S. Baker and Nicholas Howe (Toronto: University of Toronto Press, 1998), 3–24.

"little evidence that they were widely known."[63] The Old English Gospels may, suggests Liuzza, have functioned as something of a utilitarian reference book:

> The evidence is inconclusive, but does not preclude the hypothesis that the Old English Gospels in a manuscript such as Y [New Haven, Beinecke Library, 578 endleaf] or A [CUL Ii.2.11] were used as a reading-book after the recitation of the Gospels in Latin on occasions when full homilies were not preached, or preliminary to an extemporaneous homily on the Gospel. It is possible, then, that in addition to its use as a devotional book for monastic or clerical reading, the Old English version may have been adapted to meet the same need as that which drove Ælfric to publish homilies, to aid the secular priests' explication of the gospel pericope.[64]

The Gospel books, too, like other early medieval books, were at times transformed into anthologies by the practice of adding substantial marginalia or filling any blank spaces. Liuzza describes the Bath Abbey manuscript (now CCCC 140) as having been "used like a Latin gospel-book as a place record, a depository for important information, a fit container for facts which could not be altered or erased. ... The manuscript attracted relic inventories, a list of bishops and popes, an agreement of confraternity between the members of surrounding monasteries; it was a registry as well as a text."[65] Even when initially presented in a continuous sequence, books were, then, sometimes quite quickly moved into also functioning as non-sequential repositories of other information, thereby creating a challenge to the dominant sequentiality.

From a narrative as well as a material perspective, the Old English Hexateuch offers perhaps the most logical comparison book for Junius 11. Both Junius 11 and BL MS Cotton Claudius B.i (the Old English Hexateuch) offer illustrated Old Testament texts in the vernacular, with relatively close proposed dates of compilation – from the end of the tenth to the early eleventh centuries – and both show evidence of purposeful compilation structure; indeed, the sequential coherence is even stronger in the Hexateuch than it is across the Junius 11 poems, in large part, of course, because of the closer connection to biblical source

63 Ibid., 5.
64 Ibid., 14.
65 Ibid., 13.

material. Claudius B.iv also adds part of Ælfric's *Preface to Genesis* as if in introduction to the ensuing coherent unit of texts.[66]

Yet the Hexateuch is not a consistently defined book. In Oxford, Bodleian Library Laud Misc. 509, for instance, it is followed by "several other texts not found in Claudius B.iv: a homily on Judges, ... two letters dealing with the interpretation of biblical texts written by Ælfric and addressed to laymen, and a life of Saint Guthlac."[67] Indeed, Withers concludes that "Æthelweard's request that Genesis be translated indicates that it would have been much more common for an Anglo-Saxon reader to think of the Old Testament books individually than to think in terms of a compilation ranging from Genesis through Joshua."[68] If "a significant demand for several prose vernacular treatments of the Old Testament in Anglo-Saxon England" existed, in other words, that demand may have been for particular texts – influenced perhaps by liturgical uses of sections of the Bible – and not simultaneously or consistently identified with a single book form.[69]

Against such a variety of books, even if they represent only a fraction of what was once available, Junius 11 as a coherent, sequential narrative may have been more the exception than the rule, and its internal material distinctions, while notable, may have been so commonplace as to not have challenged such an approach, even while attesting to other approaches to the volume's content. Composite manuscripts provide the clearest evidence of coexisting material distinctions and unity, and

---

66 Lockett offers strong arguments for dating Junius 11 to ca. 960–90; see "An Integrated Re-examination." Peter Clemoes dates Cotton Claudius B.iv to the early eleventh century; see "The Production of an Illustrated Version," in *The Old English Illustrated Hexateuch*, ed. C.R. Dodwell and Peter Clemoes, EEMF 18 (Copenhagen: Rosenkilde & Bagger, 1974); Withers, *Old English Illustrated Hexateuch*, argues that the "earliest date that the particular combination of text and image found in Claudius B.iv could have been made is at the end of the second decade of the eleventh century" (62). See also chap. 5 below for the connection of the Hexateuch to the possible lay patron for Junius 11.

67 Benjamin C. Withers, "A 'Secret and Feverish Genesis': The Prefaces of the Old English Hexateuch," *Art Bulletin* 81 (1999): 56.

68 Withers, *Old English Illustrated Hexateuch*, 130–1, 132. Versions of the book of Genesis in Anglo-Saxon England appear to have had their own quite distinct textual history separate from the Hexateuch, an idea for which Withers sees support in such features as rubrication differences between Genesis and the rest of the Hexateuch.

69 Ibid., 56. See also Richard Marsden, "Wrestling with the Bible: Textual Problems for the Scholar and Student," in *Christian Tradition in Anglo-Saxon England: Approaches to Current Scholarship and Teaching*, ed. Paul Cavill (Cambridge: Cambridge University Press, 2004), 69–90.

"the practice of assembling booklets into compilations was already well established in the Anglo-Saxon period," as P.R. Robinson's evidence makes clear:

> For example, a tall narrow booklet (fols. 138–60) which contains homilies for Advent, Easter Day and the Assumption was added to a Worcester volume, Oxford, Bodleian Library, Junius 121. London, Lambeth Palace Library, 489 consists of two small booklets written at Exeter; the first (fols. 1–24) contains homilies for Christmas, Easter and All Saints days, while the second (fols. 25–58) contains a Sunday sermon, a sermon on the Lord's prayer and three homilies suitable for the anniversary of the dedication of a church.[70]

Even when whole booklets were not bound together, continuities that might seem disjunctions to modern readers distinguish early English books. The Bath Abbey copy of the Old English Gospels that Liuzza cites – with its opening pages "covered with manumissions" – presents unity not on the page or in the content, but in physical and, in turn, spiritual association: "In other words, copies of the translation [of the gospels] were sometimes treated like Latin gospel-books – immutable, authoritative, public, and sacral – whose power extended protection to the documents entered into them."[71] That kind of connection encourages consideration of reading practices beyond the more conventionally modern expectations of sequential coherence, as should what is broadly evident to anyone with much familiarity with early medieval books: that early medieval readers may have been at least as accustomed to material discontinuities in their books as they were to first-to-last-page, consistent presentation.

Admittedly, any attempt to consider early medieval books as a whole, specifically ones dominated by Old English, quickly "enforces an awareness of how much has been lost," as Lapidge reminds us in his study of libraries.[72] To judge, however, from the relatively large number of apparently non-sequential or at least not narratively or otherwise obviously sequential collections that survive, early medieval readers may have been willing to read any single book either sequentially or episodically, approaching books as a unified whole or as collections of

70 P.R. Robinson, "Self-Contained Units in Composite Manuscripts of the Anglo-Saxon Period," *ASE* 7 (1978): 234–5.

71 Liuzza, "Who Read the Gospels?," 13.

72 Lapidge, *Anglo-Saxon Library*, 131.

discrete units to be taken in any order and without feeling at all the need to read an entire book.

If, as Lapidge asserts, "The principle purpose for which libraries were assembled was the interpretation of Scripture and the regulation of the Church," then his notion of the "functional bias of Anglo-Saxon libraries" might best account for considering the book in practical terms. "The typical Anglo-Saxon monastic library probably owned fewer than fifty volumes," according to Lapidge, and compendia of various kinds would help make the most of such numbers.[73] At the same time, evidence for some degree of sequentiality is strong. Even in vernacular miscellanies such as CCCC MS. 201, a discernable logic seems to exist in beginning with the *Regularis Concordia* and in then having the first homily open with Adam, the first man – and material emphasis is given to the opening of the book; the start of the text has the flourish of a large green A.

Junius 11 even more clearly privileges page 1, with its frontispiece of divine majesty facing a page of text that begins at the start of Christian history – but after that? In practice, if an initial encounter was sequential, subsequent encounters, particularly for the majority of books that survive with substantial Old English content, seem far less likely to have begun at page 1. Nor does adherence to page sequence throughout a book necessarily follow from a page 1 flourish and overlapping concerns; once through the front door, a reader might wander in any number of directions within this single house and skip some rooms altogether.

The early medieval expectation of linearity in books appears, on the whole, to have been less strong than our own, and the contents of Junius 11 offer a rich array of distinctions that sit alongside the kinds of thematic coherences that other scholars have posited for the book. Junius 11 includes the same story repeated three times, with three distinct functions as well as cumulative but not narratively sequential effect. The poems in the manuscript echo each other's concerns, lending weight to thematic developments, at the same time as they participate in larger topical discussions that reach well beyond this single manuscript, so that an informed reader could create a set of thematic connections quite distinct from those that emerge within Junius 11 on its own. Perhaps most of all, the literary and material disruptions within Junius 11 encourage reading against or at least alongside thematic and chronological coherence.

---

73 Ibid., 128, 129, 127.

The chapters that follow explore the implications of reading the contents of Junius 11 sequentially or (perhaps *and*) selectively, in juxtaposition to each other, in partial sequence, and in shelf context, providing a series of models for use of this particular book in tenth- or eleventh-century England other than those focused on the posited goals of the book's compiler, its first intended audience, or the thematically unified readings that can be found. The goal is not to challenge sequential coherence in Junius 11, but to set alongside it other options that this early medieval book invites and, in so doing, to suggest a model for reading and meaning-building that might also apply to other complex collections of Old English literature.

The first chapter focuses on the Fall of the Angels story, which is repeated three times in the manuscript and is a prominent subject in the literature of early medieval England, presumably for its usefulness in explaining the existence of sin in the world.[74] If sequential coherence was the primary driver in reading Junius 11, the angelic Fall episodes cumulatively build a rich and complex understanding of God's power, divine creation and human weakness, post-lapsarian existence, and the need for obedience to divine authority. At the same time, however, each version of the story both overlaps the others and reinterprets it to suit the immediate context, so it functions effectively without reference to the other verbal and visual versions of the story in the same manuscript. God's power remains a constant in the story, of course, but each version of the Fall of the Angels effectively positions that power in the service of a point tied to the contextual narrative, whether that narrative is of Creation, human Fall, or Christ's life. Repetition of the story in a single book, whether accumulative or selective, implies interest, even if the multiple versions are accidental rather than deliberate, and the flexibility of the episode highlights the recombinatory practice evident in early medieval books; texts regularly, at least in the surviving corpus, are excerpted, adapted, interpolated into other texts, anthologized in different collections.

The reworkings of the Fall of the Angels story in Junius 11 seem to reflect both a standard approach to "text" as a malleable entity and a prominence of the story in early English culture at large. Lucifer and his fellows' fall turns up in *Vainglory, Juliana, Elene,* and *Andreas* as well as in the Junius 11 poems; it is also referenced in such authoritative

74 See Michael Fox, "Ælfric on the Creation and Fall of the Angels," *ASE* 31 (2002): 199–200.

works as the writings of Gregory the Great and of Ælfric.[75] The Fall of the Angels serves different purposes even as its basic narrative remains the same, and the variety of its contexts encourages juxtaposed readings, comparison, and analysis. The same kinds of reading work are also suggested by more subtle connections across and beyond the contents of Junius 11.

Two narratives rarely considered together by scholars are the accounts of the Fall of Adam and Eve and the conversion of Nabuchodonossor, stories that occur in the *Genesis B* and *Daniel* sections of the manuscript, respectively, and that are the focus of this study's second chapter. Although each story frames the topic in an entirely distinct narrative, both are marked by a concern with perception and discernment, and, like the Fall of the Angels repetitions, the two discernment stories build sequential meaning and yet do not rely upon manuscript sequence to convey a spiritual lesson or narrative point. When juxtaposed, these two sections of Junius 11 reveal a shared interest and an interest evident in texts outside Junius 11, one that the manuscript context obscures, to some extent, especially for readers not familiar with narratives or discussions of *discretio spirituum*. Sequentially or individually encountered, the discernment concerns of *Daniel* and *Genesis B* would be most meaningful to readers who, like King Alfred, were already interested in the "modes eagan" (eyes of the mind): presumably well-educated readers.[76]

How well educated becomes a more pressing concern when the contents of the Junius 11's implied Liber I are considered in terms of the reading skills that they seem to ask of readers. No one poetic style unites these poems; they share no single approach to "biblical poetry." For instance, "with the single exception of the concise rendition of the Song of the Three," as Remley points out, "no section of *Daniel* offers the sort of close biblical paraphrase observed in, say, the genealogical sections of *Genesis A*."[77] *Exodus* has long stood out as distinctive among surviving Old English poems, and not just those in Junius 11. In its context in Junius 11, however, the poem's attention to learned readers

75 Daniel Anlezark usefully summarizes the story's presence in Anglo-Saxon England in his article "The Fall of the Angels in *Solomon and Saturn II*," in *Apocryphal Texts and Traditions in Anglo-Saxon England*, ed. Kathryn Powell and Donald Scragg (Cambridge: D.S. Brewer, 2003), 121–33.

76 David Pratt, "Persuasion and Invention at the Court of King Alfred the Great," in *Court Culture in the Early Middle Ages*, ed. Catherine Cubitt (Turnhout, Belgium: Brepols, 2003), 213, 216.

77 Remley, *Old English Biblical Verse*, 240.

and interpretation functions as a reminder that not all Old English biblical poems are alike and nor are all early readers of Old English. Chapter 3 explores both what is known of reading practices in pre-Conquest England in general and how *Exodus* participates in a discussion of reading. The reading skills of the *boceras* – the scholars, with a clear tie to book-learning – to whom *Exodus* refers and to whom it might speak most successfully are evident in the poem itself, which also encourages those with less developed reading abilities to continue to seek understanding.

Despite the difference in the demands of reading *Exodus* and those required for the *Genesis* and *Daniel* poems that surround it, none of the poems in Junius 11 so sharply demonstrates the principle of meaning in juxtaposition as does *Christ and Satan*. As the conclusion to a sequence of Old Testament narratives, *Christ and Satan* might function as the necessary redemptive end to what Karkov and others see as "undoubtedly the cycle of Fall and Redemption that runs from the Creation to the Last Judgement."[78] Readers inclined to read in ways other than building overall consecutive meaning from this book, however, would find in *Christ and Satan*, in particular, an encouragement to connect it to texts outside Junius 11. From its opening page and lines, *Christ and Satan* differs from its companion pieces physically, structurally, and topically. This last section of Junius 11 shares connections to works of wisdom literature as much or more than it does to the biblical poems that precede it. *Christ and Satan* both participates in the book's unity and coherence and stands apart from it, with ample evidence that readers may have understood this final section as simply the last text in an aggregative rather than linear collection.

The ways in which its first readers approached and understood Junius 11 and its contents can, of course, never be determined conclusively, and, indeed, the idea that a single approach to this or any book once existed seems unlikely and too reductive. What other books a reader knew before encountering Junius 11 and, indeed, what other books sat, physically or figuratively, alongside it might help us both identify a possible early home for this manuscript and better understand how it functioned in readers' eyes (unless Junius 11 was the lone book owned or read by a layperson, which seems doubtful). With those goals in mind, the last chapter of this study attempts to contextualize Junius 11 by comparing it to the known contents of the two monastic foundations that seem most likely to have produced an illustrated

78 Karkov, *Text and Picture*, 101.

book of Old English verse, whether for a lay patron, as Anlezark has proposed, or for monastic use: those at Christ Church, Canterbury and New Minster, Winchester. As a book in England around 1000, wherever it was produced, and whether its contents were read sequentially, in juxtaposition to each other or to texts and objects outside this collection, or selectively and independently, Junius 11 participated in and was the product of a reading culture about which we still know too little.

The more we learn about early medieval books and readers, the better we can understand the texts that survive as well as how reading itself, as a process and a product, changes within and across time and culture. In his 798 letter to Æthelheard, archbishop of Canterbury, Alcuin urged, "tua quoque veneranda sapientia specialiter deducat in domum Dei lectionis studium, ut sint ibi legentes. ... et librorum exercitatio" (also let your reverend wisdom especially bring into the house of God the zeal for reading, that there may be there ... reading ... and the study of books).[79] The subsequent chapters of this study approach Junius 11 with the expectation that what Alcuin endorsed was embraced in the centuries that immediately followed, if only partially at times and if only slowly and sporadically. By the mid-tenth century or so, a rich and varied culture of reading – and a complicated perception of what to do with a book – existed in England in and beyond houses of God, and readers had enough experience to select and find wisdom, narrative pleasure, and a diversity of other things inside the boards of books, including those that held the Junius 11 manuscript.

79 Alcuin, "Alcuini Epistolae" no. 128, in *Monumenta Germaniae Historica*, vol. 4, *Epistolae Karolini aevi II*, ed. Ernst Dümmler, 190 (Berlin: Weidmann, 1895); translation from Dorothy Whitelock, ed., *English Historical Documents*, vol. 1, *c.500–1042*, 2nd ed. (New York: Oxford University Press, 1979), 857.

Chapter 1

The Thrice-Told Tale

Bec sindon breme, bodiað geneahhe
weotodne willan ðam ðe wiht hygeð[1]

A contemporary book that, without providing any rationale for doing so or even any clear evidence of intentionality, gives multiple versions of the same story would likely seem flawed to most twenty-first-century readers.[2] Our desire for a sense of progress would be thwarted, to some extent; our expectations for non-repetitive invention and development challenged. Yet in a context in which material books are not so old-fashioned, one in which readers have less regular expectations of their structure, repetition might just as well be welcomed as an analytical tool or a useful unifier – and the repetition, too, might go unnoticed, particularly if reading is done selectively. Alongside all its markers of sequential coherence, the Junius 11 manuscript includes in its pages, as they survive, multiple sets of repeated episodes: three written narrative versions of the Fall of the Angels story, two versions of the Flood story, and two of the Abraham and Isaac story, while, at the same time, the creation of Eve, told twice in the biblical Genesis, appears only once in the manuscript.[3]

1 "Books are glorious; they proclaim abundantly certain purpose to one who thinks at all," from *The Poetical Dialogues of Solomon and Saturn*, ed. Robert J. Menner (New York: Modern Language Association, 1941), 229–30.

2 Samantha Zacher, e.g., links repetition to pejorative assessment of medieval texts in a familiar way when she describes the interpolation of *Genesis B* into *Genesis A* as resulting in "some awkwardness and repetition"; see *Rewriting the Old Testament in Anglo-Saxon Verse: Becoming the Chosen People* (Bloomsbury: New York, 2013), 6.

3 See Doane, *Genesis A*, 62–3, on the *Genesis A* poet's orderliness.

In part because they do not mimic biblical structure, the repetitions in Junius 11 lend themselves to comparative study: they offer a useful starting place for assessing both the potential unity of the manuscript and the distinctions from poem to poem, and perhaps page to page, within it. The Fall of the Angels story appears in *Genesis A*, *Genesis B*, and *Christ and Satan* as well as in the book's illustrations, and the distinctions among these versions are significant enough to attest to the adaptability of a biblical story even as they demonstrate the expectation that readers of Junius 11 would have been comfortable receivers of narrative repetition and variation, if they read the entire volume, or selective readers, for whom each version of the story might be encountered on its own – although not entirely in isolation, given the currency of the Fall of the Angels story in early medieval Christian culture.

The narrative repetitions in Junius 11 have received critical attention that more often highlights their distinctions in terms of poetic skill rather than reader experiences. Francis Lee Utley, for example, in comparing "The Flood Narrative in the Junius Manuscript and in Baltic Literature," distinguishes between "the two major treatments of the Flood story in Old English," that in *Genesis A* and that in *Exodus*. His comparison rests on "three ways in which a biblical narrative may be adapted and expanded in later sophisticated and folk literature": "Dark passages may be interpreted by learned exegesis and the results incorporated by the artist, the story may be elaborated with new apocryphal narrative motifs, and the tone may be altered by new cultural elements – by 'modernization' in short." *Exodus*, asserts Utley, "offers us little that is new about the Flood, apocryphal, exegetical, or cultural, save for its humane metaphor which declares that man and the creatures are a richer treasure than the ring-gold of a Germanic chieftain." In contrast, "*Genesis A* contains a genuine Flood narrative, rather than a mere linked allusion, and with this greater scope provides some evidence of each kind of biblical expansion."[4]

Robert Creed places the manuscript's two accounts of the Offering of Isaac side by side, concluding that the comparison shows that the *Exodus* poet "is rather overfond of piling up epithets," "is given to puzzling or even embarrassing parenthesis," and is "unable to resist reminding us that God will intervene in the nick of time." The *Genesis A* version of the story, in contrast, "properly complete[s]" the poem, in Creed's estimation, and is "the high point and fine climax to a sometimes desultory

4 Francis Lee Utley, "The Flood Narrative in the Junius Manuscript and in Baltic Literature," in *Studies in Old English Literature in Honor of Arthur G. Brodeur*, ed. Stanley Greenfield (Eugene: University of Oregon Books, 1963), 208, 207, 209.

poem."[5] Thomas Ohlgren cites the Fall of the Angels repetitions in the manuscript as evidence of that story's broader cultural significance, although he chiefly focuses attention on the pictorial and textual elements in the *Genesis* section.[6]

Whatever the conclusions, each of these comparisons demonstrates that, for the manuscript compiler and for early medieval readers, two or more tellings of a single story, even a biblical one, need not be alike, even if within a thematically coherent book. Indeed, such repetition may have been expected, even commonplace, for both listening and seeing audiences, and especially useful for listening.[7] The repetition of language that appears as a stylistic feature in Old English poems might be understood in parallel to larger-scale, functional repetitions within the framework of a particular book.

While the Junius 11 repetitions of the angelic Fall may not have been surprising, why they are there and how the manuscript's compiler and its early medieval audiences might have perceived the repetitions remain in question, particularly if the manuscript was read as a sequentially purposeful unit, as Hall and others have proposed. The manuscript contains three substantial written narratives of the Fall of the Angels story in addition to two versions in the illustrations. Karkov sums up the potential power of successively reading this particular story, whether in words or images: "The result of this sequential repetition is the creation of an increasingly complex picture of hell and its inhabitants, the latter becoming more and more real and individualized with each telling. It also has the effect of reinforcing the ever-present threat of hell and damnation in the minds and eyes of the manuscript's readers."[8]

The three poetic versions are, though, quite distinct, despite their shared core events. The *Genesis A* version of the story firmly establishes God's power over the fallen angels (and, indeed, all creation), while the *Genesis B* version, in less vehement but no less powerful language,

---

5 Robert P. Creed, "The Art of the Singer: Three Old English Tellings of the Offering of Isaac," in *Old English Poetry: Fifteen Essays*, ed. Robert P. Creed (Providence, RI: Brown University Press, 1967), 73.

6 See Thomas H. Ohlgren, "Visual Language in the Old English Caedmonian Genesis," *Visible Language* 6 (1972): 253–76, especially 269*ff*.

7 "That the Fall of Lucifer is twice told [in the Genesis section of the manuscript] may have seemed no more surprising to a medieval reader than that the [biblical] Book of Genesis contains two accounts of Creation," as Hall remarked in arguing for the thematic unity of the poems in Junius 11. See Hall, "Old English Epic of Redemption," 194n34.

8 Karkov, *Text and Picture*, 67.

presents the Fall of the Angels in support of its emphasis on human obedience to God, and the third version, in *Christ and Satan*, turns the tale further outward, connecting the Fall of the Angels to how readers might live their own lives. Received cumulatively, the triple repetition moves from focusing on the central fact of divine retribution to focusing on the language of obedience and disobedience and, at the end, to focusing on punishment and redemption. The logic of such a sequence supports claims of a coherent compilation strategy for the manuscript, but the Fall of the Angels repetitions also reveal the potential for reading the poems rather like reading scripture, pericope by pericope. As texts both connected and independent, each reconstructs the angelic Fall in the service of a distinct and separable lesson, and each suggests a separate intellectual perspective on the story that a reader – and the poet – might have analytically developed with or without comparison to its companions in Junius 11 and similar texts.

More than a century ago, C. Abbetmeyer noted that a "single reading of the poetry left by the Anglo-Saxons shows that the Fall of the Angels was one of their favorite themes," a popularity that may in part be accounted for by the adaptability of the tale.[9] As the independent editions of each poem have made clear, each of the Junius 11 versions of the angelic Fall has a distinct textual background, and the three poetic Junius 11 versions alone point to what Remley describes as the high "probability [that] the compilation of the Junius collection was preceded by undocumented traditions of biblical versification that extended across three or more centuries" and that included apocryphal material in varying degrees.[10] Undocumented traditions, of course, are difficult to explore, but the Junius 11 poems themselves do suggest in their distinctness some of the diversity that those traditions might have included as well as the apparently comfortable coexistence of them.

In seeking out the biblical basis of the Old Testament Junius 11 poems, Remley finds that "few if any continuous sequences of lines in the narrative of *Genesis B* derive unambiguously from the Latin text of Genesis," while *Genesis A* derives "almost certainly" from "a

9 C. Abbetmeyer defines two major categories of the story, the "semi-dramatic" or "Plaints of Lucifer," where he places *Christ and Satan*, and the "epical," where he places the Genesis accounts – he omits reference to the illustration narrative – in *Old English Poetical Motives Derived from the Doctrine of Sin*, PhD diss., University of Minnesota (Minneapolis, H.W. Wilson, 1903). He cites instances in, as he lists them, *Genesis A, Genesis B*, Aldhelm's *De Lucifero* and *De Laudibus Virginum, Christ and Satan, Guðlac, Bi Manna Mode Vainglory, Andreas, Elene, Juliana, Prayer IV Resignation*, and *Solomon and Saturn*.

10 Remley, *Old English Biblical Verse*, 3.

continuous exemplar of Genesis I–XXII (or III–V and VIII–XXII) … [that] contain[ed] a mixed (Old Latin–Vulgate) text of Genesis."[11] The Fall of the Angels itself lacks narrative biblical basis, though it does have a long literary history, exemplified in the apocryphal texts of 1 and 2 Enoch. Other potential and more widely authoritative sources of knowledge of the story available in early medieval England include the widespread and well-developed commentaries on the angelic Fall by Augustine and Gregory, but nothing that presents a clear narrative model.[12]

Yet the angelic Fall in *Genesis A*, *Genesis B*, and *Christ and Satan* follows the same basic narrative sequence: description of the joys or powers of heaven preface the announcement of Lucifer's unwillingness to serve; this is followed by an account of the rebellion, one that focuses more on words than on actual battle, and then by God's judgment and the expulsion of the angels, which includes a view of life in hell.[13] Each poetic version, too, emphasizes pride as the chief factor in the Fall – seventeen repetitions of the words *oferhygd* or *ofermod*, or similar forms, appear in the poems – and each contrasts the joys of heaven to the pains of hell, with vivid descriptions of hell's harshness.[14] Within each poem, however, the Fall of the Angels story plays a different role and directs readers to different considerations. Together in Junius 11, the differences among the versions can make a case for both purposeful repetition and selective reading, and they suggest that neither was the default approach to reading a book in early medieval England.[15]

---

11 Ibid., 157, 148.

12 David F. Johnson, "The Fall of Lucifer in *Genesis A* and Two Anglo-Latin Royal Charters," *JEGP* 97 (1998): 500.

13 Ohlgren, "Visual Language," outlines the "fall-of-the-angels type-scene" as having "five narremic units" (269). In *Genesis A*, he defines them as follows: "(1) God and the blessed angels live harmoniously in heaven (ll. 1–18a); until (2) Lucifer, through his pride, establishes a rival throne in heaven (ll. 22a–34). God, upon hearing of the rebellion, (3) becomes angry and wrathful (ll. 34b–6a), (4) creates hell (ll. 36b–46b), and (5) drives the rebel host into hell (ll. 47a–76b)" (264). In the two subsequent repetitions of the story, "the five narremic units are [again] developed poetically, but with each iteration certain details are varied, expanded, or omitted in a manner that emphasizes different aspects of the same situation" (269).

14 Six forms of *oferhygd* appear in *Christ and Satan*, all in reference to the Fall of the Angels; three forms of it show up in the Fall of the Angels section of *Genesis A*, and in *Genesis B* are eight forms of either *oferhygd* or *ofermetto/mod*.

15 Fox, "Ælfric on the Creation and Fall of the Angels," has shown that Ælfric similarly used the Fall of the Angels story, connecting it to distinct contexts, changing parts of its chronology, and using different details of the story.

Genesis A: Authority

Genesis A opens the Junius 11 manuscript with the rather stern, didactic assertion that "us is riht micel" (for us it is very right) to praise God.[16] A brief outline of God's powers follows before the poem turns to the Fall of the Angels story, which begins at line 13 with a reference to "engla þreatas" (troops of angels) and continues until line 91, on manuscript page 5, after which the narrative turns to an account of Creation. Doane, in his edition of *Genesis A*, reads this Fall of the Angels story as part of an "'exordium,'" like that at the beginning of *Beowulf*, "an extended thematic introduction to the main narrative":

> It introduces the angelic material traditionally considered an integral part of the literal meaning of Genesis and suggests such established topics as the nature of the Godhead, time and eternity, sin and free will, etc. Traditionally, creation was considered to have taken place in two forms, the prior being that of the angels and the intelligible heavens (conventionally regarded as first in "time" as well by some commentators) and the subsequent that of the lower heavens and the earth. The exordium conforms broadly to the first part of this scheme.[17]

The preliminary placement of the angelic Fall neatly separates it from the rest of the poem, which more closely follows the biblical Genesis, a layout that Doane goes on to describe as "allow[ing] the poet to dispose of the non-biblical matter in one section at the beginning" of the poem.[18] Yet the initial location of the Fall of the Angels story – as well as the manuscript's returns to the topic – hardly implies that it was perceived as something that needed to be "disposed of" in relation to the biblical matter proper. While the *Genesis A* treatment of the tale is brief, running under seventy lines, it does not leave out what was, to judge from other versions of the story, essential matter. Nor does it lack specific connection to its immediate context, preceding the Creation paraphrase and beginning the manuscript as a whole. Instead, it uses the Fall of the Angels as the basis for a presentation of God as powerful and dangerous.

The language of *Genesis A* stresses divine power. In fairly gentle terms, the narrator early on announces that the angels demonstrated

---

16 This and all subsequent quotations of *Genesis A* are from Doane's revised edition. Translations throughout are my own unless otherwise noted.

17 Doane, *Genesis A*, 287.

18 Ibid.

nothing in heaven "nymþe riht and soþ" (except right and truth, 21b), before Lucifer, and his followers, "of siblufan / godes ahwurfon" (turned from natural love of God, 24b–25a).[19] More specifically, they turned from "blæd micel" (great glory, 14b) to "gielp micel" (a great boast, 25b), impelled by "oferhygd" (pride, 22b, 29). But a central interest in *Genesis A*'s account of the angelic Fall is God's anger, as the subsequent language of the poem makes very clear:[20]

- once "wearð yrre god" (god became angry, 34b), he "sceop þam werlogan / wræclicne ham" (shaped for those faith-breakers a wretched home, 36b–37a);
- he "heht" (commanded, 39a) the rebels to endure the sufferings of hell and "heht" (commanded, 44b) furthermore "weaxan witebrogan" (to increase dread torments, 45a);
- God "honda arærde" (raised his hand, 50b) against the unfaithful and "mod getwæfde" (took away their bravery, 53b);
- God "bælc forbigde" (abased their arrogance, 54a), then "he gebolgen wearð, / besloh synsceaþan" (he grew angry, deprived the sinful opponents, 54b–5a), "dreame benam" (took away joy, 56b), and "his torn gewræc" (avenged his anger, 58b), for their fall "hæfde styrne mod / gegremed grymme" (had fiercely enraged his stern spirit, 61a);
- God "grap on wraðe" his foes (gripped in anger, 61b) and "him on fæðm gebræc" (crushed them in his grasp, 62b);
- He "sceop þa and scyrede … / engla of heofnum, / wærleas werod" (then determined and separated the angels from heaven, a faithless troop, 65–7a) and "sende / … on langne sið" (sent them on a long journey, 67b–8).

Such power-centred constructions, and in such density – averaging about one every other line for about seventy-five lines – intensify the presence of God's power, which is central to the Fall of the Angels story as a whole and to the ensuing the account of Creation in *Genesis A* (and perhaps to the remaining poems in the manuscript), and they do so in more threatening terms than the Creation story alone might. While the narrator nowhere directly generalizes the lesson of the rebelling angels for his audience, it is unmistakably clear before the end of these

19 Doane, *Genesis A*, glosses *siblufan* as "natural love (as between kin)" – here a dative singular.

20 Abbetmeyer, *Old English Poetical Motives*, 15, similarly notes that "terms of war cluster around the expulsion," but this is generally true in all three Junius 11 examples, and he does not explore the matter further.

opening seventy lines that those who challenge God's power will fail, and miserably.

The authority with which the poem delivers this message is not at all diminished by the fact that the angelic Fall precedes the rest of the poem's biblical paraphrase proper. The poem implies an awareness of and connection to textual authority, whether directly biblical or not and whether always identifiable or not to modern or medieval readers. Twentieth-century critics noted that the *Genesis A* Fall of the Angels has foundations in hexameral literature, but it clearly does not rely so closely on that material for the Fall of the Angels story that a well-read early medieval reader would necessarily draw associational authority from it. Ambrose's authoritative *Hexameron,* for instance, passes quickly over the Fall of the Angels, interestingly but briefly noting that "the abyss" at the beginning of Creation was "a mass of deep waters" into which the fallen angels were cast after being forced "to enter into the bodies of swine."[21] Doane cites multiple parallels to Ælfric's "On the Old and New Testament" and *Exameron Anglice* as well as pointing out similarities to Augustine's *De civitate Dei,* but none of these fits neatly as the major influence on *Genesis A* or as a common likely augmentation to readers' perception of divine authority in the poem.

While the *Genesis A* poet as an educated writer was, in all likelihood, familiar with Augustine's or Augustinian interpretations of Genesis, the *Genesis A* formulation of events seems to be largely from the poet's own understanding. As David Johnson points out, *Genesis A* does not follow Augustine's organizational strategy or "Augustine's interpretation of Gen. 1: 3–4 – namely, the theory that would link the separation of light and darkness to the simultaneous creation and fall of the angels." Origen's view of the angelic Fall has much more in common with the account in *Genesis A,* in terms of its use of the replacement doctrine, but here, too, any connection is general rather than specific.[22] A reader in

21 *Hexameron* 32, 37–8: "abyssum multitudinem et profundum aquarum … ubi rogabant saluatorem daemonia, ne iuberet illis ut in abyssum irent. Sed qui docebat uoluntates daemoniorum non esse faciendas praecepit illis ut irent in porcos, porci autem se in stagnum aquarum praecipitauerunt, ut quod recusabant daemonia non euaderent, sed digno praecipitio demergerentur"; see Ambrose, *Hexameron: Sancti Ambrosii Opera,* part 1, *Exameron, De Paradiso, De Cain et Abel, De Noe, De Abraham, De Isaac, De bono mortis,* CSEL 32, ed. Carolus Schenkl (Vienna: F. Tempsky, 1896); see also Ambrose, *Ambrose: Hexameron, Paradise, Cain and Abel,* trans. John J. Savage, Fathers of the Church 42 (New York: Fathers of the Church, 1961). In Book 4.33 of the same work, Ambrose remarks in passing that Satan "may very well have fallen from heaven."

22 Johnson, "Fall of Lucifer," 506, 507, 511–2.

early medieval England who lingered over this poem may have had, though, other contexts from which to amplify or more fully understand the connection between the Fall of the Angels and authority.

The poem's attention to God's anger against his enemies and the power with which it shows him punishing them (as in "him on fæðm gebræc" in 62b) suggest the possibility of a political context as much as a historical-literary one, although pursuing such an argument would be assisted by knowing more about where and when the poem was written. Still, one persuasive intellectual context for the *Genesis A* Fall of the Angels story comes by way of two political documents. London, BL, Cotton Vespasian A.viii is King Edgar's refoundation charter for New Minster, Winchester, written c. 966 and attributed to Bishop Æthelwold.[23] The Peniarth Diploma is a Burton Abbey charter now in a thirteenth-century manuscript, Aberystwyth, National Library of Wales, Peniarth 390, that includes "every extant single-sheet pre-Conquest charter from the Burton Abbey archive."[24] Both of these Anglo-Latin charters include Fall of the Angels narratives, with parallels to the account in *Genesis A*. Johnson enumerates six important parallel aspects of these three narratives in the service of arguing that they demonstrate a distinctive, "shared cosmographical perspective" with foundations in Augustinian replacement doctrine. Johnson concludes that the overlaps point to a lost source that carried significant authority: "This 'text' could be a catechetical narrative concerning creation; it could conceivably be an elaborated liturgical text of some sort; or it could be as textually amorphous as an Anglo-Saxon preaching tradition. Whatever form this proposed source may have existed in, it presumably was an authoritative text from the point of view of the *Genesis A* poet and Bishop Æthelwold, one whose authority could be appropriated to their purposes."[25] Those purposes were not necessarily as different as the distinction between poem and charter might imply.

23 Alexander R. Rumble, *Property and Piety in Early Medieval Winchester: Documents Relating to the Topography of the Anglo-Saxon and Norman City and Its Minsters*, Winchester Studies 4, no. 3, Anglo-Saxon Minsters of Winchester (Oxford: Clarendon Press, 2002), 65–7. Rumble also provides an edition and translation of the entire document.

24 Nicholas Brooks, "A New Charter of King Edgar," in *Anglo-Saxon Myths: State and Church, 400–1066* (Rio Grande, OH: Hambledon Press, 2000), 221.

25 Johnson, "Fall of Lucifer," 512, 516–17, 519. Thomas A. Bredehoft, in *Authors, Audiences, and Old English Verse* (Toronto: University of Toronto Press, 2009), has suggested that Æthelwold may have had access not just to *Genesis A* but also to much other OE literature at Winchester, where King Alfred's library may have been housed after his death (128).

Other posited sources of textual authority for the Fall of the Angels in *Genesis A* are limited to discrete details, and most of these occur within the less directly political bounds of patristic reading. The most striking of these concerns the location of Lucifer's planned kingdom: "he on norðdæle / ham and heahsetl heofena rices / agan wolde" (he wished to possess a home and high seat in the northern part of the kingdom of heaven, 32b–4a). The basis for this geography may be Isaiah 14:13 or a patristic writer; Paul Salmon identified a parallel in Lactantius, and Thomas D. Hill argued that Jerome was a more likely source.[26] Both Johnson's hypothesized source and the possible connections to patristic material contribute to an image of a learned, careful poet, one who elsewhere in this poem quite diligently follows the biblical guide, as clearly demonstrated by Doane's presentation of *Genesis A* with the biblical book of Genesis in running parallel. While *Genesis A* may also draw on Irish texts and on other Old English or Latin literature, the poet – whether or not his readers concurred – appears on the whole to have perceived his work from the start as following, attesting to, and having substantial, easily recognized authority, even as the poem was also very much the creation of this individual poet.[27]

For sequential readers of Junius 11, the attention to authority in the *Genesis A* Fall of the Angels does not require external supplementary authority to establish divine power as the basis for understanding the manuscript's subsequent versions of the same story. The angry authority that God displays toward the rebellious angels in *Genesis A* might be understood as a counter to the seductive language of Satan in *Genesis B* and as a further warning for the consequences emphasized in *Christ and Satan*. Other than in the sequence of its contents, the manuscript itself offers no such explicit connection across its sections, and the God of *Genesis A* is powerful in isolation or in parallel with the punishment of Satan in *Christ and Satan*. None of the Junius 11 versions of the Fall of the Angels requires accompaniment by the others, and none is essential

26 See Paul Salmon, "The Site of Lucifer's Throne," *Anglia* 81 (1963): 118–23; and Thomas D. Hill, "Some Remarks on the Site of Lucifer's Throne," *Anglia* 87 (1969): 303–11.

27 Other inclusions in *GenA* have been identified, such as the names of Noah's wives and sons, listed in the *Prose Solomon and Saturn* and in *Genesis A* (lines 1543–8), which can be traced to Irish sources. See James E. Cross and Thomas D. Hill, *The Prose Solomon and Saturn and Adrian and Ritheus* (Toronto: University of Toronto Press, 1982), 86–7; and C.D. Wright, "Hiberno-Latin and Irish-Influenced Biblical Commentaries, Florilegia, and Homily Collections," in *Sources of Anglo-Saxon Literary Culture: A Trial Version*, ed. F.M. Biggs, T.D. Hill, and P.E. Szarmach (Binghamton, NY: CEMERS, 1990), 87–123.

to sequential coherence across the manuscript. Even the images that accompany much of the *Genesis* section of the manuscript both benefit from and, at the same time, do not require the text that surrounds them.

Illustrations: Cause and Effect

The significant status of the *Genesis A* Fall of the Angels story is underscored by the illustrations in its midst, but the illustrated version, like subsequent poetic tellings of the tale, can also be read on its own – or, rather, the illustrated versions can be read on their own since repetition occurs here, too.[28] In a sequential reading of the illustrations alone, an early medieval reader of Junius 11, as it now stands, would encounter an initial emphasis on authority that corresponds well – but not necessarily – to *Genesis A*. Following the manuscript's prefatory image of God in majesty appears, on the book's second page, a half-page image of God and five angels, one of whom is the focus of God's attention. Ohlgren reads the image as God "seated on a cushioned throne and flanked by two seraphim, addressed by a small, nimbed angel (Lucifer), who has announced his rebellion in heaven."[29] While this seems likely to be the case, the marginal inscription offers only "hælendes hehseld" (the lord's high hall), and the image suggests a moment of community before the angels actually fall. From his seat, however, God points with his right hand toward the largest of the standing angelic figures, and the difference in the positioning of the figures as well as in God's gesture clearly conveys an assertion of authority that functions as the first response to Lucifer's challenge.[30]

A full-page, multi-register drawing on page 3, with distinctly divided groups of figures, quickly continues the story and, reading from top to bottom, tells the events that followed that moment of community. The sequence includes images of Lucifer, crowned and surrounded by his supporters, and also a depiction of God "hold[ing] three spears in [his] raised right arm." Both present cause for the succeeding images, most striking of which is the hellmouth, which occupies the lower centre of

---

28 See the discussion by Thomas H. Ohlgren of the repetitions of the Fall of the Angels episode in text and image in "The Illustrations of the Cædmonian Genesis: Literary Criticism through Art," *Medievalia et Humanistica: Studies in Medieval and Renaissance Culture*, n.s. 3 (1972): 209; see also Ohlgren, "Visual Language," 269–71.

29 The description is from Thomas H. Ohlgren, ed. and comp., *Anglo-Saxon Textual Illustration: Photographs of Sixteen Manuscripts with Descriptions and Index* (Kalamazoo, MI: Medieval Institute Publications, 1992), 88.

30 See Karkov's discussion of the pointing finger, *Text and Picture*, 42–4.

the page. In the bottom register is shown, as Ohlgren concisely describes it, the effect of Lucifer's kingly action and God's power: "Lucifer, his angelic allies, and the broken remains of his throne are shown falling downwards into hell. At the bottom, Lucifer, now Satan, with flaming hair and clawed hands and feet, lies bound in the jaws of hell."[31] Like the *Genesis A* text, all the page's images focus on power, both Lucifer's vision of it for himself and God's fearsome response, something reiterated in quick succession in the four subsequent illustrations. Illustrations on pages 6 and 7 show God in positions of power, overlooking Creation, and those on pages 9 and 10 (after an unnumbered stub right before page 9) depict him as the superior instructor to Adam and Eve. The run of God-as-superior images is then capped by the depiction on page 11 of God in majesty, distinctively with filled-in colour, above and separate from the admiring Adam and Eve in the abundant garden. The visual presentation of the Fall of the Angels, though vivid, is thus surrounded and quickly outnumbered by images of God's power in its creative rather than its punitive form. The illustrations on their own, then, present a concise and effective but less enduring view of angry authority than does the *Genesis A* text.

Like and presumably because of the poetic contents of Junius 11, the illustrations return to the Fall of the Angels after the initial presentation and with a different emphasis. The shift suggests, in particular, that the illustrator read the surrounding text, but a reader of the (incomplete) completed manuscript can continue to read the illustrations on their own or in conjunction with the text; both convey the sequence of events. Within *Genesis B*, on page 16, one more illustration of the Fall appears, followed on page 17 by an image of the new order, with God enthroned above the now entirely walled-off fallen angels. The page 16 illustration repeats elements in the page 3 Fall of the Angels image: both show a very similar-looking hellmouth into which the damned angels are falling, although, on page 16, Satan lies enchained below the hellmouth, rather than cradled in it, as on page 3. The visual overlap serves as an explanatory reminder, repeating and emphasizing the fallen angels' punishment, this time with a cause-and-effect role that does not centre so directly on God's power.

In this second visual account of the angelic Fall, three images of hell occur in quick succession, on pages 16, 17, and 20 – with yet one more showing up a bit later, on page 36. The page 20 illustration is full page, divided by the enclosure of hell, which occupies the lower register. The

31 Ohlgren, *Anglo-Saxon Textual Illustration*, 89.

top half of the page shows Eve listening to the serpent as well as Adam and Eve pointing to a tree. The upper and lower registers – hell and earth – are straddled by a devil rising through a dark door from hell. As the only two pieces in the illustration that are not in outline form, the filled-in anchor for the fetters on Satan's wrists clearly corresponds to the door from hell through which his emissary reaches the garden, once again pointing to cause and effect: Satan's fall leads to the temptation in Paradise. This series of depictions of hell and Satan, following closely on the page 16 depiction of the angelic Fall itself, underscores not just the existence of hell but also its fundamental relationship to human events, something elaborated upon by the surrounding text (*Genesis B*) as well as by *Christ and Satan.*

While a reader's understanding of the Junius 11 illustrations, in sequence or separately, does not require elaboration from the poems, each is enriched by the other, and the illustrations themselves present a narrative that employs repeated elements and visual similarities to connect clearly the initial Fall to its first human implications. The visual narratives offer their own accounts of the Fall of the Angels, stressing cause and effect, and at the same time visually underscore and communicate with particular elements of the surrounding text.

Genesis B: Words

Genesis B begins on page 13 of Junius 11, alongside a half-page image of Eve and Adam in the garden, which effectively announces the human focus of the immediately ensuing pages. (Adam and Eve also appear in earlier illustrations, on pages 9, 10, and 11, but always accompanied by God; on page 13, they are first shown alone in the garden – God is a visually reduced, encircled, and more distant presence at the top of the scene.) For anyone reading sequentially in the manuscript, the Fall of the Angels in *Genesis A* provides a recent guide to events and theological import against which to understand the heroic speech of Satan, and understanding the angels' rebellion and Fall in the history of Creation better prepares readers to explore the significance of those events in relation to human history. They have, in particular, God's ire and retribution to guide their reactions to the rebelling angels' proud words and to the temptation of Adam and Eve that follows. *Genesis B* deals at more length with the circumstances of the Fall than does *Genesis A,* and it lays less direct emphasis on the overwhelming power of God. Read separately or in its interpolated presence within *Genesis A, Genesis B* shows marked interest in reiterative explanation and example. God's anger, the creation of hell, and the fall of the angels into it are, notes Ohlgren, "repeated in variation eight times in 42 lines. ... [But] the poet ... never repeats himself in exactly the same manner; each iteration emphasizes new details of different aspects of the same scene."[32] Within these elements, the character of Satan and, more specifically, Satan's words, rather than God's powerful anger, take centre stage.

References to Lucifer's skills with speech do appear in *Genesis A*, but in *Genesis B*, they abound, and they provoke.[33] The *Genesis B* narrator specifically defines Lucifer's duties as centred on words: "lof sceolde he drihtnes wyrcean, / dyran sceolde he his dreamas on heofonum and sceolde his drihtne þancian" (he was obliged to work praise of his lord, he was obliged to hold dear his joys in heaven and obliged to give thanks for his lord, 256b–7).[34] But Lucifer "sohte hetespræce / gylpword" (sought hate-speech, boasting words, 263b), as the abundant "he cwæð" phrases make clear.[35] "Feala worda gespæc / se engel ofermodes" (the proud angel spoke many words, 271b–2a) as he "þohte þurh his anes cræft" (thought through his own skill, 272b) how to build his own, higher throne.

Dramatically, the poem's audience gains access to the devil's words themselves or, at least, the narrator's account of them. The significance of words is itself acknowledged by Lucifer in his first, heroic speech, one that encourages his followers to rebel; Lucifer here asserts that he may use words as he wishes – he has no "'oleccan awiht þurfe / gode'" (need to flatter God at all, 290b–1a). Self-deceiving they may be, but words clearly have great power and, in turn, significant

32 Ohlgren, "Visual Language," 269.

33 In *Genesis A*, we hear that, with words, Lucifer "unræd ongan ærest fremman, / wefan and weccean" (first began to carry out evil council, to weave and to animate his followers, 30–2a). He "hæfdon gielp micel" (made a great boast, 25b); he "worde cwæð, / niþes ofþyrsted" (spoke words, thirsted for strife, 31–2a). And the rebelling angels "cwædon þæt heo rice, reðemode, / agan woldan" (said, furious in spirit, that they would possess that kingdom, 47–8a).

34 Quotations of *Genesis B* throughout are from A.N. Doane, ed., *The Saxon Genesis* (Madison: University of Wisconsin Press, 1991). Translations are my own unless otherwise indicated.

35 He "cwæð þæt his lice wære leoht and scene" (said that his body was bright and shining, 265). He "cwæð þæt hine his hige speonne" (said this his mind/heart persuaded/enticed him, 274b), "cwæð him tweo þuhte / þæt he gode wolde geongra weorðan" (said that it seemed doubtful to him that he would be God's servant, 276b–7). He even seems to speak to himself: He could not "æt his hige findan / þæt he gode wolde geongerdome" (in his mind find that he would serve God). Instead, "þuhte him sylfum / þæt he" (he thought to himself that he was greater than God, 266b–71a).

consequences. God's reaction comes in response to hearing of Lucifer's claims, not to seeing some action.[36] God hears, for instance, that Lucifer "spræc healic word" (spoke lofty words, 294b), and God reacts not just with expulsion, but with a word change: God "sceop him naman siððan" (gave him afterwards a name, 343b): he changes Lucifer's defining word to *Satan*. Yet cast into hell, Satan memorably still refuses to be silent: "þa spræc se ofermoda cyning" (then spoke the proud king, 338a), "he þa worde cwæð" (he said these words, 355b); "Satan maðelode sorgiende spræc" (Satan spoke, sorrowing said, 347). His speech in hell, still rebellious, extends for eighty-five lines (356–441) and ends with an offer to his followers that makes even plainer the power of language: "'Sittan læte ic hine wið me sylfne swa hwa swa þæt secgan cymeð / on þas hatan helle þæt hie hoefoncyninges / unwurðlice wordum and dædum / lare'" (I will let sit with me whoever in this hot hell comes to say that they (Eve and Adam) unworthily in word and deed [have forsaken?] God's teaching, 438–41).[37] As Doane notes, Satan's rebellion "was a vocal gesture only," and, in hell, Satan's words – boasts, then threats, then persuasion – continue to provide his only real power.[38]

In summary form but again in direct discourse, the story of the angels' Fall appears yet once more in *Genesis B* after the lengthier, dramatic account of the story, when the tempter rejoices after Adam and Eve have literally swallowed the devil's argument and, correspondingly, when the focus of their own words changes (733b–65a). The tempter tries to retell the tale with triumph, having just succeeded in his corrupting task. He casts Adam and Eve into the fallen angels' role – "'hie to helle sculon / on þone sweartan sið'" (they must [go] to hell on that dark journey, 732b–3a) – and sets their future in parallel to his own version of prior events: "'unc gegenge ne wæs / þæt wit him on þegnscipe þeowian wolden. / forþon unc waldend wearð wrað on mode, / on hyge hearde and us on helle bedraf'" (for us it was not appointed that

36 "þa hit se allwalda eall gehyrde" (292). He hears Lucifer "ofermede micel / ahebban" (raise up great pride, 293).

37 The last line on the page (p. 22) ends with the word "lare," although the clause then has no verb. Doane identifies a loss of two leaves and perhaps 250 lines here (277).

38 Doane, *Saxon Genesis*, 133. Doane, 134, points out, too, that the description of Satan's enchainment in hell is entirely in Satan's own words: "It is not the narrator who fashions the means of bondage but Satan himself," and "throughout this speech Satan reveals his egotistic isolation by his constant use of singular pronouns – he is not part of a rout of devils or society alone."

we wished to serve him in thaneship. Therefore our lord became angry in mind, hard in thought, and drove us into hell, 743b–6).[39]

While the tempter's words do not ultimately control the situation, this late return to his voice once more makes vivid the power of language and its ability to deceive, including oneself. The narrative delays God's reaction to the successful temptation, allowing the tempter's words to linger and thereby directing reaction to Adam and Eve's realization of their situation. They mourn and fear, expecting exactly what the tempter has outlined. Indeed, contradiction of the tempter's words does not come until *Genesis A* resumes and all devils are silenced. God speaks his punishment to Satan, but *Genesis A* allows no response from the angel-turned-snake. The shift, across poems but with narrative continuity, distinctly limits the authority of demonic speech. The fallen angels' extensive speeches in *Genesis B* focus attention on the connection between the human and the angelic Fall and the role of persuasive language in both, in turn underscoring the need for obedience to the divine Word even in the face of persistent, seductive speech from other sources. When the manuscript returns to *Genesis A*, the narrative takes up with God's voice again, effectively reasserting divine authority and obedience to it.

Such distinctions in narrative development yield much more than a simple repetition in the manuscript's first and second versions of the Fall of the Angels story, which moves from a focus on power to a focus on language and from emphasis on Creation to emphasis on an explanatory antecedent to the human Fall. As Doane describes it, the "*Genesis A* poet mythologizes the Fall of the Angels as battle. In *Genesis B* it is seen inwardly, as an individual intellectual act, a psychological state."[40] The two tellings together demonstrate the story's malleability, even while they make clear its potential independence, a status aided by the fact that the story has so little direct presence in the Bible.

39 See Ohlgren, "Visual Language," 270–3, for a discussion of the repetition of the Fall of the Angels in the illustrations and, in particular, the ways in which the p. 36 two-tiered drawing "depicts two fallen spiritual states, one human and the other demonic," with visual contrast in the possibility of salvation suggested by showing Adam and Eve already repentant.

40 Doane, *Saxon Genesis*, 121. Doane also points out that the *Genesis A* Fall of the Angels is squarely in the hexameral tradition, while the *Genesis B* version is not: "In *Genesis A*, following the tradition of Genesis commentary going back to Augustine's *De Genesi ad litteram* and before, the Fall of the Angels is treated … as part of the hexameral prelude to the verse-by-verse running commentary on the text proper. In *Genesis B*, the Fall of the Angels is treated not hexamerally, but theologically, the two Falls being causally and typologically linked" (*Saxon Genesis*, 116).

In the context of Junius 11, *Genesis A* can be read as a template, both narrative and theological, for *Genesis B*, especially for its direct-discourse elaborations. God's power governs both the angelic Fall and the Creation; disobedience, whether by angels or by Eve and Adam, leads to a fall. A reader approaching the manuscript selectively, however, could have come away with a view of the angelic Fall as primarily a lesson in God's power and stern authority or as primarily a cautionary example of how temptation works. Both readings serve well their immediate biblical context. The Bible's book of Genesis, in covering both Creation and human Fall, lends itself to the dual presence of the story of the Fall of the Angels. Its role in chronology and in an explanation of events has long been noted; Bernhard ten Brink, in 1883, pointed out that "in other mediæval renderings of *Genesis*, the revolt of the angels is twice related."[41] The early fourteenth-century (CCCC 444) poetic paraphrase known as *Genesis and Exodus*, for instance, includes two versions of the revolt, although one comes after the Creation narrative and the other comes after the creation of Eve and the Institution of the Sabbath.[42] Just how common multiple use of the story within medieval renditions of Genesis was we cannot know with certainty, but its status as common material that was not pinned into position in the Vulgate Genesis makes the angelic Fall prime for varied inclusion, for adaptation to suit moralizing goals as well as narrative desires. The distinction between the implied line of textual authority in *Genesis A* and what appears to be the murkier intellectual lineage of *Genesis B* attests to the story's particular narrative flexibility.

Genesis B ranks among surviving Old English biblical poems as one of the most unusual, and the difficulty that scholars have had in linking it to a definite source or sources may indicate that, even for audiences in early medieval England, the narrative was strikingly distinctive. Remley, following Timmer's assessment some fifty years earlier, distinguishes the poem for its adaptation of biblical material and as a text full of "peculiar features."[43] Indeed, despite an abundance of plausible speculation, relatively little progress has been made on identifying any

41 Bernhard ten Brink, *Early English Literature*, trans. Horace M. Kennedy (New York, 1883), 41n2.

42 This ME repetition of the Fall of the Angels also includes this overlap with the Junius versions: "'Min fliȝt,' he seide, 'ic wile up-taken / Min sete norð on heuene maken'" (277–8); see James H. Morey, *Book and Verse: A Guide to Middle English Biblical Literature* (Urbana: University of Illinois Press, 2000), 138.

43 Timmer, *Later Genesis*, 47; Remley, *Old English Biblical Verse*, 149.

specific context for the production of the poem.[44] Lost literary context can, of course, never be ruled out, nor should a poet's individual inventiveness be underestimated, but the poem has some textual affinities that suggest its writer's familiarity with apocryphal and perhaps Irish literature. This, in turn, suggests that the narrative might have seemed less biblical and Latinate – and yet perhaps more familiar – to early audiences.

The apocryphal literature on the Fall of Humanity often includes reference to the Fall of the Angels, and the Adambooks, in particular, include similarities to *Genesis B*. Five early lives of Adam, plus one fragmentary version, survive; these are designated the "primary Adam books" by scholars such as Michael Stone.[45] Among these, the Latin *Vita Adam et Evae*, a translation from a lost Greek text, enjoyed wide popularity in the Middle Ages.[46] Such texts offer enough parallels to *Genesis B* to support the idea of authorial familiarity, directly or indirectly, with them, but the *Vita Adam et Evae* account of the Fall of the Angels comes within the narrative of Adam's and Eve's penance, when Satan complains to Adam that he caused the angels' Fall. Adam coexists with Lucifer, whose fall from heaven comes because the rebellious angels refuse to worship man. In turn, Satan attacks Adam and Eve because they caused his fall.[47]

Such a narrative differs notably from *Genesis B* in both its positioning of Satan's fall after the establishment of humans in Paradise and its assertion of Adam's role in the angelic loss. Brian Murdoch connects the *Genesis B* Fall of the Angels instead with another apocryphal text, Enoch 2, also known as *The Book of the Secrets of Enoch*, in which "Lucifer falls simply through *superbia*. The form taken by his arrogance is shaped by the biblical death-song to the king of Babylon in Isaiah xiv, and the references to that king's fall are linked with a diabolical premundane attack on God. With this is linked another important Genesis-legend, the so-called replacement doctrine, according to which man is created in order to make up the tenth choir of angels, those that fell with

44 Remley, *Old English Biblical Verse*, e.g., remarks that "the possibility that the extant fragment (or, rather, its lost Old Saxon model) owes a special debt to otherwise unrecorded traditions of Germanic alliterative verse … cannot be ruled out" (154, 151).

45 Michael E. Stone, *A History of the Literature of Adam and Eve*, Society of Biblical Literature: Early Judaism and Its Literature 3 (Atlanta, GA: Scholars Press, 1992), 4.

46 Ibid., 14–30 and ch. 4.

47 See Brian O. Murdoch, *The Irish Adam and Eve Story from Saltair na Rann*, vol. 2, *Commentary* (Dublin: Dublin Institute for Advanced Studies, 1976), 16.

Lucifer."[48] While theologically *The Book of the Secrets of Enoch* offers the closer model, stylistically the Adambooks have more in common with the *Genesis B* angelic Fall. God himself recounts the rebellion and punishment of the angels, in sum and with brevity, in the Enoch narrative. The dramatic Satan of the *Vita*, who tells his own tale (or, at least, a version of it), sounds more akin to the Satan of *Genesis B*, as when, "with a heavy sigh," he laments, "'I was hurled out of the presence of God and banished from the company of angels.'"[49]

In associating *Genesis B* with the Adambooks and other apocryphal literature, we can also connect it to other insular, vernacular texts that draw on the same traditions and on authority markedly different from those that contribute to *Genesis A*.[50] Although also of later date than seems likely for *Genesis B*, the Irish *Saltair na Rann*, a poem that may have been composed in the late tenth century, echoes aspects of the Adambooks and, particularly in the character of the devil, *Genesis B*.[51] Both the Irish and the English narratives preface the human Fall with an account of the Fall of the Angels, and, in each, the rebelling angel uses his lively voice to declare himself high king. Satan in *Genesis B* announces that "'I mæg hyra hearra wesan, / rædan on þis rice'" (I can be their lord, rule in this kingdom, 288b–9a) and "'Ic hæbbe geweald micel / to gyrwanne godlecran stol, / hearran on heofne'" (I have great power to prepare a better throne, higher in heaven, 280b–2a), while in *Saltair na Rann* he asserts, "'bam ri reil os cach caingin. ... biam tigerna os cech drung, / ni bía rí aile húasum'" (I will be a bright king above every dispute. ... I will be a king over every people, there will be no other king above me, 851–6). Of the two motivations ascribed to Lucifer in the apocryphal examples, *Saltair na Rann*, unlike *Genesis B*, follows the Adambooks model: Lucifer rebels after God commands him, "'Tabair úait airmitiu iar sreith / do Adom, dom chomdelbaid'" (Give reverence accordingly to Adam, to the one shaped like me, *SR* 837–8). Lucifer's refusal to do so precipitates his fall, and he takes with him the

48 Ibid.

49 R.H. Charles, ed., "Vita Adae et Evae," in *The Apocrypha and Pseudepigrapha of the Old Testament in English*, vol. 2, *Pseudepigrapha* (Oxford University Press, 1913), 137.

50 Timmer, *Later Genesis*, distinguishes the narrative of *Genesis B* from other Adam and Eve stories: "We know what the mediaeval poems about the Fall of Man are like: none of them is strikingly emotional or dramatic. We also know that the prose stories in Latin and Greek are not emotional or dramatic" (48).

51 See Gearóid MacEóin, "Observations on *Saltair na Rann*," *Zeitschrift fur Celtische Philologie* 39 (1982): 1–28; and David Greene and Fergus Kelly, eds. and trans., *The Irish Adam and Eve Story from Saltair na Rann*, vol. 1, *Text and Translation* (Dublin: Dublin Institute for Advanced Studies, 1976).

"'airbri imdai archangel'" (many bands of archangels, 836) that God before granted him.

Despite the significant difference in theological history, both *Saltair na Rann* and *Genesis B* belong to the same general family, giving vernacular, dramatic accounts of the Fall of the Angels and the Fall of Humanity. The writers of both narratives seem familiar with apocryphal literature on the angelic Fall and were working in related styles and traditions that were distinct from the flavour of *Genesis A* and would presumably have been recognized as such by well-read early audiences.[52]

The similarities between *Genesis B* and *Saltair na Rann* may be due to familiarity with the same or similar sources or perhaps even to shared actual sources, or simply a more general intellectual tradition of which too few examples survive.[53] That tradition may have been Irish, an idea that Doane, for instance, supplements with the proposal that apocrypha such as the *Book of the Secrets of Enoch* and *The Gospel of Bartholomew* might have been known to the *Genesis B* poet, "possibly through Irish sources."[54] Nothing has yet been discovered, however, to substantiate such a connection.[55] And while parallels between Avitus's poem on the Fall and *Genesis B* have been well explored, Calder and Allen's assessment of its influence and others still sums up the indefinite nature of the poem's known literary context: "In short, Evans' claim that the poet depended upon a tissue of reminiscences from the Christian Latin poets is no more reasonable than Woolf's insistence on a lost apocryphal source. Although the Latin poets were known to some of the insular and continental Saxons, we cannot be sure whether they were known to the Old Saxon poet or his translator."[56]

Genesis B sits comfortably in the literary tradition of apocryphal Adam and Eve literature but has no identified single precursor. It incorporates

52 Doane, *Saxon Genesis*, 96. For an overview of Adam and Eve literature, see Stone's *History of the Literature of Adam and Eve*.

53 Michael Benskin and Brian Murdoch, "The Literary Tradition of Genesis," *NM* 76 (1975): 395.

54 Doane, *Saxon Genesis*, 98n6. Doane notes, too, that in the Gospel of Bartholomew is "Satan bound, making a speech closely resembling GenB 368ff, [and] send[ing] out emissaries" (98).

55 Benskin and Murdoch, e.g., have suggested that *Genesis B* might display Irish influences, or textual connections that came through Irish sources, although J.M. Evans, *Paradise Lost and the Genesis Tradition* (Oxford: Clarendon Press, 1968), does point out that "a fragment of the Book of Enoch has been found in a non-Irish insular manuscript of the eighth century, and a Vita Adam is listed in a catalogue of the monastic library of Regensburg dated A.D. 994" (8).

56 D.G. Calder and M.J.B. Allen, *Sources and Analogues of Old English Poetry: The Major Latin Texts in Translation* (Cambridge: D.S. Brewer, 1976), 5.

material found in the works of such standard patristic authors as Gregory I and Ambrose, and the poet or translator may have been familiar with other Old English poetry – in particular, with *Andreas*, *Daniel*, and *Christ and Satan* – although the proposed dates of composition for these poems are disputed and *Genesis B* seems likely to predate at least some of them.[57] *Genesis A*, in contrast, rests as a whole on one widely known source, the Bible, and its Fall of the Angels narrative seems to draw primarily on some other authoritative source. Whatever contexts contributed to their composition, these poems and their accounts of the Fall of the Angels possess individual perspective and presentation. Any moderately skilful reader of English ca. 1000 would, in turn, undoubtedly have recognized and understood distinct functions and imports for these two Fall of the Angels narratives.

Christ and Satan: Consequences

The adaptability of biblical narrative is perhaps made clearest in Junius 11 by the recurrence of the Fall of the Angels story outside the *Genesis* poems. The story makes its sequentially final appearance in *Christ and Satan*, the section that ends the manuscript and that in its Christocentrism is both sharply distinct from *Genesis* and typologically connected to it. The narrative units within *Christ and Satan* offer a rather homiletic overview of the actions of divine and once divine figures at three significant moments in Christian history: first, the Fall of the Angels; then the harrowing of hell and the ensuing resurrection, ascension, and anticipated last judgment; and, finally, a chronologically out-of-place account of Christ's temptation in the wilderness.[58] The Christological

57 Timmer, *Later Genesis*, 39. Thomas D. Hill ties Gregory the Great's *Moralia in Iob* to *Genesis B* in "Satan's Injured Innocence in *Genesis B*, 360–2, 390–2: A Gregorian Source," *English Studies* 65 (1984): 289–90; and Doane puts Satan's speech in parallel with a passage in Ambrose's *De Paradiso liber unus* 12.54. The lines "engelcynne ... tene getrimede" (246–8), which Doane, *Saxon Genesis*, 257, calls a "familiar medieval notion, from Pseudo-Dionysius," and which Salmon surveys the widely attested occurences of, also suggest patristic sources. See also Paul Salmon, "Die zehnte Engelchor in deutschen Dichtungen und Predigten des Mittelalters," *Euphorion* 57 (1963): 118–23.

58 The relationships among these three pieces have been variously and extensively explained as, e.g., a rhetorical display of the "incommensurate might of God"; "a demonstrat[ion of the] various aspects of Christ's power in the context of a comparison of the forces of good and evil"; a "celebration" of "Christ's long-ago victories on the planes of heaven, hell and earth"; an exemplum–exhortation; and a comparison between Christ, who abases himself and exalts humanity, and Satan, who exalts himself and earns condemnation. See, e.g., Bernard F. Huppé, *Doctrine*

context of the angelic Fall narrative in *Christ and Satan* foreshadows what may have been commonplace, to judge from later examples: in Middle English biblical narrative, as James Morey surveys it, "the Fall of the Angels is a necessary preliminary to the Passion of Christ."[59]

The Fall of the Angels tale in *Christ and Satan* focuses on existence after the Fall, mostly by way of Satan's speeches, but this time, unlike *Genesis B*, they are speeches of lament that dwell on the contrasts between hell and lost heaven.[60] Christ's role is emphasized, for the angels here rebel against Christ rather than God, and their fall from heaven is identified as the work of Christ: "Crist heo afirde, / dreamum bedelde" (Christ removed them, deprived them of joys, 67b–8a).[61] The poem's subsequent yoking of Satan's fall to Christ's redemptive acts caps the sequence begun with *Genesis A*: the first version of the Fall of the Angels story conveys the heart of the story, God's power; the second emphasizes obedience in word and deed to that power; the third, dwelling on suffering (both hopeless and hopeful), leaves readers with

---

and Poetry: Augustine's Influence on Old English Poetry (New York: State University of New York Press, 1959), 227; Constance D. Harsh, "*Christ and Satan*: The Measured Power of Christ," *NM* 90 (1989): 244; Judith N. Garde, "Junius Liber II: A Christ–Satan Retrospective; the Second Adam," in *Old English Poetry in Medieval Christian Perspective: A Doctrinal Approach*, ed. Judith N. Garde (Cambridge: D.S. Brewer, 1991), 49; as well as Charles R. Sleeth's chapter, "The Work and the Question of Its Unity," in his *Studies in Christ and Satan* (Toronto: Toronto University Press, 1982), 3–26.

59 Morey, *Book and Verse*, 2. Morey's list of ME accounts of the Fall of the Angels story includes *Fall and Passion*, *Trinity Poem on Biblical History*, Grosseteste's *Chateau d'Amour*, *Cursor Mundi* [Abbetmeyer, *Poetical Motives*, 20, thought it is "almost certain that the author knew GenB"], *The Mirour of Mans Saluacioune*, *Life of Adam and Eve*, *Canticum de Creatione*, William of Shoreham's *On the Trinity, Creation, the Existence of Evil, Devils, Adam and Eve*, etc., *Genesis and Exodus* [here definitely the Fall is repeated; Morey, *Book and Verse*, 138, says ll. 35–212 include Fall of the Angels, after "Almanac of six-day creation with relevant lore"; then ll. 269–338 are devoted to "Fall of Lucifer" and "Temptation, Fall, Curses, Expulsion"], *Cleanness*, *Pepysian Gospel Harmony*, *The Devil's Parlament*, *Book to a Mother*, *Northern Homily Cycle*, *Prose Version of Epistles, Acts, Matthew*.

60 Comparison of the presentation of Satan in *Genesis B* and *Christ and Satan* has a long history, addressed by Rosemary Woolf, "The Devil in Old English Poetry," *RES*, n.s. 4 (1953): 1–12; and Peter Dendle, *Satan Unbound: The Devil in Old English Narrative Literature* (Toronto: University of Toronto Press, 2001), especially chap. 3, "The Role of the Devil."

61 Thomas D. Hill, "The Fall of Satan in the Old English *Christ and Satan*," *JEGP* 76 (1977): 315–25, discusses the poem's focus on Christ and a potential explanation for it. All my quotations from *Christ and Satan* are from George Philip Krapp, ed., *The Junius Manuscript*, ASPR 1 (New York: Columbia University Press, 1931); translations unless otherwise indicated are my own.

lessons of damnation and redemption and advice for applying those lessons in their own lives.

As in *Genesis A* and *B*, the recognition of divine power and the role of speech in the Fall figure prominently in *Christ and Satan*, despite Satan's attempts to obscure the truth by asserting, for instance, that he is the father of Christ. By the end of the poem, Satan's lies are fully exposed and punished, and Christ's powers are, correspondingly, made clear.[62] But the angelic Fall, which fills more lines here (379) than in the two *Genesis* accounts combined, plays a more contrastive role, and a more original one.[63] Modern perception of the poem as strikingly original extends at least as far back as Merrel Dare Clubb's 1925 edition, where he asserts, "There is little evidence that the poet in [the Fall of the Angels section] was drawing from Latin documents, either Scriptural, apocryphal, or patristic."[64] Both *Genesis A* and *Genesis B* include ideas found in the writings of Gregory I, and Gregory's delineation of time in relation to the fallen angels illuminates a central distinction between the *Genesis* accounts and the one in *Christ and Satan*, as Rosemary Woolf succinctly explains:

> At the beginning, before [Satan] has been damned for innumerable centuries, he deludes himself, as in *Genesis B*, that he will be happier if he can bring about the downfall of man, but in the poems [such as *Christ and Satan*] which describe him after the coming of Christ, that is in the second period defined by Gregory I, no justification for his actions is suggested. The devil tempts because it is his nature to tempt. There is no possibility of any relief from torment.[65]

Overall, parallels in phrasing between *Christ and Satan* and the account of the Fall of the Angels in the other Junius poems are minimal, a fact that contributes to the separateness of this final section of the manuscript.[66]

62 Christ assigns Satan the task of measuring hell – and in a wonderful detail, he tells him to complete the task in two hours (see line 709).

63 The Fall of the Angels in *GenA* is about 77 lines, in *GenB* about 200; in *Christ and Satan*, more than 365.

64 Merrel Dare Clubb, ed., *Christ and Satan* (New Haven, CT: Yale University Press, 1925), xxxii. Hall, "Old English Epic of Redemption," notes that "The Lament [of the Fallen Angels (1–364) in *Christ and Satan*] serves an important role in the manuscript, but as an 'event' the material lacks a parallel in the two homilists' commentary on this portion of sacred history. In treating of the coming of Christ neither Augustine nor Wulfstan refers to Lucifer's crime and punishment. The *themes* of the lament, however, have close parallels in the final admonitions of the homilists" (204n62).

65 Woolf, "Devil in Old English Poetry," 6.

66 Emphasizing the distinction of *Christ and Satan* in relation to the manuscript's other poems, Sleeth asserts that the verbal singularity of *Christ and Satan* "cannot be more

The distinctiveness of *Christ and Satan* is confirmed by the scholarship over the years that has attempted to identify the poet's reading background and, by extension, the literary contexts that audiences in early medieval England might have brought to the poem. In *Christ and Satan,* the angelic Fall is tied directly neither to Creation nor human Fall but to judgment, perhaps the poet's invention and perhaps a response to other literature available to him. In attributing the angelic Fall to pride, *Christ and Satan,* like *Genesis B,* does follow *The Book of the Secrets of Enoch* and Gregory, but it remains dissimilar in that the rebellion is directed against Christ rather than God.[67] Robert Finnegan finds some connection for this Christocentrism in the *Epistle of Jude,* verse 6, and in Bede's commentary on the same, and he also identifies similarities to a late seventh-century Ascension Day homily, in which Christ is mentioned as Satan's opponent and punisher.[68] Sleeth notes, as well, "Interest in Lucifer's state of mind after the Fall appears in England in the Latin works of Aldhelm, Bishop of Sherborne (d. 709). In his *De Octo Principalibus Vitiis,* ll. 296–302, though not in Lucifer's words but in the poet's, Lucifer's angelic glory before his fall is set in sharp contrast with his damned state."[69] Aldhelm's riddle on Lucifer (number 81), spoken entirely in the first person, addresses a similar contrast: "O felix olim servata lege Tonantis! / Heu! post hæc cecidi proterva mente superbus" (Once I was happy, when I kept the law of God the Thunderer. But alas, I fell, wanton and proud of mind, 5–6). And the riddle's last line suggestively points to an array of textual accounts of the angels' Fall: "Gnarus quos poterit per biblos pandere lector" (As readers wise in books may best explain).[70]

To such speculative connections, Thomas Hill adds a gloss from Augustine on John 8:44, in the *Tractatus in Evangelium Ioannis,* as "the most probable source" for the Old English poetic motif of Satan's

---

than partially explained by differences of subject matter, and may well suggest to us that within the overall oral-formulaic tradition there must have been narrower streams of tradition – poetic schools, if you will – and that the *Christ and Satan* poet may have belonged to the same one of these as the authors of poems somewhat vaguely called Cynewulfian." See Sleeth, *Studies,* 62; and Clubb, *Christ and Satan,* xxvi.n35.

67 See Robert Emmett Finnegan, ed., *Christ and Satan: A Critical Edition* (Waterloo, ON: Wilfrid Laurier University Press, 1977), 37–9.

68 Ibid., 40n18, referencing Geoffrey Shepherd, "Scriptural Poetry," in *Continuations and Beginnings,* ed. E.G. Stanley (London: Nelson, 1996), 26; see also Sleeth, *Studies,* 51.

69 Sleeth, *Studies,* 52. Sleeth also notes Clubb's suggestion that the devil's speech in *Guthlac A* may have shared a source with the devil's speech in *Christ and Satan.*

70 James H. Pitman, ed., *The Riddles of Aldhelm,* Yale Studies in English 67 (New Haven, CT: Yale University Press, 1925; repr., Hamdon, CT: Archon Books, 1970), 48–9. The citations refer to the 1970 edition.

rebellion being directed against Christ, a source perhaps also used by Alcuin and Ælfric and, in turn, perhaps more widely known than surviving literature suggests.[71] The effectiveness of the Christological connection has also been noted by Judith Garde, who describes "the contrived confession of Satan" that dominates "this overtly didactic work" as a means by which the poet "cleverly juxtaposes the relationship between sin and ghastly infernal punishment, and proper Christian attitude and the celestial joys that now lie within the grasp" of the poem's audience. In *Christ and Satan*, the "roles that are prominent in the *Genesis* poems are explicitly reversed. The arrogance and bluster of the earlier Satan are replaced by a progressively detailed confession of the omnipotence of Christ and of his own guilt, envy and pride, including his regret and sorrow, and the inestimable loss of once-enjoyed celestial blessings."[72] None of these attempts to locate with precision the poem's intellectual and literary milieu, however, has been conclusive. While together they suggest something of what the *Christ and Satan* poet and early readers may have read or known, the work mostly confirms that the Fall of the Angels story could be told in a wide variety of ways. It also suggests that early sequential readers of Junius 11 may well have found the *Christ and Satan* account of the Fall of the Angels more different from, than connected to, the volume's preceding versions of the same story.

The overt didacticism in *Christ and Satan*'s version of the angelic Fall is both structural, particularly in the interspersion of dramatic and homiletic material, and verbal, in the narrator's forceful

71 Hill, "Fall of Satan," 319–20: "John 8 describes a violent and bitter encounter between Christ and those Jews who refused to accept His claims; the dialogue ends when the assembled Jews try to stone Him. At one point in the exchange, the Jews claim that they are children of Abraham, and Christ in response says that they are not children of Abraham but children of Satan. 'Vos ex patre diabolo estis; et desideria patris vestri vultis facere. Ille homicida erat ab initio, et in eritate, not stetit: quia non est veritas in eo: cum loquitur mendacium, ex propriis loquitur, quia mendax est, et pater eius' (John 8:44). The phrase 'in veritate non steti' as a rationale for the fall of Satan interested Augustine, and he glossed the phrase in terms of its Christological resonances. In John 14:6, Christ defines Himself as the 'Truth' ('ego sum via, et veritas, et vita'), and hence the phrase that the devil stood not in the 'truth' could be taken to imply that the devil rebelled against Christ, and this is the interpretation that Augustine proposes. ... This remark is echoed by Alcuin in his commentary on John, and Ælfric alludes to the gloss succinctly when he writes (in the preface to his translation of the *Heptateuch*) that Satan 'nolde þa habben his Scippend him to hlaforde, ne he nolde þurhwunian on ðære soþfæstnisse ðæs soðfæstan Godes sunu, þe hine gesceop fægerne.'"

72 Garde, *Old English Poetry*, 49.

exhortations. The poem's initial, summary account of the Fall is followed by Satan's articulations of its horrors. Satan's words here are not to explore the mechanism of disobedience, as in *Genesis B*, but to make a more immediate point. In the service of this, the narrator admonishes:

Forþan sceal gehycgan hæleða æghwylc
þæt he ne abælige bearn waldendes.
Læte him to bysne hu þa blacan feond
for oferhygdum ealle forwurdon.
Neoman us to wynne weoroda drihten,
uppe ecne gefean, engla waldend. (193–8)

Therefore must each of men consider, so that he does not anger the Son of the Ruler. Let it be as an example to him how the dark fiends all perished because of their pride. Let us accept as a joy the Lord of hosts, aloft, everlasting gladness, the Ruler of angels.

The two "let" constructions here are the first in a series in the poem, six of which are first-person plurals ("let us").[73] Only one such direct comment appears in the *Genesis B* account of the angelic Fall, when the narrator asserts that Satan "sceolde … þa dæd ongyldan, … his wite habban. … Swa deð monna gehwilc / þe wið his waldend winnan ongynneð" (must pay for that deed, … have his punishment. … So does each of men who attempts to fight against his lord, 295b, 296b, 297b–8). The *Christ and Satan* narrator's exhortations, by contrast, punctuate Satan's laments, intruding emphatically and often at some length, supplanting, as Sleeth puts it, "words directly expressive of combat," as in *Genesis A*.[74] The optative reappears, for instance, in a section of *Christ and Satan* that consists, in R.K. Gordon's dismissive description,

73 The six are *neoman* 197; *gemunan* 201, 205; *ceosan* 202; *beoran* 204; and *uta cerran* 215. Finnegan notes: "The "forþan" in line 193 has the same syllogistic function as the "forþons" in the *Blicking Homilies*, and the form "uta" + infinitive, line 215, is also familiar. The … verbs are [often] in the subjunctive mood, a hortatory technique employed by both Anglo-Saxon and Latin writers" (*Christ and Satan*, 23). See also Sleeth, *Studies*, 75, 22–3.

74 Sleeth, *Studies*, 106, notes that the narrator of *Christ and Satan* "observes a similar parsimony in the use of words directly expressive of combat, to a degree that it is conspicuous in a poem whose whole overt subject matter is the archetypal struggle between Christ and Satan. The strongest verbs of this kind refer to the Harrowing of hell."

"of further lamentation on Satan's part, and of conventional moralizing, in which the joys of heaven are contrasted with the torments of hell." (Gordon finds it so conventional that he chooses not to include the section in his translation of the poem.)[75] The narrator's expositions on his story here begin with a directive summation of Satan's speech: "Swa gnornedon godes andsacan / hate on helle. Him wæs hælend god / wrað geworden for womcwidum" (So lamented God's adversaries, hot in hell. The saviour God had become angry with them for their evil words, 279–81).

What follows is more assertive, a combination of optatives and promises:

- "Forþon mæg gehycgan … / þæt he him afirre frecne geþohtas, / laðe leahtras, lifigendra gehwylc" (Therefore should each living person be mindful … that he put away from himself dangerous thoughts, hateful offenses, 282–4);
- "Gemunan symle" (Let us remember always, 285a);
- "gearwian us" (let us prepare, 286a);
- "us befæðman wile freobearn godes, / gif we þæt on eorðan ær geþencað" (the noble Son of God will wish to embrace us if we on earth beforehand think about that, 288–9).

Then, after a list of what Christ "tæceð us" (teaches us, 293a), the narrator fairly shouts: "Uton cyþan þæt!" (Let us make that known!), specifying that "Deman we on eorðan, ærror lifigend, / onlucan mid listum locen waldendes, / ongeotan gastlice!" (We must consider on earth, beforehand, living, [how to] unlock with skills the Ruler's locks [or stronghold], to understand [this] spiritually!, 297b–300a).[76] That Satan has, despite his attempts, so utterly failed to unlock the Ruler's locked-up knowledge is demonstrated not just in his punishment and in hell itself but also in the contrast of his lack of understanding with what the readers are to understand.[77] As Satan looks around hell, he almost

75 R.K. Gordon, trans., *Anglo-Saxon Poetry* (New York: E.P. Dutton, 1926), 131. S.A.J. Bradley, ed. and trans., *Anglo-Saxon Poetry* (London: Everyman, 1982), translates up to 314, then dismissively writes, "Lines 315–64 (section VIII) are here omitted. They contain a further reiteration of the horrors of hell contrasted with the joys of heaven" (95).

76 See Finnegan, *Christ and Satan*, 103–4.

77 Satan's fiendish companions accuse him, "'þu us gelærdæst ðurh lyge ðinne'" (You convinced us through your lying, 53); "'Segdest us to soðe þæt ðin sunu wære / meotod mancynnes'" (You told us as a truth that your son was the creator of mankind, 63–4).

hesitatingly comments, "'Ne mæg ic þæt gehicgan hu ic in ðæm becwom, / in þis neowle genip'" (I cannot understand that, how I came into that, into this obscure darkness, 178–9a).[78] Few readers or listeners could surely resist at least a mental response, an explanation to counter Satan's apparent confusion, and the narrative shortly after models just such a response with the directives in lines 193 and following. The narrator demands that his audience contrast themselves with the fallen angels, knows they understand full well how Satan came into that obscure darkness, and presses the reward of Christ's redemption.[79]

The hortatory content throughout *Christ and Satan* led Finnegan to assess its structure in homiletic terms, but, remarked Sleeth, while placing "the work firmly in the homiletic tradition … [was] a service of permanent value," Finnegan focuses so much on the connections to Christ that his "argument runs the risk of denying the poet any adequate justification for making Satan the focus of so much attention."[80] Sleeth, in turn, suggests that a gospel passage – "Whosoever exalteth himself shall be abased; and he that humbleth himself shall be exalted" (Luke 14:11; compare Matthew 23:12 and Luke 18:14) – functions to unify the sections of the poem. The didactic firmness in *Christ and Satan*, whatever its source, obviously encourages the perception of connections to sermon style, but sermon habits may also have influenced the use and reception of the Fall of the Angels in *Genesis A* and *B*.

The triple reworkings of the angelic Fall in Junius 11 are not perhaps so thoroughly governed by impulses, which Hall calls "basically narrative, not catechetical," that they are "a different genre" entirely than the sermons.[81] Instead, the Fall of the Angels reconceived and recontextualized suggests a distinctly functional and open-ended view of this narrative, one distinct from modern traditions of genre: it is both homiletic and narrative poetry, available both in each of its separate contexts and cumulatively across the Junius 11 manuscript, used as a

78 Or "how I came to be there," as Clubb, *Christ and Satan*, 76, translates it; the reference is presumably to the *laðan ham*, which Satan mentions just before (177). All that is now clearly revealed to him is the enormity of his action and his distance from heaven: "Nu is gesene þæt we syngodon / uppe on earde" (Now it is apparent that we sinned in the dwelling above, 228–9a).

79 See Ruth Wehlau, "The Power of Knowledge and the Location of the Reader in 'Christ and Satan,'" *JEGP* 97 (1998): 1–14, esp. 3–4.

80 Sleeth, *Studies*, 8. Finnegan, *Christ and Satan*, 17, notes, "If we investigate the Latin and vernacular homilists with whom our poet may have been familiar, tracing in their devotional prose the use of the exemplum as a pedagogical device, then the mixture of verse kinds in Christ and Satan is seen to be a problem more apparent than real."

81 Hall, "Old English Epic of Redemption," 26.

counter-example for Creation, human Fall, and redemption. As is common in homilies, each writer has adapted a single, probably familiar, narrative to suit a distinct didactic goal, however the compiler conceived the poems' relationship in this manuscript.[82] What the three versions have perhaps most in common is the perception of functional applicability in the Fall of the Angels story, something that writers such as Alcuin expressed directly. He asks, in the *Interrogationes* III, "Hwi wæs þæra engla synn forsuwod on þære bec genesis, 7 þæs mannes wæs gesæd?" (Why was the angels' sin left out of the book of Genesis, and man's was recounted?) The answer he provides is, in sum: "For þon þe god / gemynte þæt he wolde þæs mannes synne gehælon, / na þæs deofles" (Because God intended that he would heal man's sin, not the devil's).[83] Even God, it seems, had ideas about selectively structuring narrative to suit a particular goal in a particular context.

Together or Separate

Multiple versions of a single story may have been an intentional aspect of compilation, and whether or not the Junius 11 compiler paid any particular attention to the Fall of the Angels repetitions in selecting and arranging the book's contents, audiences in early medieval England seem likely not to have perceived them at all as flaws in this collection. Each version of the story in its separate context functions purposefully and offers much for independent consideration. At the same time, if initial audiences encountered these three versions of the same basic narrative within the framework of consecutive reading, they may have recognized in the accounts of the Fall of the Angels an even stronger, cumulative encouragement to consider the story's intellectual and spiritual implications.

A tenth- or eleventh-century English audience for Junius 11 might have had experience of such repetitions, too, in the context of homilies.

---

82 The relationship among the Junius versions of the angelic Fall was long ago established as not one of source material: Clubb, in his edition of *Christ and Satan*, xxvi, comments, "The verbal correspondences between *Genesis A* and the whole of *Christ and Satan* are so few, so scattered, and generally so insignificant as to make it doubtful whether there was any vital relationship at all between the two poems, even though both treat the themes of the Creation, the fall of the angels, and the fall of man." And while more connections have been made between *Genesis B* and *Christ and Satan*, exact connection has never been persuasively argued.

83 Ælfric, *Interrogationes Sigewulfi*, 27–9, in "Ælfric's Version of *Alcuini Interrogationes Sigeuulfi in Genesin*," ed. George E. MacLean, PhD diss., University of Leipzig (Halle: E. Karras, 1883), 60.

A familiar story could be adapted not only to suit a particular homiletic purpose but also to improve the story itself for a particular telling. Paul Szarmach, in a discussion of three versions of the Jonah story "in certain Rogationtide homilies," argues that "seeing the narrative potential of his material, the redactor is attempting to rework [the story of Jonah] to make it a better narrative. He is a narrator as well as a homilist."[84] The poets of the narrative poems in Junius 11, to judge from their use of the Fall of the Angels story, seem to have functioned partly as homilists, with distinct goals that comfortably coexist within the framework of this coherent compilation.

The flexibility and wide appeal of the Fall of the Angels story seem incontestable given so many returns to it within a single book – six in total. In addition to the three relatively extensive narrative developments of the story are the two illustrated versions, plus the tempter's summary account at the end of *Genesis B*. So many versions in such relatively close context may also indicate a particular kind of reading that could be done within this collection or beyond it, one focused on comparative analysis and evaluation. Comparative presentation may "reflect an interest in the study of dialectic" and "the multiplicity of senses of scripture," which Parkes outlines from a booklist written in the second half of the eleventh century: "Alongside copies of familiar texts like the *Dialogi* of Gregory the Great, Orosius, the *De consolatione Philosophiae* and Sedulius, we find copies of 'Kategorie Aristoteli,' 'Commentum Boetii in categorias' and 'Boethius in perihermenias.'"[85] The relative independence of the multiple Fall of the Angels versions in Junius 11 works against any necessity for sequential reading and, indeed, amplifies the possibility that partially sequential or episodically selective reading was a familiar approach to books.

We cannot know with any certainty how readers in tenth-century England approached a book such as Junius 11. The multiple accounts of the Fall of the Angels should, however, make us question the priority of sequential reading and assumptions about the relationships between repetition and coherence that are based on our own experiences with books. The presence of multiple accounts of a single story implies a wider cultural interest in that story, and it also demonstrates that even when this particular book was begun, as an amply illustrated collection of biblical poetry in the vernacular, repetition was not avoided – and too many of the repetitions of the Fall of the Angels occur in the earlier,

---

84 Paul Szarmach, "Three Versions of the Jonah Story: An Investigation of Narrative Technique in Old English Homilies," *ASE* 1 (1972): 192.

85 Parkes, "*Rædan, areccan, smeagan*," 20, 13.

illustrated pages of the manuscript to ascribe the repetition to a falling off of interest in the book. The Fall of the Angels both binds together the contents of Junius 11 and amplifies distinctions and discontinuity across its parts. The result provides multiple, sometimes competing, avenues for reading and for *enarratio* – in particular, the kind of trained reading that focuses on accessing meaning, whether within a linear and continuous structure or not.

Chapter 2

Seeing and Believing in *Daniel* and *Genesis B*

7 nu we magon geseon 7 witan witodlice ... swa us oft sægdon ða ðe ure lareowas 7 ure boceras wæron[1]

The triple repetition of the Fall of the Angels both ties together and disrupts the pages of Junius 11. A sequential reader reaching the second iteration is inevitably drawn back to the first to some extent; repetition invites comparative analysis. At the same time, the Fall of the Angels repetitions point outward, attesting to a wider currency for the story, perhaps prompting some readers to link the Junius 11 tellings, or even just one of them, to other uses of the story, such as those Ælfric employs in sermons and letters.[2] If we consider that all the poems in Junius 11 had pre-existence, that the four narrative units now visible were not composed as collection companions and that they survive only in this particular book as an accident of history governed by vagaries of textual survival and the choices of one or more compilers, the push to look for non-sequential connections, overlaps, and interests shared outside Junius 11 rises.

While now received largely in terms defined by the manuscript's date, the poems' histories attest to a greater span of time and place, and presumably of readership. *Genesis A* may be the oldest of the poems in the book, if Doane is right that archaisms in it attest to "an absolute date for the earliest written copy to be pre-750," although he and R.D.

1 "And now we are able to see and truly understand, ... just as those who were our teachers and our scholars often said to us": Vercelli Homily 15.100–3; see D.G. Scragg, ed., *The Vercelli Homilies and Related Texts*, EETS 300 (Oxford: Oxford University Press, 1992), 257.

2 Fox, "Ælfric on the Creation and Fall of the Angels," 175.

Fulk find evidence for substantial revision of *Genesis A* when it was combined in about 900 with what was the "recently or simultaneously west-saxonized *Genesis B*." Doane argues for a pre–Junius 11 compilation that featured *Genesis A/B* with *Exodus* and *Daniel*, although the latter two poems seem quite clearly to have originated separately, perhaps before the first quarter of the ninth century: the idea that *Exodus* and *Daniel* "were added to the complex post-900 and from a different line of transmission is guaranteed by the fact that they show virtually no early West-Saxon forms and at this time they may have still retained a predominantly Anglian linguistic character."[3] In their editions of *Christ and Satan*, Clubb and Finnegan suggest a 790–820/830 composition date for that poem, while Sleeth puts it slightly later, around 850, and Fulk concludes only that "the metrical practice of the poem is not as archaic as that of *Beowulf*, but the evidence is too meager to suggest where it ought to be placed in the chronology."[4]

We do not know when and why the poems in Junius 11 were first brought together, and books of exclusively Old English verse are not plentiful survivals, leaving Junius 11 difficult to situate among such companions, if, indeed, very many such companions ever existed.[5] If the poems of Junius 11 did not survive in this context – or in any collection so clearly defined by subject matter and traditional chronology as this is – what might we perceive as their emphasis, or in what framework might we assess them? Certainly some early medieval audiences received the poems sequentially as they appear in Junius 11, but the poems' separate histories make it likely that other audiences, seeing or hearing the text, received *Genesis B* (or its Saxon predecessor) before receiving *Daniel*, or encountered the Junius 11 poems, or indeed just some aspect or section of them, outside their collection in this manuscript as well singly within it.

If the contents of Junius 11 survived only in separate contexts, biblical chronology might be the least of what connected them, and the Junius 11 compiler's interests might be replaced or redirected by some other major strand of intellectual attention in early medieval England. One such strand is the Fall of the Angels narrative, as the multiple presentations of it even within the boards of Junius 11 attest. Another,

3 Doane, *Genesis A*, 39–40. See also, on the dating, R.D. Fulk, *A History of Old English Meter* (Philadelphia: University of Pennsylvania Press, 1992), 391–2, 332; and Bredehoft, *Authors, Audiences*, 141–2.

4 Clubb, *Christ and Satan*, lx; Finnegan, *Christ and Satan*, 63; Sleeth, *Christ and Satan*, 48–9; Fulk, *History of Old English Meter*, 394–6.

5 See Bredehoft, *Authors, Audiences*, 47.

and one with more varied narrative contexts and presentations outside Junius 11 as well as with confirmation in the material record, is sensory perception and, in particular, sight as it relates to spiritual condition, a topic addressed by both *Daniel* and *Genesis B*. The reader's work in understanding spiritual sight as addressed in the contents of Junius 11 is more complicated, more subtle, and has fewer apparent sequential possibilities for building meaning than do the Fall of the Angels repetitions. The topic might, indeed, have been one more readily accessible from outside the bounds of this particular book than within it, as a subject familiar especially among the most experienced readers. Although not as neatly established in narrative as is Lucifer's fall, the connection between what is seen and what is understood is one that educated readers – especially of Latin – could have encountered in *Daniel* and in *Genesis B*, in other vernacular texts, and in Anglo-Latin and patristic texts as well as in other forms of art.[6]

While we know little about the original contexts of either *Daniel* or *Genesis B*, one a possibly eighth-century production (according to Fulk) and the other derived from a Saxon predecessor that came to England between roughly 850 and 900 (according to Doane), both poems had an existence outside Junius 11. Across or outside Junius 11, *Genesis B* and *Daniel* might have been understood as participants in the long conversation in early medieval England about the relationship between spirituality and sight.

The material evidence for attention to sight alongside these Old English texts includes a series of coins from the first half of the eighth century, as Anna Gannon has identified them, which seem to share a thematic connection in representing each of the five senses. Among these coins is one that features a face framed by two loops, which may be "wreath ties" or hair. Citing related images on St. Cuthbert's coffin and on "sculptural fragments from Hoddom and Rothbury," Gannon postulates that "the figure with large eyes that now turns to face us is Christ: we are now *seeing Salvation*."[7] Either this representation of sight or a representation of speech on a sixth coin seems to be defined as having primacy in relation to the other senses. Speech, "as the 'sixth sense,'

6 Katherine O'Brien O'Keeffe, "Hands and Eyes, Sight and Touch: Appraising the Senses in Anglo-Saxon England," *ASE* 45 (2016): 105–40, explores the cultural understanding of eye/sight (as well as hand/touch), including reference to "*De consolatione Philosophiae*, when Philosophy wishes to teach Boethius that anything known is comprehended according to the ability of the perceiver" (117).

7 Anna Gannon, "The Five Senses and Anglo-Saxon Coinage," *Anglo-Saxon Studies in Archaeology and History* 13 (2006): 100.

the quality that distinguishes man from animals, may be equated with wisdom, or reason, which would allow the Senses to be controlled. … Both interpretations, through the *mind's eyes* or through Speech as synonymous to Reason, are highly sophisticated and ultimately multivalent," Gannon argues, and she notes in support of this sophistication the fact that Tatwine's riddle figuratively presenting the five senses was produced at about the same time as the coins were.[8]

Interest in the senses and the emphasis on sight are not, however, limited to the early centuries of Christian Germanic England. The late ninth-century Fuller Brooch, perhaps most notably, also seems to depict the five senses and to elevate sight, in particular.[9] David Pratt has linked the brooch to the court of King Alfred and to Alfred himself, and he describes an intellectual context for the brooch that corresponds to interests evident in the Junius 11 poems. At the centre of the brooch, surrounded by smaller depictions of four figures that have been linked to hearing, taste, smell, and touch, a large-eyed figure stares directly at the viewer, appearing to represent the sense of sight.[10] Pratt suggests that the image may represent both primacy of the "mind's eyes," which "have the ability to perceive wisdom," and the "five 'outer senses,' which perform an analogous role in perceiving the material world alone." Patristic and exegetical interest in the five senses fostered centuries of discussion of the "mind's eyes" (*oculi mentis*). Isidore, for instance, explains in the *Etymologiae* the superiority of sight – "Sight (*visus*) is so called, because it is livelier (*vivacior*) than the other senses" – and Pratt identifies a more immediate and local context for the Fuller Brooch iconography, one linked to Alfred's interest in the acquisition of wisdom: "Although these 'mind's eyes' are a patristic commonplace, favoured particularly by Gregory the Great, it is striking that they should be employed by Alfred in his translations at every available opportunity."[11]

One such example comes in Alfred's Old English version of the *Pastoral Care*, with the claim, "Đurh ða gesceadwisnesse we tocnawað good & yfel, & geceosað ðæt good, & aweorpað ðæt yfel" (Through that

8 Ibid., 101. Tatwine's riddle, *De quinque sensibus*, is in Tatwine, *Tatuini Opera Omnia*, ed. Maria De Marco and F. Glorie, CCSL 133 (Turnhout, Belgium: Brepols, 1968).

9 David Pratt, "Persuasion and Invention." See also O'Brien O'Keeffe, "Hands and Eyes, Sight and Touch," 129–31.

10 Leslie Webster and Janet Backhouse, in *The Making of England: Anglo-Saxon Art and Culture AD 600–900* (Toronto: University of Toronto Press, 1991), 280–1, provide a good image and overview of the brooch.

11 Pratt, "Persuasion and Invention," 215–16.

discernment we recognize good and evil, and choose the good, and reject the evil).[12] But more extensive attention to the mind's eyes appears in the Old English translation of Augustine's *Soliloquia*, Book 1 of which, as Pratt points out, "is dominated by the distinction between sense perception, on the one hand, and the analogous process of perceiving God and eternal truths with the intellect." Pratt, in turn, reads the Fuller Brooch "as a sophisticated iconographic representation of Alfredian thought," one that "would seem to convey a familiar didactic message about the need for wisdom and the means of acquiring it."[13] Similar imagery and meaning may attend the Alfred Jewel, with its large-eyed figure.[14] Both Pratt and Leslie Webster argue for the distinct appropriateness of the emphasis on sight to Alfred's role and his aims in stimulating vernacular literacy, and for the possibility that such art played a significant role in the development of Alfredian and subsequent manuscript culture. Junius 11 contributes support to that claim, particularly if we lift some of its contents out of their current presentation sequence.

Daniel and *Genesis B* are tagged by critics with the term "interpolation." Within Junius 11, both poems appear to be somehow incomplete relative to an implied existence outside this manuscript, a status that further encourages consideration of them as representatives of ideas tied to, but not distinctly restricted by, their potential sequential meaning in Junius 11. Both poems also have external witnesses to a less closely related existence: *Genesis B* partly overlaps the Old Saxon Genesis in a Vatican manuscript, Bibliotheca Apostolica, Palatinus Latinus 1447, and *Daniel* partly overlaps the Exeter Book *Azarias* (or *The Three Youths*), although the precise nature of the relationships in these pairs remains elusive.[15] The *Genesis B* repetition of the Fall of the Angels, already presented in *Genesis A*, might or might not be additional evidence for interpolation. Certainly the tone of *Genesis B*, particularly in the characters' speeches, yields some disjuncture in its present context that even a relatively inexperienced reader would probably note, and, as a separate poem, *Genesis B* now seems likely to be missing lines at its beginning and end. Similarly, a long-standing debate continues over whether *Daniel* as it appears in Junius 11 is complete or not, especially in its conclusion, and the relationship among its parts has not been firmly settled.[16] Despite such disagreement, and even if, as Doane has

12 Gregory, *King Alfred's West-Saxon Version of Gregory's Pastoral Care*, 64.

13 Pratt, "Persuasion and Invention," 213, 216.

14 See Egil Bakka, "The Alfred Jewel and Sight," *Antiquaries Journal* 46 (1966): 277–82.

15 See, e.g., Remley, *Old English Biblical Verse*, 24.

16 Ibid., 336.

argued, *Genesis, Exodus,* and *Daniel* circulated together as a unit before Junius 11, features of both *Daniel* and *Genesis B* strongly encourage consideration of their possible roles outside Junius 11 and across it in a non-linear way.

The place of these two poems in relation to larger cultural interests extends across continents and centuries before their late tenth-century appearance as book companions. The Saxon Genesis, *Genesis B*'s continental ancestor, "seems to be centered on certain topics that were of lively interest in the mid-ninth century," in Doane's view. "The intellectual concern with the role of devils and their deceptions is," for instance, "central to the work against popular superstitions of Agobard of Lyon (d. 840)."[17] In England, Alfred's concern with the mind's eye(s) might have encouraged attention both to *Daniel,* which Fulk argues is likely to have been available at the latest by roughly the same period as the continental "lively interest" to which Doane refers, and to *Genesis B,* which may well have come into English as "a translation of the Alfredian period" and which includes Eve's misperception of the nature of the tempter and of her post-lapsarian vision.[18] Fundamentally, both *Genesis B* and *Daniel* are concerned with material and spiritual perception and with the acquisition and application of wisdom, a topic addressed in other vernacular poetry and more widely in texts that pay particular attention to the role of seeing in relation to understanding.[19]

In the Exeter Book poem known as *The Order of the World,* for instance, a description of the glory of seeing the sun with "eagna gesihð" (sight of the eyes, 66b) turns to the spiritual dimension of seeing with an assertion about the rewards of seeing correctly:

Hy geseoð symle hyra sylfra cyning,
eagum on wlitað, habbað æghwæs genoh.
Nis him wihte won, þam þe wuldres cyning
geseoþ in swegle. (93–6a)[20]

(They see always their own king, with their eyes gaze on him, have enough of everything. Not for them is anything lacking, for those who see the king of glory in heaven.)

17 Doane, *Saxon Genesis,* 101.

18 Fulk, *History of Old English Meter,* 391–2 and 280.

19 See also Yun Lee Too, "The Appeal to the Senses in the Old English 'Phoenix,'" *NM* 91 (1990): 229–42.

20 George Philip Krapp and Elliot Van Kirk Dobbie, eds., *The Exeter Book,* ASPR 3 (New York: Columbia University Press, 1936), 166.

The poet seems, as Robert DiNapoli comments on this section of the poem, "obsessed ... with opening his hearers' or readers' eyes to hitherto unseen dimensions of 'ordinary' reality," and the sun "provides a convenient symbol for God's omnipresence and for the universal accessibility of the divine vision, to which, in theory, any believer may attain."[21]

Somewhat more mundane but still linking sight to understanding is a reference in the Exeter Book's *Riddle 59*. The rather obscure lines might more specifically have to do with literacy, the ability to transfer visible marks into understood meaning:

Him torhte in gemynd
his dryhtnes naman dumba brohte
ond in eagna gesihð, gif þæs æþelan
goldes tacen ongietan cuþe. (7b–10)

([The ring] showed to him in his mind the name of its lord, the dumb one brought it forth into the sight of his eyes if he knew how to understand the sign [made] of noble gold.)[22]

Maxims I, also in the Exeter Book, includes a rather more cryptically phrased passage that might refer to spiritual blindness, an image, in James Earl's estimation, "too common to require a footnote":[23] "blind sceal his eagna þolian" (the blind must dispense with his eyes, 39b), although "Waldend him þæt wite teode, se him mæg wyrpe syllan, / hælo of heofodgimme, gif he wat heortan clæne" (the Ruler made that torment for him, who could give him relief, health for the head's gem, if he perceived a pure heart, 43–4).[24] Such references suggest, at the least, that thinking about the power of eyes might not have been unfamiliar and that readers in England ca. 1000 might have been particularly receptive to more complex explorations of the significance of sensory perception. Jeremy DeAngelo posits just such an exploration for *The Whale*. In its Exeter Book context, *The Panther* poem precedes *The Whale*, which positions sequential readers as "fac[ing] the same dilemma

21 Robert DiNapoli, "The Heart of Visionary Experience: *The Order of the World* and Its Place in the Old English Canon," *English Studies* 79 (1998): 105.

22 Krapp and Dobbie, *Exeter Book*, 209–10. The translation is Elisabeth Okasha's, from her article on the material evidence for reading these rings as finger-rings, "Old English 'hring' in Riddles 48 and 59," *Medium Ævum* 62 (1993): 61–9.

23 James W. Earl, "Maxims I, Part I," *Neophilologus* 67 (1983): 279.

24 Krapp and Dobbie, *Exeter Book*, 158.

confronted by the beings of the two poems: how to distinguish between behaviours and sensations that in appearance and description appear entirely analogous."[25]

Perceptive ability is available in some degree to everyone, but, as Pratt notes, Alfred's amplification of St. Augustine's *Soliloquies* also outlines a hierarchy of ability:

> So also it is regarding wisdom: everyone who desires him and is eager for him can come to him and abide in his household and dwell in his company, yet some are nearer to him, some further from him, just as it is with the estates of every king: some live in the chamber, some in the hall, some on the threshing floor, some in prison; and yet they all live by the favour of one lord, just as all men live under one sun and by its light see what they see.[26]

Not everyone, then, sees equally clearly, and the ability never sits entirely securely in an individual. Gregory's *Moralia in Iob*, which was available in England by at least the early 700s, stresses the ability of the "antiquus hostis" (old enemy) to interfere with seeing and judging:[27]

> Quasi lucet dies iste mentibus hominum cum prauitatis eius persuasio propera creditur, et qualis sit intrinsecus non uidetur. Sed cum iniquitas illius sicut est, agnoscitur, dies falsae promissionis quasi quibusdam ante iudicii nostri oculos tenebris obscuratur; quia uidelicet qualis est ex merito talis perspicitur in blandimento. In tenebras ergo dies uertitur, quando aduersa intellegimus, etiam quae prospera suadendo pollicetur. In tenebras dies uertitur quando antiquus hostis qualis est saeuiens, talis a nobis perspicitur etiam sub blandimentis latens; ne fictis prosperitatibus quasi ex diei lumine illudat et ueris miseriis ad peccati tenebras pertrahat. (4.ii.7)

> He shines like the day in the minds of men when his persuasive wickedness succeeds in winning our belief and we fail to understand what he is like within. But when his iniquity is realized for what it is, the day of false

25 Jeremy DeAngelo, "*Discretio spirituum* and *The Whale*," *ASE* 42 (2013): 272.

26 Pratt's translation, in "Persuasion and Invention," 193; for the OE, see Augustine, *King Alfred's Version of St. Augustine's Soliloquies*, ed. Thomas A. Carnicelli (Cambridge, MA: Harvard University Press, 1969), 77.5–78.2.

27 A copy of Gregory's *Moralia in Iob* that is partially preserved in Beinecke Library, Yale University, New Haven, MS 516 dates to the first half of the eighth century and was written at Monkwearmouth-Jarrow. See Rosalind Love, "The Library of the Venerable Bede," in *The Cambridge History of the Book in Britain*, vol. 1, *c.400–1100*, ed. Richard Gameson (Cambridge: Cambridge University Press, 2012), 606–32.

> promise is covered with darkness in the sight of our judgment and we see him as he really is even in his soft words. Day is turned into darkness, then, when we understand that the things whose goodness he had promised us and persuaded us to seek are in fact bad for us. Day is turned into darkness when the ancient enemy is seen by us just as he is, savage with rage even when hiding under soft words. Then he will no longer deceive us with his false promises of success, as if by the light of day, and lead us to true misery in the darkness of sin.[28]

The diversity and number of references linking sight to understanding implies that the subject was indeed one of extended interest in early medieval England, and, as Karkov has shown, Junius 11 as a whole foregrounds sight, perception, and acts of interpretation. The narratives of *Daniel* and *Genesis B* specifically develop around central acts of physical and intellectual seeing, and both involve a hierarchy related to perception, although the poems approach the topic from different directions. *Genesis B* encourages the rejection of false visual presences, and *Daniel* emphasizes the power of true ones; *Daniel* focuses more directly on a distinction between external and internal sight, which is both addressed in other literature and more closely follows its biblical base text, while *Genesis B* follows a pattern of action attested in didactic discernment of spirits narratives as it builds a link between visual signs and wisdom. The two narratives indirectly speak to each other and, as with the Fall of the Angels story, invite cross-evaluation, particularly to the reader who recognizes the narratives' participation in discussions of seeing and understanding. That possibility is heightened if the texts were received communally and with comparative discussion. Indeed, in some ways, the role of visual and spiritual discernment in *Genesis B* stands out more clearly when read after rather than before the more direct attention in *Daniel*.

Daniel

The story of *Daniel* turns on the ability to see. In the Old English poem as it appears in Junius 11, Nabochodonossor and his followers are set in clear contrast to Daniel as well as to the three youths, so that those

28 Gregory, *Moralia in Iob*, edited by Marc Adriaen, 3 vols, CCSL 143, 143a, 143b. Turnholt, Belgium: Brepols, 1979, 143:168. The translation here follows James J. O'Donnell's, from a "draft translation, made in the early 1980s and never satisfactorily revised," but still very helpful and easily accessed, http://www9.georgetown.edu/faculty/jod/gregory.html.

who cannot perceive fully stand distinct from those who can – one, in particular, within the story and the one who tells it. The distinction is made in references to both perception with the eyes and perception with the mind. The poem's narrator repeatedly draws attention to sensory and intellectual perception, and the poem does not allow the king to speak for himself until the narrator's authority has been established, which begins with the narrator's voice in the poem's first line, as it now stands: "Gefrægn ic" (I heard, 1a).[29] Attention to the narrator's authority is then reiterated with what seems like an attestation of an eyewitness, "geseah ic þa gedriht in gedwolan hweorfan" (I saw that people turn to error, 22), before retreating to "ic … gefrægn" again (57a). These assertions of sense-supported authority come well before Nabochodonossor speaks for the first time, when he chastises his advisers for their inability to understand his dream (136–44).

The narrative thus provides a basis on which to judge the king's ability to perceive and to judge perception, and from his introduction into the poem, the poem calls attention to Nabochodonossor's limited understanding: his attack on the Israelites comes after "he secan ongan sefan gehygdum" (he began to seek in the thoughts of his mind, 49). His first action after conquest is complete is to seek out youths among the Israelites "þæt him snytro on sefan secgan mihte" (so that to them he could deliver the wisdom of his mind, 84), neatly contrasted with the youths' possession of "wisdom … þurh halig mod" (wisdom … by means of a holy mind, 96, 98) and driven home just six words later by reference to Nabochodonossor as "swiðmod cyning" (arrogant king, 100).

The poem focuses on perceptive ability more than it does on what is actually seen or even what occurs to make Nabochodonossor perceive truth, and the truthfulness of the narrator's representation of perception serves as part of its argument. Reiterated mid-poem and again near its current conclusion, the narrator distances himself from Nabochodonossor's inability to understand the youths' survival of the fire and aligns himself – and, in turn, the reader attending to this narrator – with clearer sight, as he appears to see the protecting angel ascend (440–1) and he understands the authority of his sources, "Þa ic … gefrægn" (Then I … heard, 458), in the "soðum wordum" that the king seeks (true words, 458). Still more pointedly, the narrator's position of understanding is confirmed when he understands what others could

29 Quotations of the Old English *Daniel* are from Krapp's ASPR edition of Junius 11. Except where noted, translations are my own.

not, "Ne mihton arædan runcræftige men / engles ærendbec, æðelinga cyn" (ones skilled in mysteries, the offspring of nobles, were not able to understand the angel's message, 733–4), which, again, notes the narrator, "ic … gefrægn" (I heard, 738).

In contrast to the narrator, the unreformed Nabochodonossor and his councillors do not hear true words. They are denied the understanding of dreams, and the narrator's language implies active divine agency in restricting perception. Nabuchodonossor, at first in sleep, is shown truth, "soð gecyðed," presumably by God, but awake can longer remember it (113). Nor are his councillors allowed the perception of truth. The narrator bluntly asserts, "næs him dom" (judgment [or interpretation] was not for them, 128) and "hit forhæfed gewearð" (it was refused, 147) that they interpret the king's dream. Without internal perception, the king's powers of external perception remain limited. His sense of sight cannot really be trusted, whether he sees when asleep or awake.

Marking still further the distinction between physical sight and true understanding, the narrative presents the king as failing to understand fully even when he sees correctly. After witnessing the three youths' safety from fire as well as the injuries of the servants who stoke it, Nabochodonossor is again identified in terms of his mind or spirit as "swiðmod cyning" (the strong-minded king, 268a) who "his sefan ontreowde, / wundor on wite agangen" (trusted his senses, a wonder [or miracle] took place in [that] torture, 268b–9). When the angel then arrives to further bless the three youths, Nabuchodonossor sees now or admits now to seeing four individuals in the furnace: "'Nu ic þær feower men / geseo to soðe, *nales me selfa leoge*'" (Now I see in truth four men there, I do not at all deceive myself, 414b–15; emphasis mine).[30] As if in answer to and again distancing the narrative voice from Nabochodonossor's lingering hesitations, the narrator asserts shortly afterwards that the youths with many tokens of truth ("soðra tacna," 446) encourage Nabochodonossor to trust what he has seen. Even these tokens, however, do not permanently convince Nabochodonossor to reform, and, in this, the narrator stresses that the king saw but lacked understanding: "beacen onget, / swutol tacen godes. Ne þy sel dyde, / ac þam æðelinge

30 This is a disputed emendation from *leogeð*. See R.T. Farrell, ed., *Daniel and Azarias* (London: Methuen, 1974), who translates, "I do not (at all) deceive myself" and notes, "Krapp and other editors emend MS. *selfa* to *sefa*, retaining leogeð" (73n). R.M. Liuzza, ed. and trans., in *Old English Poetry: An Anthology* (Peterborough, ON: Broadview Press, 2014), translates: "my senses do not deceive me." Nabuchodnossor goes on to remark, "þæt we ðær eagum on lociað" (that we look on there with eyes, 418).

oferhygd gesceod" (he saw the beacon, God's clear token. Yet for that he did no better, but pride harmed the prince, 487b–9).

While tokens meant to verify the truth of what was seen also appear in *Genesis B* (four times), they function there as part of deception. In *Daniel,* the tokens are part of conversion. In both contexts, however, the one who offers the token asserts its value, and the receiver must perceive that value correctly; neither Eve nor Nabochodonossor does so, nor does either fully accept interpretive assistance from one who sees more clearly.[31]

The import in both *Daniel* and *Genesis B* is that God provides either the ability to see directly and understand what is true or, since such an ability is a rare gift, an authority on whom to rely for guidance. While both Eve and Nabochodonossor have difficulty correctly interpreting what they see, only *Daniel* includes a counter-example of true discernment. In *Daniel,* that authority is two-fold, external and internal: the narrator serves the role of interpretive authority for the poem's readers (perhaps problematically claiming for himself the gift of spiritual sight), and Daniel's power to see truly and fully makes him the interpretive authority for Nabuchodonossor. Both Daniel and Nabochodonossor see the same dream, but understanding of it and memory of it are restricted to Daniel, which helps identify him as possessing spiritually supported sight. In addition, the poem twice names Daniel, in identical phrasing, as the "drihtne gecoren, / snotor and soðfæst" (lord's chosen, wise and truthful, 150b–1a, 735b–6a), and twice, too, the narrator connects Daniel's powers of perception to a gift from God. When Daniel is called upon to interpret Nabochodonossor's dream, the narrator firmly ascribes Daniel's perceptive ability to divine rather than human control: "Him god sealde gife of heofnum / … þæt him engel godes eall asægde / swa his mandrihten gemæted wearð" (To him God gave a gift from heaven … so that to him an angel of God told all as his lord dreamed, 154–7).

Daniel's encounter with Baldazar is similarly framed with the remark that "Ðam wæs on gaste godes cræft micel" (God's great skill was in his spirit, 737; Farrell's translation). Within the narrative, the power to perceive clearly is at least recognized, if not understood, by those who value written text enough to try to pay Daniel "þæt he him bocstafas /

31 John F. Vickrey, "Adam, Eve, and the *Tacen* in *Genesis B*," *Philological Quarterly* 72 (1993) has noted, "In number and proximity within a single text these four instances of *tacen (-)iewan* are not equaled in Old Saxon or Old English" (2). See also Janet Schrunk Ericksen, "Legalizing the Fall of Man," *Medium Ævum* 74, no. 2 (2005): 205–20.

arædde and arehte, hwæt seo run bude" (so that he might decipher and interpret the letters for them, what the mystery might mean, 739b–40; Farrell's translation). The poem's distinctions between those who possess divinely inspired, "interior" perception and those who are denied it follows a tradition of identifying Babylon and its rulers as being distinctly without it. Gregory's *Moralia in Iob* offers perhaps the most immediate model for understanding the emphasis on perception in the Old English *Daniel*, for not only does Gregory identify two kinds of vision, exterior and interior, but he also links both kinds explicitly to the city of Babylon and thus to Nabochodonossor, the "wulfheort ... Babilone weard" (wolfheart, guardian of Babylon, 116–17a).[32] The narrator of *Daniel*, however, also advances the role of narrative as a guide for discernment.

Without the gift of true seeing – what the narrator labels as "snytro cræft" (535b, 594b, and "snyttro cræftas," 485b) – vision remains external and untrustworthy, a point the poem returns to again and again, in both the narrator's expression of his authority and the struggles of the story's actors. The narrator positions readers with Daniel as he tries to help the king see power beyond his own, centring us with language and, by extension, on text, "soðra worda þurh snytro cræft" (of true words through the skill of wisdom, 594). In sharp contrast, Nabochodonossor stubbornly perceives only the limited glory of what he has built and what requires no representation in words, "Babilone burh, on his blæde geseah / ... þæt se heretyma / werede geworhte þurh wundor micel" (saw in its splendour the city of Babylon ... that the leader of armies had made for the people with great marvels, 600–3). Not until after his period of suffering are sight and understanding finally united in Nabochodonossor: "him frean godes in gast becwom / rædfæst sefa,

32 Harry Jay Solo, "The Twice-Told Tale: A Reconsideration of the Syntax and Style of the Old English *Daniel*, 245–429," *Papers on Language and Literature* (1973): 361–2. As Solo has shown, Gregory "establishes clearly the connection between carnal, exterior vision, the vision that cannot see beyond things of this world, and the confusion of Babylon. Babylon, he says, is the glory of this world, the golden cup that shows its temporal beauty and inebriates foolish minds with concupiscence so that they desire deceitful temporalia and despise the invisible, spiritual things of beauty. This was the case with [the biblical] Eve, who, seeing that the fruit of the tree of knowledge was beautiful to look at" – a feature notably and entirely absent from the *Genesis B* narrative – "desired and finally took it. Thus Babylon, showing a vision of exterior beauty, takes away the internal sense of right." Gregory articulates similar views in his *Homilie on Ezechial*, and, adds Solo, his perspective is consistent with "a standard catalogue of the meanings of Babylon, such as that found in the *Allegoria in Sacram Scripturam* of Rabanus Maurus" and similar to comments made by Augustine in both the City of God and the *Enarrationes in psalmos.*

ða he to roderum beseah" (to his soul came from the Lord God a wise mind, when he looked to the heavens, 650–1).

The narrative addresses the topic of split sight and text one last time with the account of Baldazar and the angelic "worda gerynu, / baswe bocstafas" (mysteries of words, bright red letters, 722b–3a). Pauline Head points out that the clause structure itself in Daniel's actions here links internal and external sight: "The verbs have two objects, and two concepts of reading converge: '[H]e him boctafas / arædde and arehte, hwæt seo run bude' (739b–40). Daniel is both reading a text ("bocstafas") and deciphering the implications of a mystery. Both activities create an interpretation that embraces a passage of special significance and brings about its inclusion in the narrative."[33] Karkov extends to the audience the poem's focus on perceptive ability: if the content of the writing on the wall, which ends the poem, was to be in one of the planned illustrations, readers would have been positioned "alongside Daniel and Baltasar looking at the letters." If the letters had been actually readable in an illustration, readers then "would have been given the choice between ignorance and knowledge, depending on whether or not we were able to interpret them properly."[34]

Even without such a visual reinforcement, the narrative of *Daniel* asks the audience whether they are among those who can see and understand. Readers of Latin who encounter this message might draw on additional textual authority in positioning themselves alongside Daniel, and reading the poem as something other than the next chapter after *Genesis* might amplify the hope that spiritual perception is accessible, either directly or, more frequently, by following the right authority.

Discernment

The *Daniel* narrator's controlled definition of who does and who does not read signs properly implies authority on the matter external to the text as well as within it, as if the narrator has access to information that supports confidence in the narrative judgment evident in the poem. Such contextual grounding may rest on the apostle Paul's explanation in 1 Corinthians 12:10 that "there are diversities of gifts" extended by the Holy Spirit, including "operatio virtutum, alii prophetatio, alii discretio spirituum" (the working of miracles; to another, prophecy; to

33 Pauline Head, *Representation and Design: Tracing a Hermeneutics of Old English Poetry* (Albany: State University of New York Press, 1997), 71.

34 Karkov, *Text and Picture*, 140.

another, the discerning of spirits).[35] The gift of discerning provides a means of testing the nature of a spirit, of ascertaining whether a presence is divine or demonic, and also refers to the ability to see correctly, to match external sight with internal understanding. Origen, in his third homily on Exodus, simultaneously stresses the rareness of dispensation of the gift and heightens its value by referring to its usefulness in dealing with evil:

> Unde mihi non uidetur esse paruae gratiae intelligere os quod aperit diabolus. Non est sine sancti Spiritus gratia huiusmodi os et uerba discernere; et ideo in diuisionibus spiritalium gratiarum additur etiam hoc quod datur quibusdam *discretio spirituum*? Ergo spiritalis est gratia per quam spiritus discernitur, sicut et alibi dicit Apostolus: *Probate spiritus, si ex Deo sunt*.[36]

> It seems to me to be no small gift to perceive the mouth which the devil opens. Such a mouth and words are not discerned without the gift of the Holy Spirit. Therefore, in the distributions of spiritual gifts, it is also added that "discernment of spirits" is given to certain people. It is a spiritual gift, therefore, by which the spirit is discerned, as the Apostle [Paul] says elsewhere [1 John 4:1], "Test the spirits, if they are from God."[37]

Daniel discerns the nature of the king's dreams, accurately reading the divine message, and enough references to this kind of discernment occur in the literature available in early medieval England, either directly or through secondary references, to claim reading-based interest in the topic. Daniel's ability echoes, for instance, Augustine's discussion in Book 12 of *De Genesi ad litteram*, which explores and explains Paul's vision of a third heaven and distinguishes between spiritual and physical sight, including in dreams. Book 12 includes, in Chapter 11, an explanation of Baltassar's and Daniel's contrastive external and internal seeing, and the whole book immediately follows

---

35 See Robert Weber, ed., *Biblia Sacra Iuxta Vulgatam Versionem* (Stuttgart: Deutsche Bibelgesellschaft, 1969).

36 Origen, *Homélies sur l'Exode*, 3.2, ed. Marcel Borret, Sources Chrétiennes 321 (Paris: Éditions du Cerf, 1985), 93.

37 Origen, *Origen: Homilies on Genesis and Exodus*, trans. Ronald E. Heine, Fathers of the Church 71 (Washington, DC: Catholic University Press, 1982), 248. In the homily ("On that which is written: 'I am feeble in speech and slow in tongue'"), Origen begins with a discussion of Moses's response when confronted with divine communication and moves to presences whose words are guided by the devil.

Augustine's discussion of how Adam fell. The last chapter of Book 11 links discernment to Adam and then extends to a wide audience a lack of discernment:

> Hanc autem proprie seductionem appellauit apostolus, qua id, quod suadebatur, cum falsum esset, uerum putatum est ... non tamen eum arbitror, si iam spiritali mente praeditus erat, ullo modo credere potuisse quod eos deus ab esca illius ligni inuidendo uetuisset. Sed quid plura? Persuasum est illud peccatum, sicut persuaderi talibus posset; conscriptum est autem, sicut legi ab omnibus oporteret, etsi a paucis haec intellegerentur, sicut oporteret.
>
> According to Saint Paul, a seduction in the proper sense occurs when one is persuaded to accept as true what in reality is false. ... I do not think that Adam, if he was endowed with a spiritual mind, could have possibly believed that God had forbidden them to eat the fruit of the tree out of envy). But enough of these speculations. Adam and Eve were induced to commit this sin in accordance with the way in which such persons can be tempted. The account was written as it must be read by all, although the content would be understood as it ought by only a few.[38]

The medieval understanding of discernment of spirits was developed primarily by authors concerned with monastic spirituality. Among their works, those that circulated widely in the early Middle Ages include Rufinus's translations of Origen and Athanasius's *Vita Antonii* – an authoritative text on discernment – which offers this summary advice: "Orandumque prorsus est, uti supra dixi, ut accipiamus gratiam discernendorum spirituum; ut, quemadmodum scriptum est non omni spiritui credamus" (Certainly one must pray ... to receive the gift of discernment of spirits, so that we might not, as Scripture says, *believe every spirit*).[39] Understanding of the term *discretio* evolved after

---

38 Augustine, *De Genesi ad litteram*, CSEL 28.1, ed. Joseph Zycha (Vienna: F. Tempsky, 1894), 378; *St. Augustine: The Literal Meaning of Genesis*, trans. John Hammond Taylor, Ancient Christian Writers 42 (New York: Newman Press, 1982), 176–7.

39 Athanasius, *Vita Antonii* sec. 38, ed. J.P. Migne, *PG* 26 (Paris, 1857), 898. See also Athanasius, *The Life of Antony and the Letter to Marcellinus*, trans. Robert C. Gregg (New York: Paulist Press, 1980), 60. Clare Stancliffe, *St. Martin and His Hagiographer* (Oxford: Clarendon Press, 1983), in the section "The Egyptian Ascetic Background" in the chapter "Martin's Spiritual Powers," discusses the influence of the *Vita Antonii* in discernment theology. On the importance of Athanasius's work to Felix's *Life of Guthlac*, see Henry Mayr-Harting, *The Coming of Christianity to Anglo-Saxon England* (University Park: Pennsylvania State University Press, 1972), 237–9.

the fifth century from referring to the ability to perceive the nature of an independent, visually substantial spirit to describing the reaction of prudence in response to a more psychological manifestation, but both senses of the term survived as long as the works that contained them remained authoritative, for the latter understanding does not contradict the former.[40] In the *Moralia in Iob*, for instance, Gregory refers, perhaps figuratively, to the older, more substantial sense of discernment of spirits, while, in the second of the *Dialogues*, he praises Benedict's *Rule* for its newer, charismatic sense of discernment (*discretio*).[41]

Among all these works, lack of discernment is as much a topic as is the exemplary use of the rare gift, and the absence of the gift is important to understanding the human Fall as recounted in *Genesis B*. Cassian, in particular, describes a hierarchical response to deter seduction into sin for those who, like Adam and Eve, cannot discern the nature of the spirit confronting them. In general, in these suggested responses to temptation, the two understandings of discernment conform.[42] The hierarchical behaviour for reacting to an unfamiliar spirit and the hierarchical behaviour for reacting to an unfamiliar internal temptation are identical: turn for help to others who may be better able to deal with the situation. Bede might well have suggested the Irish bishop Aidan as one of those to whom a person could have turned for such assistance: in the *Ecclesiastical History* 3.5, he describes Aidan as one "qui gratia discretionis, quiae uirtutum mater est, ante omnia probabatur inbutus" (who had proved himself to be pre-eminently endowed with the grace of discretion, which is the mother of all virtues).[43]

---

40 J.T. Lienhard, "'Discernment of Spirits' in the Early Church," *Studia Patristica* 17, no. 2 (1982): 519–22. See also Jacques Guillet et al., "Discernment of Spirits," trans. Sister Innocentia Richards from *Dictionnaire de Spiritualité* (Collegeville, MN: Liturgical Press, 1970); Günther Switek, "'Discretio spirituum': Ein Beitrag zur Geschichte der Spiritualität," *Theologie und Philosophie* 47 (1972): 36–76; and Rachel Burchard, "Angel or Devil? Visionary Dilemmas in the Egyptian Desert," *Essays in History* 32 (1989): 69–84.

41 Exegesis of the Pauline passage in the later Middle Ages is dominated by Bernard, who, as in his *Sermo 88, De diversis*, on the diverse gifts of the Holy Spirit, is chiefly interested in the charismatic aspect of the discernment of spirits and an individual's ability to distinguish between good and evil inspirations.

42 See Stephen Lake, "Knowledge of the Writings of John Cassian in Early Anglo-Saxon England," *ASE* 32 (2003): 27–41. Surviving Anglo-Saxon manuscripts of Cassian's *Collationes*, or, rather, those with excerpts of the work include London, Lambeth Palace Library, 414, fols. 1–80; Oxford, Bodleian Library, Hatton 23; and Salisbury, Cathedral Library, 10. See the *Handlist*.

43 Bede, *Bede's Ecclesiastical History of the English People*, ed. Bertram Colgrave and R.A.B. Mynors, Oxford Medieval Texts (Oxford: Clarendon Press, 1969), 228–9. My thanks to Dabney Anderson Bankert for the connection.

Discernment of spirits texts and ideas offer a particularly adaptable framework for a variety of narrative contexts. DeAngelo's reading of *The Whale* explains how the poem "depicts in vivid metaphor the necessity of *discretio spirituum* for proper Christian metaphor." It links the whale to "figures such as Leviathan, Jonah's *piscis grandis*, and Aldhelm's *balenus* [to] create a consistent symbolism" that uses discernment to emphasize "pride as the downfall of those who go astray."[44] Pride, of course, also plays a central role in the temptation and Fall story, and the essential hierarchy of discernment of spirits – those who can discern and those who cannot – would likely have resonated with a secular as well as a monastic audience.[45] The fundamental pattern of a discernment tale is the same as the basic narrative in the *Genesis B* temptations of Adam and Eve by the devil: a person is confronted by an unknown spirit and, if discernment does not follow, either turns for help in discerning to someone hierarchically superior or does not. Sulpicius Severus's *Vita Martini* offers the example of an imperially dressed devil claiming to be Christ, whom Martin resists after he appears to Martin in his cell and says,

> Martine, quid dubitas? Crede, cum uideas! Christus ego sum. Tum ille, reuelante sibi spiritu ut intellegeret diabolum esse, non Dominum: non se, inquit, Iesus Dominus purpuratum nec diademate renidentem uenturum esse praedixit; ego Christum, nisi in eo habitu formaque qua passus est, nisi crucis stigmata praeferentem, uenisse non credam.
>
> "Martin, why do you hesitate? Trust your eyes! I am Christ." Then Martin, prompted by a revelation of the Spirit to perceive that it was the devil, not the Lord, said: "The Lord Jesus did not predict that he would come clothed in purple, and wearing a glittering diadem. I shall not believe that Christ has come unless he does so in the clothing and appearance of his passion, bearing the marks of the cross."[46]

---

44 DeAngelo, "*Discretio spirituum* and *The Whale*," 279, 287.

45 Doane, in *Saxon Genesis*, and Thomas D. Hill – in "The Fall of the Angels and Man in the Old English *Genesis B*," in *Anglo-Saxon Poetry: Essays in Appreciation of John C. McGalliard*, ed. Lewis E. Nicholson and Dolores Warwick Frese (Notre Dame, IN: University of Notre Dame Press, 1975), 279–90 – argue that the narrative sophistication of *Genesis B* suggests an elite audience with listening leisure.

46 Sulpice Sévère, *Vie de Saint Martin*, ed. and trans. Jacques Fontaine, 3 vols., Sources Chrétiennes 133–5 (Paris: Éditions du Cerf, 1967–9), 25.6–7 (1:308). The translation here is from Stancliffe's *St. Martin*, 236.

Clare Stancliffe points out that such a story is "clearly related to stories told of eastern monks to illustrate their gift of discerning between good and evil spirits."[47] Martin receives the gift of discernment of spirits, but in his sudden remembrance of and deference to the instructions of Christ, he undertakes the same action required of those who do not receive the gift: subordination to proper authority.

Those who both lack discernment of spirits and do not submit to higher wisdom are unlikely to have successful encounters with unknown spirits. Cassian recounts a pointed story about the lack of discernment and one that highlights the fact that virtuous, even holy, people can be misled if they act on their own:

> senem uidelicet Heronem ante paucos admodum dies inlusione diaboli a summis ad ima deiectum, quem quinquaginta annis in hac heremo conmoratum singulari districtione rigorem continentiae tenuisse meminimus et solitudinis secreta ultra omnes hic commorantes miro feruore sectatum. Hic igitur quo pacto quaue ratione post tantos labores ab insidiatore delusus grauissimo conruens lapsu cunctos in hac heremo constitutos luctuoso dolore percussit? Nonne quia minus discretionis uirtute possessa suis definitionibus regi quam consiliis uel conlationibus fratrum atque institutis maiorum maluit oboedire?[48]

> Remember the old man Hero who was cast down from the heights to the lowest depths because of a diabolical illusion. I remember how he remained fifty years in his desert, keeping to the rigors of abstinence with a severity that was outstanding, loving the secrecy of the solitary life with a fervor marvelously greater than that of anyone else dwelling here. After such toil how and why could he have been fooled by the deceiver? How could he have gone down into so great a ruin that all of us here in the desert were stricken with pain and grief? Surely the reason for it was that he had too little of the virtue of discernment and that he preferred to be guided by his own ideas rather than bow to the advice and conferences of his brethren and to the rules laid down by our predecessors.[49]

Even before such stories of Martin and Hero, the idea that Adam and Eve fell because of a problem with discernment was noted by the

---

47 Stancliffe, *St. Martin*, 236.

48 John Cassian, *Conférences*, in E. Pichery, ed., Sources Chrétiennes 42 (Paris: Éditions du Cerf, 1955), 2.5, 116–17.

49 John Cassian, *Conferences*, trans. Colm Luibhéid (New York: Paulist Press, 1985), 64.

third-century Irenaeus, Bishop of Lyon, who asserts in the *Epideixis* that Adam fell because "his [discernment or] discretion [was] still undeveloped, wherefore also he was easily misled by the deceiver."[50]

Collectively and perhaps part of more than one good early medieval library, such texts provide a framework for the kinds of seeing with which both *Daniel* and *Genesis B* are concerned. The limited reach of Latin texts – primarily available only among those who read well and so might have thought that they possessed some discernment – may imply a particularly academic interest in ways of seeing. Both the Latin and the Old English examples, however, demonstrate the narrative adaptability and, in turn, broader reach of physical and spiritual sight as a central plot element – that is, as the mystery or challenge of a story and the element that distinguishes one kind of character from another. Discernment, especially discernment of spirits, connects narrative to theology, Latin to English, book to experience. As such, it is a tool and a topic exceptionally well suited not just to biblical narrative in general but also to the foundational Christian narrative of the human Fall.

Genesis B

While reading and misreading have significant consequences in Nabochodnossor's Babylon, they matter still more at the moment when temptation arrives in Paradise, as might be especially evident to a reader familiar with other discussions of discernment or with its presentation in the *Daniel* poem. In *Genesis B*, the framework of discernment includes both a spirit and words. The narrator, one who, like the narrator of *Daniel*, serves as an interpretive guide for readers, presents in Adam's and Eve's responses to the devil two opposing models for dealing with temptation by an unknown spirit. The narrator also, as an authoritative figure, functions in concordance with discernment of spirits principles. The extent to which the narrator steps in to reiterate

50 Irenaeus's *Epideixis*, which Eusebius refers to in the *Historia ecclesiastica* 5.26, was supposed lost until an Armenian version was discovered in 1904. This text appears in Irenaeus, *Epideixis: Patrologia Orientalis*, vol. 12, no. 5 (655–731), ed. and trans. Karapet ter Mekerttschian and S.G. Wilson (Paris: Firmin-Didot, 1919). It is also known as the *Demonstratio apostolicae praedicationis*, or the *Proof*, and as such appeared as *Irenaeus: Proof of the Apostolic Preaching*, trans. Joseph P. Smith, Ancient Christian Writers 16 (Westminster, MD: Newman Press, 1952), 55. See also J.H. Crehan, "Devil," in *A Catholic Dictionary of Theology* (New York: Nelson, 1962–7), 2:169. Daniel Anlezark argues that Irenaeus is the direct source for *Genesis B*'s predecessor, the Saxon Genesis; see "The Old English *Genesis B* and Irenaeus of Lyon," *Medium Ævum* 86 (2017): 1–21.

and comment on the characters' speech corresponds to a character's defined need for higher wisdom: Adam's interaction with the devil is largely unmediated; Eve's is heavily mediated. The result is that Adam, who in first encountering the devil chooses correctly, appears a relatively autonomous character, even as he subordinates his will to God's law. Eve's guilty actions, on the other hand, are largely presented with interpretive guidance from the narrator. The description of Satan is a combination: the fallen angel speaks for himself, but his words are buffered by critical commentary from the narrator.

Such presentations enable the narrator to draw subtle distinctions – in particular, between Eve, guilty but good, and Satan, guilty and evil by choice. Satan may be the more seemingly autonomous character of the two, but surrounding each of Satan's speeches is emphatic critical commentary, explicitly condemning character and events. Before ever quoting Satan's speech, the narrator sums up its nature of revolt and blames the arrogant angel, "ne meahte he æt his hige findan / þæt he gode wolde geongerdome" (He could not find it in his heart that he was willing to be in allegiance to God, 266b–7).

The interpretive support from the narrator becomes, with Satan's speeches, a doubly strong condemnation of the character. The narrator makes perfectly clear that Satan was in error and that pride is the central feature of his fall – variations on the word *ofermod* (pride) occur eight times in reference to him.[51] Pride is not, however, mentioned in conjunction with Eve. That Eve's error is of a different nature is emphasized by the laudatory formulaic definitions of her character as "idesa scenost" and "wifa wlitegost" and (brightest of women, most beautiful of women, 626–7), terms that draw attention to what is visible about her, and by the narrator's contrastive stress on the evil nature of temptation and the devil's ability to deceive. Instead of allowing Eve as much self-revealing speech as Satan has, the narrator does not give Eve voice – does not quote her – until after she has eaten the fruit, and both the devil's temptation speech to her and his speech urging her to tempt Adam are followed by lengthy sections of narrator commentary.[52]

51 In lines 262b, 272a, 293b, 328a, 332a, 337a, 338a, and 351a. See also the word-study of *ofermod* by Helmut Gneuss in *Die Battle of Maldon als historisches und literarisches Zeugnis* (Munich: Verlag der Bay, 1976).

52 Direct speech by female characters is rare in surviving OE poetry; it appears in the female saints' lives and in *Wulf and Eadwacer* and *The Wife's Lament*. See Patricia A. Belanoff, "Women's Songs, Women's Language," in *New Readings on Women in Old English Literature*, ed. H. Damico and A.H. Olsen (Bloomington: Indiana University Press, 1990), 193–203. Stephen G. Nichols, "An Intellectual Anthropology of Marriage in the Middle Ages," in *The New Medievalism*, ed. Marina S. Brownlee,

Readers are distanced from Eve's actions and character as they are not from the Fall of the Angels or the temptation of Adam scenes, where characters speak for themselves, often extensively. The account of Eve's Fall is instead firmly controlled by the narrator's commentary, which positions Eve as culpable but more redeemable than Satan.

Adam's fictive autonomy and Eve's lack of independent voice in the devil's temptations mean both that Adam's scene is dealt with relatively briefly and that attention is focused on Eve. Adam's actions are exemplary. When the tempter approaches him, Adam is wary, mindful of what God previously told him. He tells this messenger,

Þu gelic ne bist
ænegum his engla þe ic ær geseah
ne þu me oðiewdest ænig tacen
þe he me þurh treowe to onsende,
min hearra þurh hyldo. Þy ic þe hyran ne cann
ac þu meaht þe forð faran. (538b–43a)

You are not like any of his angels whom I saw before, nor have you shown me any token that he, my lord, has sent to me through truth and favour. Therefore I cannot obey you, and you may go forth.

In essence, Adam asks, why don't you look like other angels I've seen, and what proof of your identity do you bring from God?[53] His questions echo those that a story of St. Anthony suggests:

Cum quaedam aderit visio, ne statim pavore concidas, sed qualiscunque illa sit, fidens primum interroga: Quisnam tu es, et unde? Tum si sanctorum

Kevin Brownlee, and Stephen G. Nichols (Baltimore: Johns Hopkins University Press, 1991), notes that "both in the original texts of Genesis 2 and in Patristic literature, we find a direct link between the marginalization of woman and hostility towards her speech. … Adam's authoritative discourse [in the Vulgate] distinguishes the woman only as type, not individual" (71, 75).

53 That the tempter does not look like a devil is suggested by lines 427–30, in which Satan asks his minions to "think about this, how you might beguile" Adam and Eve, and by lines 442–5, in which the devil-messenger puts on a *hæleðhelm*, literally a "hero's helmet" but perhaps a *heoloðhelm*, a "helmet of invisibility." Doane, *Saxon Genesis*, 277–8, provides a note on the word that summarizes previous readings of it and persuasively argues that the best translation is "helmet of deceit," "for in all the OE and OS instances the issue is not invisibility, but true and false seeing." In the context of discernment of spirits teachings, the precise nature of the devil's disguise becomes irrelevant since the procedure in dealing with any unfamiliar spirit remains the same.

> sit visio, certiorem te facient, atque terrorem tuum in gaudium vertent; sin diabolica illa sit, statim debilitatur, perspecta animi firmitate: nam imperterriti animi signum est, vel sic interrogare: Quis tu es, et unde?
>
> Whenever some apparition occurs, do not collapse in terror, but whatever it may be, ask first, bravely, "*Who are you and where do you come from?*" If it is a vision of holy ones, they will give you full assurance and transform your fear into joy. But if it is someone diabolical, it immediately is weakened, finding your spirit formidable. For simply by asking, "Who are you and where do you come from?" you give evidence of your calmness.[54]

Although Adam interrogates the devil from the standpoint of not discerning his true form, his questions repeat this kind of discernment-based prudence. His final choice not to obey Satan's messenger is based on the instructions that he knows God gave him previously; it is a choice to trust a higher authority when he cannot discern the nature of the spirit confronting him, and his verbal response to the tempter makes plain the wisdom of that choice, at least to the narrator, who does not elaborate on it. The narrator allows readers to hear and judge both what the devil says to Adam and Adam's response. In introducing Adam's quoted response, the narrator says only, "Adam maðelode þær he on eorðan stod, / selfsceafte guma" (Adam spoke where he on earth stood, a self-created man, 522–3a).[55] This is the only episode in the poem as we have it in which the narrator loosens control over the narrative, a shift that implies that right actions speak for themselves. Adam's approved response yields rage from the tempter, and its brevity strikingly contrasts with the quantity of narration that accompanies the devil's temptation of Eve.

Readers are initially presented with Eve's temptation in the same way as Adam's, in the direct discourse of the devil. The subsequent narration in this episode, however, describes Eve and her actions rather than allowing her to speak for herself. The narrator, in a move that echoes the narrator of *Daniel*, describes Eve as neither interrogating Satan's messenger nor deferring to Adam's or God's authority, though her hierarchical position has been clearly established in the poem: she is the "seo betste" (the best, 578b) of women – although that praise comes from the tempter's mouth and at a time when she is the *only* woman – but Adam

54 Athanasius, *Vita Antonii* 43, 906–7; Athanasius, *Life of Antony*, 64.

55 On the phrase "selfsceafte guma," see John Vickrey, "*Selfsceafte* in *Genesis B*," *Anglia* 83 (1965): 153–7; and John Vickrey, "Some Further Remarks on *Selfsceafte*," *Zeitschrift für deutsches Altertum und deutsche Literatur* 110 (1981): 1–14.

is clearly defined as her lord, "frea min," as she calls him (655a). If logic is allowed a role, she, like Adam, cannot recognize the messenger as a devil – still knowing only good, they do not know fallen angels – but she can further examine the devil's offer of mastery, "Meaht þu Adame eft gestyran" (you can guide Adam afterwards, 568). When the devil says that Eve must help Adam by taking the fruit, she apparently decides that she is in a position to judge better than Adam did in the same situation; the devil has no qualms about stressing Adam's earlier refusal to act upon his message, yet still Eve does not turn to Adam for advice.[56] In the context of discernment narratives, her acceptance of this offer not only makes her culpable of pride but also provides a didactic example of what happens when a person does not carefully examine spirits and seek help in doing so (an especially apt lesson if the story is received communally). The poem even turns this hierarchical point outward, generalizing it for readers: "bið þam men full wa / þe hine ne warnað þonne he his geweald hafað" (It is a great woe to one who does not guard himself when he has the power, 634b–5).

In short, Eve becomes a lesson in the results of subverting hierarchy, a role that might be amplified or affirmed by the example *Daniel* offers: self-reliance has dangers, and higher authority can provide practical as well as spiritual insight.[57] Eve is not, however, Nabochodonossor, and neither the narrator nor Eve herself explains, beyond the assertion of her "wacran hige" (weaker or yielding mind, 590b), why "hire on innan ongan / weallan wyrmes geþeaht" (within her began to well up the serpent's thought, 589b–90a).[58] Her actions indicate that either she did not mistrust the messenger or she suppressed that mistrust. The omission of Eve's verbal response and the narrator's inclusion only of the fact that the temptation consisted of lies – rather than recapitulating the content of the ongoing temptation – direct attention not to the particular sin that seduced Eve but to the circumstances of sin in general: weakness and deceptive appeal.[59] Eve, like anyone else, is

56 In psychological terms, as Doane, *Saxon Genesis*, 144, puts it, Eve is "in the position where she must identify her welfare with what the snake dictates rather than with the word of God as interpreted by Adam."

57 Susan Burchmore, "Traditional Exegesis and the Question of Guilt in the Old English 'Genesis B,'" *Traditio* 41 (1985): 117–44, argues that the text presents Eve as guided by her senses and thus not cognizant of her guilt, while Adam is more guilty because he has the rational power of discernment.

58 Translation of "wacran hige" is complicated. For particular relevance here, see Katherine DeVane Brown's discussion of the phrase in "Antifeminism or Exegesis? Reinterpreting Eve's *wacgeþoht* in *Genesis B*," *JEGP* 115 (2016): 141–66.

59 Indeed, Hill has suggested that the whole poem focuses on the "subversion of hierarchical order which is involved in the commission of any sin." The particular

deceived because when confronted with a spirit she does not recognize, she allows appeals to her own authority to take precedence over a hierarchically based and gendered prudence. The narrator takes pains to emphasize the anti-hierarchical deception – the same explanation of events, that she was deceived by lies, occurs twice in quick succession, immediately before and after she eats.[60] Too, the narrator stresses Eve's positive attributes, including her beauty and her ignorance of the result of her actions.[61]

A fine person who does not suspect an assault is not, however, excused from guilt.[62] At least some in an early medieval audience – the best read, especially – could have drawn such an understanding from a discernment discussion in the *Moralia in Iob* 9.13.20, where Gregory warns against just such situations:

> Et tamen saepe mens, dum de uirtutis suae securitate resoluitur, insidiante aduersario, inopinatae culpae telo perforatur; et inde a Deo in aeternum longe fit, unde ei ad tempus sine cautelae custodia propinquauit.
>
> Yet it often happens that whilst the mind is made to sit loose by self-security in its virtues, from the adversary plotting against it, it is pierced with the weapon of unexpected sin, and is for ever put far away from God

---

sin that led to Eve's fall has traditionally been assumed to be pride, though *Genesis B* does not name it as such (though it does for Satan); see "Fall of the Angels and Man," 285. For a cross-section of such readings, see Burchmore, "Traditional Exegesis," 130–4; Doane, *Saxon Genesis*, 143–6; and Gillian R. Overing, "On Reading Eve: *Genesis B* and the Readers' Desire," in *Speaking Two Languages: Traditional Disciplines and Contemporary Theory in Medieval Studies*, ed. Allen J. Frantzen (Albany: State University of New York Press, 1991), 35–63.

60 See lines 588 and 647. After Eve's speech of temptation to Adam, in lines 699–703a, the narrator repeats for a third time this essential information that the devil deceived Eve, "idese sciene, wifa wlitegost" (the fair woman, the most beautiful of wives).

61 Ambrose, for instance, also explains Eve's weakness as evidence of the need for hierarchy, but he is much less interested in Eve's positive attributes than is the *Genesis B* poet. See, e.g., *De paradiso* 14, in Ambrose, *Sancti Ambrosii Opera*, part 1, 329–30.

62 Robert Emmett Finnegan argues that even if Eve herself does not perceive the implications of her actions – she acts with loyal intent – the sequence of events in the poem presents her as culpable. Since Eve is, in particular, present for God's command concerning the tree, and the devil admits to her that he has already tried and failed to tempt Adam, still she does not use this in judging the devil; "the moral quality of her actions comes under the heading of 'vincible' or 'culpable' ignorance," as defined in Augustine's *De civitate Dei*, 14.13–14, 335. See "Eve and 'Vincible Ignorance' in *Genesis B*," *Texas Studies in Literature and Language* 18 (1976): 329–39; and Augustine, *Sancti Aurelii Augustini De ciuitate Dei XXII*, ed. Bernhard Dombart and Alfonsus Kalb, 2 vols., CCSL 47–8 (Turnhout, Belgium: Brepols, 1955).

> by the very means whereby for a time it was brought near to Him without the action of heedfulness.[63]

Both Gregory and the *Genesis B* narrator see the threat of sin as great when people think themselves most secure.[64] In succumbing to an unforeseen weakness – the narrative, at least, gives no earlier, clear indication of her pride – Eve is characterized as someone who not only lacks the ability to discern accurately the nature of spirits but also fails to discern the right response to a spirit she cannot identify.

Eve's initial error, then, might have been understood as less in finding the devil persuasive than in not turning to the defined authority. As in the discernment stories told by the Desert Fathers and in the Fall of the Angels narratives in Junius 11, the submission to the will of another is in *Genesis B* construed as a virtue. That point is amplified by contexts within, across, and outside Junius 11.[65] The devil's approach to Eve, in particular, echoes an example from the *Vita S. Martini*, summarized by Stancliffe, in which one Anatolius "initially claimed that angels spoke with him; then, that he was a 'virtus Dei,' and that God would give him a gleaming white garment to prove his claim and convict those who disbelieved in him."[66] The next day, one of the brothers, suspicious of Anatolius's claims, attempts to lead Anatolius to the clear-seeing Martin himself: "adprehensum dextera ad Martinum trahere uolebat, bene conscius inludi illum diaboli arte non posse" (taking him by the hand, he wished to lead him to Martin, well aware that [Martin] could not be deceived by the arts of the devil).[67]

63 Gregory, *Moralia in Iob*, 143: 471; Gregory, *Morals on the Book of Job*, 3 vols., Library of Fathers 18 (Oxford: J.H. Parker, 1844), 1:509.

64 Gregory attributes the problem specifically to the post-lapsarian condition: "Seclusum quippe ab internis gaudiis genus humanum, exigente culpa, mentis oculos perdidit, et quo meritorum suorum passibus graditur nescit" (For the human race being shut out from the interior joys, in due of sin, lost the eyes of the mind; and whither it is going with the steps of its deserts, it cannot tell): *Moralia in Iob*, 9.13.20, CCSL 143: 471; *Morals*, 1:509). The comment implies that Eve should have been able to discern the devil, for Eve's mind, when she first meets the tempter in her pure state, is not clouded; yet without knowledge of good and evil, without ever having met a devil, she does not recognize the nature of the being before her. The central concern of *Genesis B* is less a recovery of Eve's pre-lapsarian motivations than a post-lapsarian lesson derived from her actions and their contrast to Adam's.

65 See Graham Gould, *The Desert Fathers on Monastic Community* (Oxford: Clarendon Press, 1993), particularly the chapter "The Abba and His Disciple" on discernment as a teaching tool.

66 Stancliffe, *St. Martin*, 235. See also Sévère, ch. 23, "*Vie de Saint Martin*," 1:302–6.

67 *Vie de Saint Martin*, 1:304–6.

Cassian, too, believed in the necessity of seeking guidance when faced with an indiscernible spirit. In the second of his *Conferences*, he gives "rules" for *discretio* that focus on humility and the need to trust "one's own judgment in nothing," to submit "everything done or thought of" to the "scrutiny of our elders." Though Cassian's emphasis is on the monastic world, early medieval readers may easily have found relevance in reading Eve's situation, not least because of reference to a snake:

> ualebit ignoranti eius callidus hostis inludere, qui uniuersas cogitationes in corde nascentes perniciosa uerecundia nescit obtegere, sed eas maturo examine seniorum uel reprobat uel admittet. Illico namque ut patefacta fuerit cogitatio maligna marcescit, et antequam discretionis iudicium proferatur, serpens teterrimus uelut e tenebroso ac subterraneo specu uirtute confessionis protractus ad lucem et traductus quodammodo ac dehonestatus abscedit.
>
> The skill of the enemy will not be able to delude the ignorance of a man who does not, out of dangerous shame, conceal the thoughts arising in his heart and who rejects or accepts them following upon their quick examination by older men. An evil thought sheds its danger when it is brought out into the open, and even before the verdict of discernment is proffered the most foul serpent which, so to speak, has been dragged out of its dark lair into the light by the fact of open avowal retreats, disgraced and denounced.[68]

In the context of such discussions, Eve, no matter what intentions she had and no matter what her intellectual capacity, is guilty of relying on herself alone. Like Adam, Eve cannot be familiar with angels or snakes bringing word of God's change of mind; like Adam, she should have been wary. Eve's "wacran hige" in *Genesis B* has, it appears, more to do with her independence from authority than with her intelligence.

Only after Eve eats the fruit does she acquire a discernment of sorts, and then it is a false discernment falsely given by the devil:

> Þa meahte heo wide geseon
> þurh þæs laðan læn þe hie mid ligenum beswac,
> dearnenga bedrog þe hire for his dædum com
> þæt hire þuhte hwitre heofon and eorðe

68 Cassian, *Conférences*, 2.10; Cassian, *Conferences*, 67–8.

and eall þeos woruld wlitigre, and geweorc godes
micel and mihtig þeah heo hit þurh monnes geþeaht
ne sceawode Ac se sceaða georne
swicode ymb þa sawle þe hire ær þa siene onlah
þæt heo swa wide wliten meahte
ofer heofonrice. (600b–9a)

Then she could see far and wide through the loan of the evil one, he who with lies deceived her, insidiously beguiled her, by which it came about on account of his deeds, that to her heaven and earth seemed brighter, and all the world more beautiful, and God's work great and mighty, though she did not see it by means of human perception, but by the devil who eagerly deceived her being, who had given her that vision, so that she could see so widely over the heavenly kingdom.

The "laðan læn" of false discernment is an inversion of the divine gift of true discernment from the Holy Spirit. Eve herself confirms her lack of prior discernment when, in tempting Adam, she asks, "'Who else could give me such understanding, or discernment (*gewit*), if God, heaven's ruler, did not directly send it?'" (671–4a).[69] In her post-lapsarian state, for the moment guided by the devil, the question is to her rhetorical, and the narrative pointedly does not show her "testing the spirit" before accepting the fruit.[70] Instead, Eve's description of the tempter as "'þes boda sciene / godes engel god'" (this bright messenger, God's good angel, 655b–6a) – in her first direct speech – highlights her lack of true discernment. By trusting her own judgment, she has lost the chance to discern the true form of the messenger.

69 Bede's reference to the *discretio* of Aidan is translated in the *Old English Ecclesiastical History* 3.5 as *gesceades*, one of the bishop Aidan's "gastlicum mægenum"; see Bede, *The Old English Version of Bede's Ecclesiastical History of the English People*, ed. Thomas Miller, EETS, o.s. 95, 96, 110, 111 (London, 1890–8; repr., London: Oxford University Press, 1959), 1:164. Among modern editors, Bradley, *Anglo-Saxon Poetry*, 31, translates *gewit* as "discernment," though *witan* can also mean "to know, have knowledge of, be aware," according to Bosworth-Toller, or "to understand, observe, perceive, ascertain, learn," according to J.R. Clark Hall's *A Concise Anglo-Saxon Dictionary*, 4th ed., Medieval Academy Reprints for Teaching 14 (Toronto: University of Toronto Press, 1960).

70 Doane, *Saxon Genesis*, 151, describes this shift in Eve's perception as the poet "brilliantly reus[ing]" the "old motif, available from Pauline and apocalyptic traditions" of devils disguised as angels of light.

Her actions are a direct inversion of those advocated in discernment texts such as this pseudo-Macarian homily (translated from the Greek):

> The [person] who loves virtue must exercise great discernment in order to recognize the difference between the good and the evil, to examine and understand the varied ruses of the wicked one, who is accustomed by means of specious imaginings to pervert many. ... Do not give yourself over too quickly through lightness of mind to the promptings of spiritual beings, who might deceive you, even if these are angels from heaven; remain prudent, make a careful examination, accepting what is good, rejecting what is evil.[71]

This is exactly what Adam does, and what Eve does not do. Yet the homily also notes that, to protect against evil, a person must study it, learning to understand its disguises and its complexities. *Genesis B* offers good ground for an audience to do so. The dual temptations of Adam and Eve, the dramatic, mixed characters, and the extensive narrator commentary demonstrate subtle mendacity at work and suggest how to guard against it. Instead of a simplistic, didactic account of either refusing or submitting to temptation, the poem shows and tells about both. The apparent duality in Eve's character – those elements that have been read as potentially heterodox – might then be read as part of a sophisticated, if also gender-inflected, exploration of how evil works and who might fall prey to it.

Eve both subverts the established hierarchy by her actions and is contained again in it by the narrator's commentary on those actions, which offers her as a negative example of the limits of good intentions. In that example, neither the devil's strategy nor Eve's response is presented simplistically. Where Adam can seize on the messenger's lack of a *tacen* verifying his angelic status, Eve is given a token, in the form of a seemingly divine vision, that she does not perceive for what it actually is. The devil uses lies; he manipulates "hyge Euan" (the mind of Eve):

> wifes wac geþoht   þæt heo ongan his wordum truwian,
> læstan his lare   and geleafan nom
> þæt he þa bysene from gode   brungen hæfde
> þe he hire swa wærlice   wordum sægde,

71 Pseudo-Macarius, *Homilies* 1 and 3, PG 3.876b, trans. in Guillet et al., "Discernment of Spirits," 17.

iewde hire tacen and treowa gehet,
his holdne hyge. (649–54a)

the woman's weak thought, so that she began to trust his words, to follow his counsels, and took faith that he had brought from God that command that he to her so carefully in his words declared, showed her a token and promised faith, his loyal intent.

When Eve then turns to tempting Adam, the narrator repeats the assertions of her ignorance of the devil's wiles:

                idese sciene,
wifa wlitegost, ... heo on his willan spræc,
wæs hi*n*e on helpe handweorc godes
to forlæranne ... .
heo dyde hit þeah *þurh holdne hyge,* nyste þæt þær hearma swa fela,
fyrenearfeða, fylgean sceolde
monna cynne, þæs heo on mod genam
þæt heo þæs laðan bodan larum hyrde
Ac wende þæt heo hyldo heofoncyninges
worhte mid þam wordum þe heo þam were swelce
tacen oðiewde and treowe gehet. (700b–14; emphasis mine)

The brightest of women, the most beautiful of wives, ... she spoke according to his [the devil's] wishes, the handiwork of God was a help to him in seducing [Adam]. ... She did it, though, with loyal intent; she did not know that so many injuries, terrible sufferings for humankind, would follow that which she in her mind accepted, so that she obeyed the teachings of the evil messenger; but she thought that she worked with those words the favour of the King of heaven, so that she showed [Adam] such tokens and promised faith.

Eve's own words are not given for readers to judge for themselves. The narrator instead repeatedly declares her a good creature misled by subtle trickery. Yet even in the narrator's claim, Eve's intentions are less praiseworthy than her position as the first woman since the devil, too, claims to have "holdne hyge" himself, and the narrator repeats his claim.[72] The connection modifies any hints of exculpation; that Eve,

72 The devil asserts that "wæs seo hwil þæs lang / þæt ic geornlice gode þegnode / þurh holdne hyge" (it was not long since I eagerly served God with loyal intent, 584b–6a).

moreover, subsequently "remedies" the devil's failed temptation of Adam, even producing some kind of token in her persuasion, highlights the fact that thoughts or intentions alone are not sufficient when outside the ordained hierarchy.[73]

Eve's story is a calculated balance between mediated praise for her good qualities and criticism for her lack of proper subordination to a defined hierarchy, a lack that both the Fall story and discernment of spirits teachings can help others avoid. The narration of Eve's actions recounts her Fall, precedes the quotation of the words she uses to tempt Adam, and is interposed between her speech and the devil's celebratory speech as well as beginning the subsequent episode. The structure reduces Eve's presence as an autonomous individual but also limits her culpability. The narration, in large part, presents Eve's worst moments indirectly and ensures that the audience knows that, despite Eve's actions, she has laudable aspects and her sin is less stark and more complicated than Satan's.[74] And when Eve does again speak for herself, her words carry heavy contrition. The final description of Eve encapsulates the narrator's attitude toward her:

> Ða spræc Eue eft, idesa scienost,
> wifa wlitegost – hie wæs geweorc godes
> þeah heo þa on deofles cræft bedroren wurde:
> "Þu meaht hit me witan, wine min Adam,
> wordum þinum. hit þe þeah wyrs ne mæg
> on þinum hyge hreowan þonne hit me æt heortan deð." (821–6)

> Then spoke Eve again, fairest of women, most beautiful of women, – she was created by God, though she had come then into the devil's power: "You may blame me for it, my friend, Adam, with your words, yet you cannot sorrow more deeply for it in your mind than do I in my heart."

Eve speaks as both God's beautiful creation and the devil's corrupted instrument, and her words are matched and mediated by a roughly

---

73 Doane, *Saxon Genesis*, 295, argues that "holdne hyge" "plays on the idea that Eve as the inferior of Adam ought to be 'loyal,' i.e., obedient, but as one usurping authority, she thinks of herself as 'gracious,' i.e. as bestowing a favor on her inferior. Her 'loyalty' is now to her new lord, the devil."

74 Vickrey, in "Adam, Eve, and the *Tacen*," argues on philological grounds that "Eve, as well as Adam, subverts the created hierarchy" (10). The poem carefully establishes degrees of guilt in succumbing to temptation, but, he concludes, the "verbs *nyste* '(she) knew not' [in 708–9] … and *wende* [in 712–13]" do not offer exoneration of Eve.

equal number of the narrator's words. Adam's lengthier response to her is, in contrast, introduced only by "Hire þa Adam andswarode" (Adam then answered her, 827).[75] Here and throughout the poem, the narrator, in effect, subordinates audience interpretation to narrator commentary and contains Eve's words and actions within the hierarchy that she transgressed. In doing so, the poem offers an example of what discernment discussions teach: the situation that is harder to read, Eve's, requires more authoritative guidance. Adam's response to the devil is important, but Eve's situation offers a theological object lesson – one that validates the authority of patristic commentary as well as endorses the narrator's own discernment – in the results of trusting too much one's own strength in a difficult-to-discern situation.

Whether or not audiences were familiar with Latin discernment narratives, the attention to characters' and readers' perception – to seeing and understanding – in *Genesis B* and *Daniel* seems likely to have resonated with the broader interest in the topic. This remains true if these poems were read independently but even more so if they were read in conversation with each other or with other literature or material culture on the subject. Within the bounds of the Junius 11 manuscript, the poems function separately or in sequence as part of the Old Testament chronological narrative. The first instance of human action based on faulty perception, in *Genesis B*, lays the groundwork for the events and concerns found in *Daniel*. But, as the sequence in this chapter's discussion – *Daniel* before *Genesis B* – emphasizes, the topic of spiritual perception is also enriched by a reversed order and by otherwise juxtaposed reading. A reader of *Genesis B* already familiar with the *Daniel* poem, whether from reading it within or outside Junius 11, would be far more likely to read Eve as needing to rely on a divine or divinely gifted interpreter of discourse. For a sequential reader of Junius 11, the divine authority so emphatically defined by *Genesis A* is tested in *Genesis B* and then is explored in *Daniel* within post-lapsarian, human spheres of perception and understanding.

However approached, the concern with spiritual perception in *Genesis B* and *Daniel* indicates participation in a rich, enduring cultural context outside the manuscript itself, one evident in other texts and

75 Adam when he does fall gives in not to an unknown spirit but to Eve, to her words as influenced by the devil. Once Adam weakens and begins to submit to temptation by Eve, the narrator takes away his voice; not until after he eats the fruit does the narrator allow Adam to speak for himself again. Even then, however, the narrator focuses his comments on Eve, stressing both her error and her remorse (765b–77a).

other art, and one that might provide its own reasons for reading these particular sections of Junius 11 aside from, or in addition to, reading them within the manuscript's sequential coherences. Discernment in *Daniel* and *Genesis B* models and encourages careful reading with an authoritative guide. The same topic is addressed more explicitly in their companion poem *Exodus*, by accident or intention, and whether readers noted such an overlap or not.

Chapter 3

Boceras and *Exodus*

Nis þis nan leas spel! Hit stent on Leden þus on ðære bibliothecan. Þæt witon boceras þe þæt Leden cunnon þæt we na ne leogað.[1]

Across its topical overlaps and interests, Junius 11, on its pages and in its texts, presents visible as well as textual disruptions. Readers who approach the manuscript as a consecutively ordered whole encounter places where connection between parts is at some distance – intellectual or physical – or is implied by an understanding of other sequences, such as biblical or liturgical. If opening with *Genesis A* establishes a reader's or audience's expectations of literary style as well as content and presentation, reaching *Genesis B* seems likely to lead to an adjustment of expectations, as would continuing to read through and beyond *Genesis A*. Although Irving asserted that "there is no positive evidence that the [Junius 11] scribe considered *Exodus* to be a separate poem," *Exodus* seems likely to have significantly challenged most of any reader expectations established by the preceding Genesis poems. Among the distinctive features of *Exodus* is what Lucas describes as the "sheer brilliance of its writing," evident, for instance, in its diversity of styles, including passages with "allusive condensation of meaning," as well as "vivid metaphors" that bring together "the animate and the inanimate, the concrete and the abstract."[2]

1 "This is no lying story. It stands in the Latin, thus in the Bible [or library]. Scholars who know Latin know that we are not lying at all"; see Ælfric, *Judith,* in *Ælfric's Homilies on Judith, Esther and The Maccabees*, ed. Stuart D. Lee, 1999, 404–6, http://users.ox.ac.uk/~stuart/kings/; as well as Paul E. Szarmach, "Ælfric's *Judith,*" in *Old English Literature and the Old Testament*, ed. Michael Fox and Manish Sharma (Toronto: University of Toronto Press, 2012), 82.

2 Lucas, *Exodus*, 43, 47–8, 50.

The poem, too, shows a remarkable attention to audience. The poet, as Samantha Zacher argues, "employs a range of mnemotechnical devices that encourage personal reflection and meditation upon the covenant as personal contract. The aim is to create a meditative template that allows each of its readers to experience the terms of the covenant individually."[3] Readers of *Genesis B* attuned to *discretio spirituum* and accustomed to reading with attention to issues of interpretation and understanding may have welcomed *Exodus*, and they may have read the Israelites' reliance on the learned guidance of Moses as yet more evidence of understanding achieved with the assistance of the right authority. *Exodus*, however, asks *all* readers to consider how well they read. Like *Daniel*, in particular, it also presents the narrator as a guiding authority for those who lack sufficient interpretive ability on their own. As such, *Exodus* might have functioned particularly well in communal reception, where authoritative guidance could be stressed and presumably provided.

Readers in tenth- and eleventh-century England have often been invoked *en masse* as a single body of textual interpreters, ones who frequently possess familiarity with patristic literature and Latin poetry as well as with Old English prose and poetry. The elusiveness of evidence for actual readings of Old English texts in early medieval England fosters such generalization, particularly for those who recognize that understanding the text means understanding its reader, a point made perhaps most emphatically for critics in the last half-century by Wolfgang Iser: "The involvement of the reader is essential to the fulfillment of the text. ... The literary text, then, exists primarily as a means of communication, while the process of reading is basically a kind of dyadic interaction."[4]

The problem, of course, is that knowing how any one early medieval reader read on the page or aurally received an Old English poem is forever out of reach, and even making generalizations about a particular kind of reader or reading requires leaping across gaps in knowledge. Still, the desire to know the other half in that dyadic interaction persists, tied to the pursuit of understanding the text in historical terms and fostered by glimpses of particular readers and meaning-building practices around texts. Howe cites two particularly good examples of such glimpses, that which Bede provides in recounting the history of Cædmon and that which Asser provides in his account of Alfred's life.

3 Zacher, *Rewriting the Old Testament*, 49.

4 Wolfgang Iser, *The Act of Reading: A Theory of Aesthetic Response* (Baltimore: Johns Hopkins University Press, 1980), 66.

The Cædmon story, particularly in its account of Cædmon's ongoing ability to transform scriptural text into vernacular poetry, represents reading "as a skill reserved to an elite group pledged to spread the truth as contained in a Latin text." Reading words on a page remains a distinctive skill in Alfred's time, one that Alfred achieves for himself slowly and, according to Asser, only after years of being read to and after "knowing absorption of the ideas and workings of a literate culture – that is, of written texts in Old English and in Latin."[5]

Alfred's program of translation helped to make reading one step more accessible for readers in tenth- and eleventh-century England, but it did not remove the idea of reading as a restricted skill or of readers of Latin as being more skilled. George Hardin Brown describes, in general terms, the "distinction drawn in the Middle Ages between the *litteratus* (in Latin) and the *idiota*, competent in the vernacular or local language but not in schooled Latin, the language of cultural and political power."[6] Any gap that existed between Latin and English reading comprehension would have diminished somewhat in distinctly Latinate Old English texts, but even alongside a growing availability of books in Old English, the idea of reading as a particularly skilled activity that requires ongoing work still had firm support from writers such as Augustine. In Book Seven of the *Confessions*, Augustine describes reading both as potentially dangerous and as a journey toward understanding. Reading the Platonists was an experience like that of an unsuccessful traveller, one who as if "from a wooded summit [were] to catch a glimpse of the homeland of peace and not to find the way to it, but vainly to attempt the journey" (de silvestri cacumine videre patriam pacis et iter ad eam non invenire et frustra conari per invia circum obsidentibus, 7.21.27). In contrast is the journey achieved through scriptural reading:

> coepi et inveni, quidquid illac verum legeram, hac cum commendatione gratiae tuae dici, ut qui videt non sic glorietur, quasi non acceperit non solum id quod videt, sed etiam ut videat (quid enim habet quod non accepit?) ... , et qui de longinquo videre non potest, viam tamen ambulet qua veniat et videat et teneat. (7.21.7)

> I began reading and found that all the truth I had read in the Platonists was stated here together with the commendation of your grace, so that

5 Howe, "Cultural Construction of Reading," 71–72.

6 George Hardin Brown, The Dynamics of Literacy in Anglo-Saxon England," *Bulletin of the John Rylands Library* 77, no. 1 (1995): 110.

> he who sees should "not boast as if he had not received" both what he sees and also the power to see. ... So also the person who from a distance cannot yet see, nevertheless walks along the path by which he may come and see and hold you.

Augustine was initially "subdued by books" – "cum postea in libris tuis mansuefactus essem" – and only afterwards learned to read the right books the right way, with greater understanding.[7]

Augustine's framing of reading as a journey toward understanding has long resonance, with explicit development in, for instance, Isidore's *Etymologiae*: "Letters (*littera*) are so called as if the term were *legitera*, because they provide a road (*iter*) for those who are reading (*legere*), or because they are repeated (*iterare*) in reading."[8] In an explanation that echoes Isidore, to some extent, Howe notes that the development of the Old English word *rædan* "has no etymological basis in the idea of collecting or gathering together letters and words to form the text as a whole, as do [Gothic] *lisan*, [modern German] *lesen*, or the Latin *legere*." Instead, the word's history lies in the act of explaining or interpreting. Howe, laying out the connection between giving counsel (*ræd*) and reading (*rædan*), identifies Ælfric's translation of *Exodus* as "a neat example" of the development of meaning and, at the same time, the continued connection between guiding and reading:

> In translating Exodus 18:19, *sed audi verba mea atque consilia* (*Biblia Sacra*: 60), he offers *ac gehyr min word ond minne ræd* "but hear my word and my counsel" (Crawford 1922: 258). Here, as one would expect, *ræd* is used for *consilio*. In translating Exodus 24:7, *legit audiente populo* (*Biblia Sacra*: 65), however, Ælfric offers the extended sense of *rædan*: *rædde his boc þam folce* "he read his book to the people" (Crawford 1922: 272).[9]

With its texts, guides, and journeys, the narrative of the biblical Exodus offers particularly rich ground for exploring notions of reading, and the Old English poem on Exodus, even more than in Ælfric's rendering

7 All the quotations from Augustine are from *Augustine: Confessions*, ed. James J. O'Donnell, 3 vols. (Oxford: Clarendon Press, 1992); the translations here are from *Saint Augustine: Confessions*, ed. and trans. Henry Chadwick (New York: Oxford University Press, 1991). Five manuscripts of the *Confessiones* survive from early medieval England; all, however, are late (see the *Handlist*).

8 1.iii.3, in Isidore, *The Etymologies of Isidore of Seville*, ed. and trans. Stephen A. Barney et al. (Cambridge: Cambridge University Press, 2006), 39.

9 Howe, "Cultural Construction of Reading," 62, 65.

of the story, offers glimpses of readers and reading practices. The poem possesses a narrator self-conscious about his position, which he expresses as one of a learned guide, much as does the narrator of *Daniel* in asserting his alliance with "runcræftige men" (733b). But in *Exodus*, the rune-craft becomes more literal. The narrator's authority is explicitly tied to reading rather than more generally to interpretation, and, as a result, the act of reading functions as both a pathway and a goal in the poem. Indeed, the poem sketches a meta-narrative on reading that defines two kinds of readers – those who are practised, accomplished readers and those who are not – and, correspondingly, two kinds of reading. The narrative offered alongside that of the Jews crossing the Red Sea is one in which both the learned narrator of *Exodus* and the poem itself, in its language and allusions, challenge readers to understand the need for interpretive guidance as part of moving toward the enduring rewards of heaven.[10]

Exodus opens with an invitation of sorts before making an explicit connection between the guidance of God and that of learned readers. Like *Genesis A*'s opening reference to what is appropriate for "us," the *Exodus* narrator opens with a first-person plural, observing that "we feor and neah gefrigan habað" (we, far and near, have learned, 1) of the commandments.[11] The phrase seems to extend the example of the Israelites to a general audience who already understands its significance and who shares, to some extent, the narrator's perspective and understanding, but the narrator's subsequent invitation to consider the acts of reading and interpretation implies a division between a trained and an untrained readership, or between those who choose or choose not to hear the story in the right way. From summary reference to the story of the laws of Moses, the narrative turns to the "langsumne ræd" (lasting counsel, 6b) that the story offers, and the opening lines end with a challenge: "gehyre se ðe wille" (listen who will, 7b).

That phrase, formulaic or not – a closely similar phrase also appears in the opening to the *Meters of Boethius* – provides a foundation of individual choice for the audience, although, at the same time, it puts

---

10 Sarah Elliott Novacich has also discussed the "reminders of literary prowess [that] hang about the Old English *Exodus* even though Moses's two inscribed tablets make only fleeting appearances"; her reading focuses on more on "Moses as a reader of the sea," "align[ing] him primarily with the reader confronting the difficult text of *Exodus*"; see "The Old English *Exodus* and the Read Sea," *Exemplaria* 23 (2011): 51, 59.

11 Throughout this chapter, the citations of *Exodus* are from Lucas's edition. The translations are my own unless otherwise noted.

forward no acceptable alternative.[12] The poem's opening asserts the power of narrative to reveal "in uprodor eadigra gehwam / æfter bealusiðe bote lifes, / lifigendra gehwam langsumne ræd – / hæleðum" (the reward of life in heaven above for each of the blessed after baleful journey, a lasting counsel for all the living, 4–7a). The immediately following phrase, "gehyre se ðe wille," implicitly notes that while some may choose not to hear (including, in other words, not to be educated by the poem that follows), a rejection of reading, whether heard or seen, would be imprudent and improvident.

The journey of the Israelites that occupies the majority of the ensuing narrative is marked by references not just to Moses's knowledge but also to the narrator's learnedness, which establishes the narrator's authority as a guide for readers in parallel to Moses's role as a guide for the Israelites. Moses is introduced as divinely favoured; he is "leof Gode" and "horsc ond hreðergleaw" (loved by God, quick-witted and wise, 12a, 13a). Moses is above other men, even those who also possess great wisdom. Following the biblical book of Exodus 6:2–3, the narrator explains that God told Moses "soðwundra fela" (many true wonders, 24b), which even the wisest men – presumably Abraham, Isaac, and Jacob – did not before know. Not so evident in the biblical base is the narrator's accompanying comment on the patriarchs that they did not know the name of God "þeah hie fela wiston" (although they knew many things, 29b). The *Exodus* poem condenses much in comparison to the biblical book, as Irving and others have shown, including, at this point, two separate conversations between Moses and God, but the inclusion of the "þeah hie fela wiston" remark allows the narrator to stress the wisdom of the patriarchs as well as to imply how much more the narrator knows and might have said about them.[13]

That the *Exodus* narrator knows a great deal and is presenting important knowledge is nowhere made clearer than when, late in the poem, the work of scholars is directly connected to the work of God. In reaction to Moses's speech just after the crossing of the Red Sea, the narrator expresses, in one of the most frequently discussed passages in the poem, not so much awe at the events just narrated as expectation regarding understanding:

Gif onlucan wile   lifes wealhstod,
beorht in breostum,   banhuses weard,

12 The proem to the *Meters of Boethius* cautions, "hliste se þe wille" (10b).

13 Irving, *Old English Exodus*, 68.

ginfæsten god gastes cægon,
run bið gerecenod, ræd forð gæð;
hafað wislicu word on fæðme,
wile meagollice modum tæcan,
þæt we gesne ne syn godes þeodscipes,
metodes miltsa. He us ma onlyhð,
nu us boceras beteran secgað,
lengran lyftwynna. (523–32a)

If the interpreter of life, the guardian of the bone-house, bright in breasts, wishes to unlock ample good with the keys of the spirit, the mystery will be explained, wisdom will go forth. He has wise words in his grasp, earnestly seeks to instruct our minds so that we will not be lacking the community of God, the maker's mercies. He grants us more, now scholars tell us of the better, longer-lasting joys of heaven.

The passage "makes a sudden leap from the decrees of Moses to the poet's present in what would appear to be a quick lesson on the interpretation of scripture," as Dorothy Haines describes it.[14] Haines also acknowledges that the passage stands out so much in its immediate context that modern readers' responses have included "baffled dismissal" as well as reorganization and removal.[15] As the poem exists on the page, however, the comment underscores the poem's attention, here and throughout, to the narrator and the act of storytelling, naming the *boceras* and the act of telling as key elements on the path toward God.

The narrator's role as a learned source and clear, knowledgeable interpreter of the story begins to be established early in the poem, even as God is defined as the most powerful guide on this journey. The account of the Israelites' journey begins with their navigation through hostile, narrow, unknown, and fierce lands and their reliance upon the knowledge of their guide. At each encampment on the way out of Egypt, the poet maintains the power of God over the individual – this is a remarkably passive army. When Moses (or God) first commands the fleeing Israelites to camp (63–105), militaristic language describes the people as "a most powerful force" (mægnes mast, 67a), yet they are also, for now, happy and comforted by God, who demonstrates his favour with the protecting cloud, the "dægsceldes hleo" (protection of the day shield,

14 Dorothy Haines, "Unlocking *Exodus* ll: 516–532," *JEGP* 98 (1999): 481.

15 Ibid., 482. Irving, e.g., moves the passage to near the end of the poem in his edition, and W.J. Sedgefield, ed., excises it altogether in *An Anglo-Saxon Verse Book* (Manchester: Manchester University Press, 1922).

79b). The company has been pushed by danger ("nearwe genyddon on norðwegas," difficulties forced [them] on the ways north, 68) rather than being described as taking a bold course, and their "lifweg" (way of life, 104b) is guided by God and Moses. Three times in this passage, the poet references the active role of God: holy God shields the people ("halig god / wið færbryne folc gescylde," 71b–2), wise God unfurls the metaphorical sail ("witig god / sunnan siðfæt segle ofertolden," 81b–2), and the Lord of Hosts himself comes to make camp ("drihten cwom, / weroda drihten, wicsteal metan," 91b–2). Lucas suggests that "these lines refer to the real presence of God in the Tabernacle suffused with the cloud. Numbers 9.15–23 explains how the stopping-places were indicated to the Israelites by the cloud."[16]

Real or figurative, such emphasis on divine involvement reinforces the leadership of Moses, the "tirfæstne hæleð" (glorious warrior, 63b) and "mære magoræswa" (renowned leader, 102a), and would surely encourage any audience to mimic the Israelites and serve, as do fire and cloud, in the high service of the Holy Spirit ("heahþegnunga haliges gastes," 96). As the journey progresses with these powerful guides, the narrator quietly establishes himself as also an excellent, if less powerful, guide.

In the description of the passage of the Israelite tribes across the parted sea, the narrator comments that all the tribes have "an fæder" (one father) who "cende cneowsibbe" (brought forth a nation, 353b, 356a): "swa þæt orþancum ealde reccað, / þa þe mægburge mæst gefrunon, / frumcyn feora, fæderæðelo gehwæs" (in this way the ancient ones skilfully explain, those who learned most about ancestries, about the origin of people, about each lineage, 359–61). Irving and Lucas read the reference and the passage as a whole as referring to Abraham (although Jacob is also a possibility), and both agree that mention of the skilful ancient writers "is a reference to the detailed and numerous genealogies in the Pentateuch, as usual adapted to a prominent feature in Anglo-Saxon tradition."[17] While indeed that seems the case, the phrasing also marks the poet's familiarity with those who "orþancum … reccað." In particular, *orþancum* – "skilfully," as well as "intelligence" or "understanding" – implies that the speaker not only understands his scriptural sources but also possesses awareness of the intellectual work, and perhaps too the literary skill, displayed within them. The "swa" that opens the passage aligns with those esteemed

16 Lucas, *Exodus*, 91.
17 Irving, *Old English Exodus*, 89.

sources of both the presentation of this particular information on lineage and the poem more generally. Similar comment soon follows, acknowledging authority while employing a present-tense verb that simultaneously positions the narrator alongside or dependent upon those who have done what the narrator himself is now doing: "swa þæt wise men wordum secgað / þæt from Noe nigoða wære / fæder Abrahames on folctale" (so wise men say in their words, that from Noah the ninth in lineage was Abraham's father, 377–9).

In *Genesis A*, Enos is "gleawferhð" (prudent, 1152a), Enoch and Noah are similarly labelled (1195b, 1370a), and Abraham is "wishydig" (sagacious, 1816b, 2257a; or wise, 1958b) and "gleaw" (prudent, 2375a). In *Exodus*, likewise, characters receive praise for their intellect, as when the narrator describes Solomon, "se snottra sunu Dauides" (the wise son of David, 389) and "se wisesta on woruldrice" (the wisest in the worldly kingdom, 393), but *Genesis A* does not offer praise for the *producers* of its sources or, by extension, the use of those sources in the poem itself. In the "gastes cægon" (keys of the spirit, 525b) passage, in particular, *Exodus* links wisdom, interpretation, and instruction to interpretation and interpreters, the "boceras" (scholars, 531a) who "onlucan wile" (wish to unlock, 523a) meaning.

Lucas understands *boceras* as most likely to be a reference to "the Church Fathers (rather than just the evangelists) who, after Christ has ensured the salvation of mankind (nu), can teach the rewards of heaven (beteran) through the interpretation of the scriptures."[18] Whether the term refers to a specific set of writers or not, the poet's invocation of them amplifies the authority of his own education and the role that learned interpretation can play in Christian life, presumably including the *Exodus* poem itself as both an interpretation of biblical text and a text in itself, also to be interpreted.[19] The fact that the most direct

18 Lucas, *Exodus*, 143.

19 Were the passage alone in the poem in its promotion of learned achievement, it might be less striking, but the comment reflects both the construction and the requirements of reading the poem, as noted in other readings of *Exodus*, such as Ellen E. Martin's: "It is fitting ... that, in a poem self-conscious enough about its figurativeness to refer to the 'boceras,' one of the poem's more puzzling figures [the African woman] not only should partake of the complication and artifice that characterize it, but also should represent the indirect and symbolic way that the poet has designed, and that the reader must read, this work." See Ellen E. Martin, "Allegory and the African Woman in the Old English 'Exodus,'" *JEGP* 81 (1982): 15; as well as the more recent studies of allegory and interpretation in *Exodus* by Novacich, "Old English *Exodus*," and by Audrey Walton, "'Gehyre se ðe Wille': The Old English Exodus and the Reader as Exegete," *English Studies* 94 (2013): 1–10.

instruction regarding reading comes at the end of the poem may seem somewhat counterintuitive, but only if we imagine a reader who reads the poem just once. The placement of the unlocking/*boceras* passage functions as a summative evaluation of the enduring value of the poem; it also might well change how a reader understands what has come before and encourage a repeat reading because it asks the reader whether the mysteries of the poem have indeed been understood. For a well-trained reader who has followed the guides at hand, wisdom can now go forth. For those for whom the mysteries remain locked, however, the work is unfinished.

Well-trained monastic readers in early medieval England, however few or many such readers were, probably followed a careful, multistep approach to reading, one tied explicitly to understanding and contemplating. Parkes has explored the evidence for this process at some length, and his examples include a note, probably written at Winchester in the first half of the tenth century, in a fragment from Bede's *Ecclesiastical History*, that frames reading in terms of the classical tradition of grammatical studies. The note begins, "Grammaticae officia sunt [quattu]or: lectio, enarratio, emenda[tio], iudicium." Brief explanations of these four stages of reading – *lectio, enarratio, emenda[tio], iudicium* – follow, and a similar account of the same principles appears in at least one earlier manuscript, "the preface to the treatise known as the *Anonymus ad Cuimnanum*," probably also from southern England but from the seventh or eighth century. Parkes summarizes the four aspects as follows:

> *Lectio* was the process whereby a reader had to identify elements of a text ... in order to read it aloud according to the accentuation required by the sense (*pronuntiatio*). *Emendatio* ... required a reader (or his teacher) to correct the text in his copy. ... *Enarratio* was the process of examining features of vocabulary, rhetorical and literary form, and above all interpreting the subject matter of the text (*explanatio*). *Iudicium* was the process of exercising judgement of the aesthetic qualities or the moral and philosophical value of the text.[20]

Additional evidence for this kind of reading can be found in manuscript glosses, corrections, comments, and the texts themselves. Among Parkes's explanations of the principle of *enarratio* – that is, "what was necessary to clarify a text in order to understand it" – is the example in *Exodus*, where the "unlocking" passage articulates the process and

20 Parkes, "*Rædan, areccan, smeagan,*" 1.

reward: "If the individual reader is willing to apply the intellective capacity of the soul (lifes wealhstod ... in breostum) to unlock the lasting riches of the text of the scriptures with the keys of the Holy Spirit, a mystery will always be explained and advantage come from it."[21] In a poem as densely written as *Exodus*, the placement of such direction seems either congratulatory, to the reader who has worked through the text to this point, or, as the *gif* more strongly implies, directive, to the reader who must keep trying to unlock the poem's riches.

While the *boceras* passage endorses a particular and contemplative style of learned reading, the preliminary qualification – "Gif onlucan wile lifes wealhstod" (If the interpreter of life wishes to unlock, 523) – indicates that such an approach to text is not universal, and other writers make clear that not everyone possessed the kind of reading skills that Parkes describes. In the preface, his first series of homilies, for instance, Ælfric famously criticizes "mycel gedwyld on manegum engliscum bocum. ðe ungelærede menn ðurh heora bilewitnysse to mycclum wisdome tealdon" (much error in many English books, which unlearned men, through their simplicity, have esteemed as great wisdom).[22] Byrhtferth takes a somewhat more encouraging stance when, as Howe recounts, he "explains in his *Manual* that he is writing for the benefit of *iunge mynstermen* 'young monastic students' and bids *þa boceras ond þa getydde weras* 'scholars and learned men' not to be impatient with his elementary exposition."[23] The implied expectation of impatience from expert readers (those skilled in *enarratio*) underscores the *Exodus* passage's emphasis on limited access and potentially heightens the role of *boceras* in transmitting learning.

The scorn that some skilled readers might have had for those less well prepared for the challenges of poetry such as *Exodus* is also suggested by three Anglo-Latin poems preserved in CUL MS., Kk.5.34, probably from Winchester ca. 1000, and edited by Lapidge. The poems include a dialogue in which a student, speaking for himself and his peers, accuses his teacher of "praising poetry to us such as not even schoolboys would deign to look at. ... And he glorifies his own muddy composition": "nobis laudare poesim / qualem nec pueri dignantur cernere scolis. ... sinthecam ... suam comit lutulentam" (35–6, 41).[24]

21 Ibid., 14.

22 Ælfric, *Catholic Homilies* 1, 51–2.

23 Ælfric, *Old English Version of the Heptateuch,* 132, quoted in Howe, "Cultural Construction of Reading," 67.

24 Michael Lapidge, "Three Latin Poems from Æthewold's School at Winchester," *ASE* 1 (1972): 112–13.

A subsequent remark by the *discipulus* acknowledges education that involves composing as well as recognizing good verse, although the students still appear to show some scepticism of their poetry teacher:

credere ni uis
quod pueri sic
edere metrum
(improbe!) possunt
hic resident qui
dogmate docti
pontificali,
ut neque sensum
prodere murcum
siue poema
non fore rectum:
indice quibus
rite loquelis,
temet adhortor.

And unless you wish to believe (you scoundrel!) that we boys who live here and are taught by the bishop's teaching can compose verse in such a way as neither to give a mutilated sense nor an incorrect poem, show us properly by what words [we err], I urge you. (55–68)[25]

The bishop referred to here may well be, as Lapidge suggests, Æthelwold, bishop of Winchester from 963 to 984, and the poems may correspond to the kind of literate and literary education Æthelwold encouraged.[26] The students' grounding would lie in Latin, of course, but at Winchester, at least, their education would presumably extend to Old English. Æthelwold's own skill in Old English is evident in his influential translation of the Benedictine Rule and in the work of his pupil, Ælfric. Such students, like the voices in the poems, would learn sophisticated reading skills as well as, presumably, a critical awareness of poetry.

Within *Exodus*, the language and style with which the narrative is delivered play at least as large a role as the narrator's self-referential comments do in establishing the idea that reading requires learning and guidance. The language of *Exodus* "is at times startlingly different

25 Ibid., 124–5.

26 See Michael Lapidge, "The Hermeneutic Style in Tenth-Century Anglo-Latin Literature," *ASE* 4 (1975): 90–1.

from that of" other Old English verse, in part because of features that Roberta Frank suggests might come from Scandinavian influences. She identifies, for instance, language characteristic of Norse skaldic poetry: in one twelve-line passage of *Exodus* (2. 71–85) "are six different metaphors for the same object," the cloud-pillar, an elaborateness of figurative language that suggests a poet "apparently unconcerned about the possibility of losing his audience."[27] Biblical references, aside from the primary narrative itself, also suggest the poet's conscious alliance of reading and learning. Hall identifies, for instance, connection between the *gastes cægon* passage in *Exodus* and "Paul's discussion of the letter and spirit of Scripture" in 2 Corinthians: "It is appropriate that the poet, in stressing the need to view the Mosaic Law in light of the Spirit and in characterizing the nature of life on earth, should borrow from Paul's discussion and should want the audience to recognize the fact."[28] Thomas Hill, who characterizes *Exodus* as "extraordinary if cryptic poetry," links the poem's biblical and Germanic backgrounds to suggest "the possibility that 'hermeneutic' Latin and 'hermeneutic' Old English reflect a similar literary sensibility":

> If one defines *Exodus* as "barbarian" poetry then the poet's interest in extravagant and sometimes obscure poetic language, his parade of seemingly esoteric Biblical learning, and his delight in traditional Germanic poetry, all reflect an essentially similar sensibility. In suggesting this definition of the art of the *Exodus* poet, I do not mean to imply that the poet was necessarily naïve or was himself "barbarian" in the pejorative sense of that term. Many of the identified authors of Latin hermeneutic texts were capable of writing classical as well as hermeneutic Latin, and *Exodus* might similarly be an extravagant set piece of an otherwise more conservative poet.[29]

Certainly the poem has long been understood as the work of a sophisticated and learned poet, a perception that has led modern readers of the middle sections of the Junius 11 manuscript to tend to esteem *Exodus* over *Daniel*. Irving put the distinction in stark terms: "Fundamentally and inescapably, the important difference between *Daniel* and *Exodus* is the difference between the inferior and superior in poetic quality."[30]

27 Roberta Frank, "Did Anglo-Saxon Audiences Have a Skaldic Tooth?," *Scandinavian Studies* 59 (1987): 339–40.

28 J.R. Hall, "Pauline Influence on Exodus, 523–548," *ELN* 15 (1977): 85, 88.

29 Thomas D. Hill, "The *virga* of Moses and the Old English *Exodus*," in *Old English Literature in Context*, ed. John D. Niles (Cambridge: D.S. Brewer, 1980), 57, 64.

30 Irving, *Old English Exodus*, 27. Irving echoes, for instance, an earlier editor of *Exodus*, Francis A. Blackburn, who places the poem "much above either the *Genesis A* or

Even a more moderate sense of poetic quality, for modern readers as well as early medieval ones, if indeed it existed for them, may derive, at least in part, from the context of Latin examples. The poetry of Alcuin, for instance, offers a base against which to measure the kind of intellectual flamboyance evident in *Exodus*. Lapidge cites a poem written by Alcuin and addressed to Charlemagne that begins "nix ruit e caelo" (snow falls from the sky) and seems to explain circuitously "that Charlemagne and his daughter have not responded sufficiently warmly to one of Alcuin's epistles." "These lines," remarks Lapidge, "are so oblique as to be impenetrable."[31]

While the Old English *Exodus* does not quite reach such a level of elite discourse, its language, even in the vernacular, suggests a poet with the kind of language comfort that we now associate with extensive reading. The first note in Lucas's and in Irving's editions of *Exodus* identifies the characteristic style of the ensuing poem: the "general meaning" of lines 1 to 7 of *Exodus* "is fairly clear," writes Irving, "but the syntax presents a puzzling problem"; Lucas cites Pamela Gradon's comment to label the lines "'a peculiarly elaborate example' of 'the complex type of parallelism' favoured in some OE poems."[32] Throughout the poem, figurative descriptions, words used in what Lucas calls "unusual collocations," and striking and unusual repetitions and compounds in what most modern readers see as a densely allusive poem have led to labelling *Exodus* as *hermeneutic* poetry, which Lapidge defines as "a style whose most striking feature is the ostentatious parade of unusual, often very arcane and apparently learned vocabulary."[33]

Among the most often noted of the *Exodus* poet's figures of speech is *hypallage*, or "transferred epithet," a device used by esteemed Latin poets such as Vergil, Lucan, Juvencus, and Alcimus Avitus. Works by the latter two writers were clearly known by Bede and Aldhelm, and they are among those that Lapidge, on the basis of booklists and surviving manuscripts, identifies as part of the school curriculum in early medieval England.[34] Indeed, Lapidge has argued that "the metaphorical diction of the Old English *Exodus* can best be understood in the context of the Latin verse which literate Anglo-Saxons studied as part of their

---

the *Daniel* in poetic worth": *Exodus and Daniel: Two Old English Poems* (Boston: D.C. Heath, 1907), xxi.

31 Michael Lapidge, "Artistic and Literary Patronage in Anglo-Saxon England," in *Anglo-Latin Literature, 600–899* (Rio Grande, OH: Hambledon Press, 1996), 62–3.

32 Irving, *Old English Exodus*, 67; Lucas, *Exodus*, 75; Pamela Gradon, *Form and Style in Early English Literature* (London: Methuen, 1971), 157.

33 Lucas, *Exodus*, 46–7; Lapidge, "Hermeneutic Style," 67.

34 Michael Lapidge, "Hypallage in the Old English *Exodus*," *Leeds Studies in English* 37 (2006): 32–3.

school curriculum."[35] Remley adds to the arguments for the *Exodus* poet's evident comfort with Latin, noting that the poet's knowledge of the Bible seems to have extended well beyond the book of Exodus: "No other single work of Old English biblical verse has occasioned as much speculation about verbal parallels within the canon of scripture as has *Exodus*."[36] Strong connections exist, too, between *Exodus* and the Latin poetry of Aldhelm: "Almost every span of lines in *Exodus* – from start to finish – finds some parallel of content in the writings of Aldhelm."[37] The distinctive and complicated language of the poem – Latinate seems an apt description, if not entirely sufficient – has attracted extensive attention from modern scholars trying to work out allusions, wordplay, and meanings, and the same aspects of the poem's language would presumably communicate to any early medieval audience the learning of the *Exodus* poet and the sophisticated literacy of *boceras*.[38]

The manuscript context of *Exodus* heightens the power of its assertion of the need for interpretive guidance: sequential reading from *Genesis A* to *Exodus* involves a shift in poetic style, in narrative emphasis, and in relationship to canonical text, whether or not an audience associates the changes with any heightened display of learning. Where *Genesis A* offers a model for behaviour that involves choosing faith and obedience, *Exodus* presents a vision not just of surrender to God but also of individual agency controlled by God; across the poems comes a move from tracking a heroic individual blessed by God to following a militant people wholly dependent on God. Reading *Exodus* against *Genesis A* highlights the almost overwhelming number of words associated

35 Ibid., 31–9. See also Roberta Frank, "What Kind of Poetry Is *Exodus*?," in *Germania: Comparative Studies in the Old Germanic Languages and Literatures*, ed. Daniel G. Calder and T. Craig Christy (Woodbridge, UK: D.S. Brewer, 1988), 191–205; as well as the introduction to Lucas's *Exodus*.

36 Remley, *Old English Biblical Verse*, 177.

37 Paul G. Remley, "Aldhelm as English Poet: *Exodus*, Asser, and the *Dicta Ælfredi*," in *Latin Learning and English Lore: Studies in Anglo-Saxon Literature for Michael Lapidge*, ed. Katherine O'Brien O'Keeffe and Andy Orchard, 2 vols. (Toronto: University of Toronto Press, 2005), 1:94. See also Andy Orchard, *The Poetic Art of Aldhelm*, CSASE 8 (Cambridge: Cambridge University Press, 1994), 68.

38 See, e.g., Manish Sharma, "The Economy of the Word in the Old English *Exodus*," in *Old English Literature and the Old Testament*, ed. Michael Fox and Manish Sharma (Toronto: University of Toronto Press, 2012), 172–94; Sharma describes the *Exodus* poet as likely to be one "intent on differentiating the illimitable word of God and limited human words" (186). See also, among many others, J.R. Hall, "Old English *sæborg*: *Exodus* 442a, *Andreas* 308a," *Papers on Language and Literature* 25 (1989): 127–34; and J.R. Hall, "Old English *Exodus* and the Sea of Contradiction," *Mediaevalia* 9 (1986 for 1983): 25–44.

with power in *Exodus*, although the *Genesis A* emphasis on divine power differs from the more human-centred show of power here. At least eighteen instances of the word *mægen*, meaning either "strength" or "a military force," or a related compound such as *mægenheap* (powerful troop), *mægenrof* (powerful), *mægenþreat* (powerful troop), and *mægenþrymm* (might or power) appear, as well as twenty-three forms of *micel*, *mara*, or *mæst*.

Although Moses functions as the leader in the poem, he does so not through his own powers but through God's. God "endowed him with his own power / and put mighty deeds into his hands," and, in keeping with commentaries that align the pharaoh with the devil, the pharaoh is "godes andscacan." Only after that division between divine power and accursed enemy is clearly established does the narrative progress to any account of action. The delay has run fifty-three lines into what survives as a 589-line poem. Indeed, Lucas asserts, "In no other OE poem is God's power so dynamically presented."[39] When the journey actually does begin, then, the audience has been well primed: God can and will destroy his enemies; God can and will endow a leader and his army with extraordinary might; God "us ma onlyhð, / nu us boceras beteran secgað, / lengran lyftwynna" (grants us more, now scholars tell us of the better, longer-lasting joys of heaven, 530b–2a).

Such emphasis on divine power yields a point of comparison particularly accessible to a sequential reader of Junius 11. Readers used to the detail-oriented, slow reading of *enarratio* and its predecessor processes – like readers trained to make the inherently comparative evaluation of "mutilated sense" and "incorrect" poetry in Latin, as the "*Responsio discipuli*" describes it – also seem particularly likely to note and comparatively assess material that occurs in both *Genesis A* and *Exodus*. Not long before (a missing page makes it difficult to know exactly how long before) the glorious and grisly account of the destruction of the pharaoh's army in *Exodus*, the poet turns to lineage and descriptions of Noah, Abraham, and Solomon, and then a version of the Abraham and Isaac story, which also appears in more extended form at the end of *Genesis A*.[40] As Creed phrases it in his comparison of these Abraham and Isaac stories, the speaker in *Exodus* "appears to be unable to resist reminding us that God will intervene" and that "Abraham will become murdered only *gief hine Meotod lete* 'if God should let him.'"[41]

---

39 Lucas, *Exodus*, 64.

40 One leaf is missing from the manuscript between the account of the patriarchs and that of the destruction of the Egyptian army; see ibid., 9, 131.

41 Creed, "Art of the Singer," 73.

In *Genesis A*, Creed points to repetitions of the word *self* at the same narrative moment and to the dialogue between Abraham and Isaac on their path to the altar to argue that the poem tells the tale more effectively than does *Exodus*, emphasizing the experience of the event by creating high drama and intense emotion for the individualized figure of Abraham.[42] Karkov reads the repetition of the tale in connecting rather than contrasting terms. She situates the patriarchal line and Abraham's test in *Exodus* in terms of potential audience association: "The references back to Noah and Abraham embedded in *Exodus* and *Daniel* serve in part to establish a genealogical and biological line running from the Creation to the Last Judgement and ultimately expanding to incorporate the audience of the manuscript. … [In particular,] as Abraham and Isaac were tried in *Genesis*, the Israelites will be tried in *Exodus*, and they will all triumph." In this framework, argues Karkov, the crossing of the Red Sea functions as "a type of baptism, and here, at the point of total immersion, their progress towards salvation begins."[43]

Resolving which of these readings best represents that of any early medieval audience remains impossible, but without making sweeping claims about all readers, we can guess that well-read audiences in England ca. 1000 would probably have been capable of making both assessments, of reading for thematic and spiritual coherence as well as for poetic style and narrative perspective. At the same time, the reiteration of the story attests, as do the multiple versions of the Fall of the Angels discussed in Chapter 1, to the range of approaches to the book suggested by Junius 11: for sequential readers, the repetition functions as a counterpoint to the earlier version of the Abraham and Isaac story, and, even on its own, the Abraham and Isaac story functions as one more piece of the rich network of allusions that attests to the authoritative narrative voice at hand in *Exodus*.

In moving from *Genesis A* to *Exodus* in Junius 11, readers would have found themselves negotiating differences that include a striking repositioning of vernacular poetry in relation to its biblical base and its preceding companion in the manuscript. In terms of narrative continuity, the biblical book of Genesis ends with a focus on Joseph and his descendants. Joseph tells them to expect a message from God after his death and divine guidance for travel out of Egypt "to the land which he swore to Abraham, Isaac, and Jacob," and he makes them swear that they will

42 Ibid. Lucas, however, finds "little individual characterization in *Exodus*" (*Exodus*, 63).

43 Karkov, *Text and Picture*, 144, 147.

carry his bones with them when they leave Egypt (Genesis 50:23–4).[44] The promise sets up neatly the events of the Exodus, and perhaps such a transition either once existed in the Junius 11 manuscript or the reader supplied it, aloud or by silent reference to the known biblical sequence, but it is not now part of the book. Instead, *Genesis* in Junius 11 ends near the top of page 142 – the rest of the page is left blank, apparently by design – with Abraham giving thanks to God, having sacrificed the ram instead of his son. *Exodus* then begins at the top of page 143 with a decorated initial *H* and with an adult Moses ready to lead his people. A thematic connection can be made between the happy ending of Abraham's story and the opening confidence in heavenly rewards attached to the laws of Moses, but the visual gap and decorated initial, as well as the notoriously difficult first seven lines of *Exodus*, immediately set the poem apart from its predecessor.

Visual markers of separation between *Genesis* and *Exodus* are reinforced by textual distinctions. At its base, *Exodus* has a more complicated relationship with biblical text than does *Genesis A*, a distinction available to readers familiar by ear or by page with the Vulgate text of the first two books of the Bible. The re-presentation of the biblical narrative in *Genesis A* maintains close connection to its primary source text, refashioning but largely adhering to the Bible's narrative. *Exodus* takes a distinctly different position. Doane argues, for instance, that "what sets the [*Genesis A*] poet apart is his ability to see Genesis *as a text*, as a fixed form of words which must be reproduced as entirely as possible," while "*Daniel* does not conceive of the text as a whole and the *Exodus*-poet cannot be said to be dealing with the words of his source at all."[45] Remley, in his detailed examination of the relationship between *Exodus* and the Bible, concludes that the Old English poem acknowledges deep familiarity with the Bible at the same time that it displays distance from the biblical version of Exodus: "The verse of the main narrative of [the OE] *Exodus* offers a treatment of the departure of the Israelites that stands in all probability at one or more removes from canonical scripture. Despite the apparently comprehensive knowledge of the Bible manifested by its text, there are only a few points at which it is possible to associate the words of *Exodus* convincingly with specific readings in Old Latin or Vulgate scripture."[46]

44 *Holy Bible: Douay-Rheims Version*, ed. Richard Challoner (Rockford, IL: Tan Books, 2000).

45 Doane, *Genesis A*, 54.

46 Remley, *Old English Biblical Verse*, 195; see also 175–95, where Remley reviews "The Latin Background of *Exodus*."

The degree to which *Exodus* may follow a now lost exemplar remains difficult to gauge, although Remley acknowledges that even if the poem's narrative does follow an existing model (one Remley believes likely to have been an excerpted liturgical version of the biblical book), the Old English poem's inclusion of the section on Noah and Abraham "clearly involves a change of scriptural exemplar" and may derive from "first-hand knowledge of an Old Latin–based liturgical lection by an Anglo-Saxon poet."[47] Whatever its source, the poem's account of the tribes of Israel's passage across the parted sea is both distinctive and difficult. As Cross and Tucker years ago argued, "The poet is not 'following rather ignorantly the allegorical tradition' [as Irving had described other critics' views]; he is conditioned by it, and re-acts to events or parts of an event, as would any well-read Christian."[48] Being already well read would undoubtedly help a reader trying to understand *Exodus* for, in Clare Lynch's summation, "the poem both expresses the importance of an allegorical approach to texts and is composed in a manner that necessitates intellectual engagement with the text in a process of decipherment."[49]

The poem's triumphant account of the Israelites gathering the treasures washed ashore after the destruction of the pharaoh's army provides both a narrative climax and, as Audrey Walton shows, a striking visual "metaphor for the practice of interpretation" for which the poem calls: "The plundering of the shore is narrated in terms most commonly used to describe biblical teaching and exegesis. The Israelites *heddon*, 'heeded,' the war-booty (l. 584), and they share out treasure among *segnum*, 'standards' or 'signs' (l. 585). Even the word *bote*, 'recompense' (l. 583), has linguistic associations, having been used earlier to describe the decrees of Moses." Walton argues that, in *Exodus*, the "*topos* of text as 'gold out of Egypt'" marks the poem's allegory as "not a quality that merely inhabits texts, intact and inert; instead it is a latent textual possibility that yields its treasures only to particular activities of reading and listening."[50] Readers of *Exodus*, in other words, are asked in multiple ways by the poem itself to work at reading and understanding it, and the responses of modern critics suggest the rich array of such work that medieval readers may have undertaken.

---

47 Ibid., 441.

48 J.E. Cross and S.I. Tucker, "Allegorical Tradition and the Old English *Exodus*," *Neophilologus* 44 (1960): 124.

49 Clare Lynch, "Enigmatic Diction in the Old English *Exodus*" (PhD diss., Cambridge University, 2000), 12.

50 Walton, "'Gehyre se ðe Wille,'" 2, 4.

The most highly literate of early medieval readers might have rejoiced to encounter such a poem if they moved sequentially through the redemption-oriented poems of Junius 11. For any reader, however, the shifts from *Genesis A* to *Exodus* and the demands of reading *Exodus* seem likely to have elicited a recognition of *Exodus* as a piece aimed at more elite, more practised readers. The modern counterpart is what one scientific study classifies as "strategic readers," those who "know how to activate prior knowledge before, during, and after reading, to decide what's important in a text, to synthesize information, to draw inferences during and after reading, to ask questions, and to self-monitor and repair faulty comprehension."[51] For the early medieval version of such readers, *Exodus* simultaneously flashes its hermeneutic style, its confidence in re-imagining the events of the journey out of Egypt, and its vision of the ultimate power of the divine, all presented in an imagistic, declarative poem that contrasts the more literal narrative in the preceding *Genesis A*.

For less experienced readers, encountering *Exodus* may have stimulated appreciation of the *boceras* and the process of interpretation or stages of reading. The level of literacy held by the compiler's or the book's patron, if it had one, would inform perception of the shifts from text to text within this book as it was being produced, but at some level and probably at multiple stages in the manuscript's production and reception, the disunities in Junius 11 must have been noted. Unless poems were selected on thematic or topical grounds alone – and we do not know what resources, what books, the compiler had to work with – the compiler of the Junius 11 manuscript must have expected the book's audience to navigate into and out of *Exodus*. The compiler offered, by accident or intention, a poem to meet the most elite of the book's potential readers. The book as a whole shows clear signs of careful planning, from its various kinds of unity to its planned cycle of illustration, and, again, whether accidental or intentional, the variety of difficulty among the poems seems unlikely to have gone unnoticed or unremarked by tenth- or eleventh-century audiences.

What an early reader of *Exodus* would have brought to the poem remains difficult to gauge with any precision, but it seems clear that those with training in the kinds of reading processes described by Parkes would have been unlikely to read for thematic coherence or liturgical connection alone. By the time readers of *Exodus* arrive at the *boceras* passage, they have already negotiated much of the language

51 Wolf, *Proust and the Squid*, 138.

of the poem and presumably formed some opinion of what Remley so aptly calls the "refractory qualities of the verse of *Exodus*."[52] Unfortunately, as Parkes's extensive work with the surviving manuscripts underscores, "Anglo-Saxon readers have not left annotations in the margins of surviving manuscripts which would reveal their responses in assessing the value of a text."[53] Certainly *Exodus* is rich enough and its early readers had varied enough literary experiences to bring to it a range of responses, although all must have recognized the poem's complexity and, if reading the whole Junius 11 manuscript, its difference from its companion pieces, even while perhaps recognizing that its endorsement of scholarship concurred with and underscored the treatment of authority in *Daniel* and *Genesis B*. "Like *Genesis*, *Exodus* opens itself up to a complex and nuanced allegorical interpretation by the knowledgeable reader, as scholars from J.E. Cross and S.I. Tucker to James Earl have shown," writes Trilling, who goes on to note: "But also, like *Genesis*, *Exodus* does not demand this kind of interpretation, and the basic elements of the narrative coexist comfortably in the kind of historical framework familiar to readers of heroic poetry."[54]

The poem could well have spoken to many medieval audiences, but it seems likely to have spoken most favourably to those trained and well experienced in reading, those familiar with the kinds of judgments about literature and Latin poetry expressed in the *"Responsio discipuli."* These "strategic readers" clearly existed in the late tenth century, and perhaps the Junius 11 compiler was one of them. Such readers seem likely to have found distinctive pleasure in *Exodus*, both for its language and its explicit and implicit embrace of advanced reading skills. As a whole, too, Junius 11 encourages moving toward such skills. A reader in England who worked through the entire book of Junius 11 – particularly if that reading occurred at a contemplative pace, whether aloud during a meal, for instance, or in the kind of private reading time outlined by the Benedictine rule – would have become a better reader, one who understood well the varieties of readers and of texts, at least in the realm of vernacular biblical poetry, even if still requiring the assistance of *boceras*.

52 Remley, *Old English Biblical Poetry*, 178.

53 Parkes, *"Rædan, areccan, smeagan,"* 19.

54 Renée R. Trilling, *The Aesthetics of Nostalgia: Historical Representation in Old English Verse* (Toronto: University of Toronto Press, 2009), 101–2.

Chapter 4

Wisdom Literature at the Back of the Book[1]

Sume boceras weorþað wisfæste[2]

The disruptions of *Exodus* come in the midst of the biblical chronology that helps tie together the first three narrative units of Junius 11. Visually, the book to this point also shares a single scribal hand and evidence of a planned, though not fully executed, illustration cycle. What is now considered the last line of *Daniel* appears as the last line of text on page 212, a page that matches the preceding page layouts by having twenty-six lines, and the final line of text runs all the way to the standard right margin, even tidily meeting the book standards of a thousand years later by ending with a punctus.[3] Page 213 faces 212 but does not continue it, nor does it continue what was established across *Genesis, Exodus,* and *Daniel.*

The last section of Junius 11 is known as *Christ and Satan,* an editorial title that alone sets it apart from its companions by acknowledging that it has no comparable single association in the Bible. This section pushes the boundaries of biblical chronology by leaping into the subject matter of the Gospels and, rather than providing a prominent continuous narrative, offering examples of Christ dealing with Satan. Sequentially accumulated understanding can nevertheless be found, as Karkov, Hall, and others have shown, "especially if the concern with salvation

1 A version of this chapter, entitled "The Wisdom Poem at the End of MS Junius 11," appeared previously in R.M. Liuzza, ed., *The Poems of MS Junius 11: Basic Readings* (New York: Routledge, 2002), 302–26.

2 "Some [people] become wise scholars" (71b–2a); see *Fortunes of Men,* in Krapp and Dobbie, *Exeter Book,* 154–6.

3 The verso of that leaf, page 211, is blank and follows an unnumbered stub.

history implicit in a Christian treatment of the Old Testament is seen to anticipate the matter of *Christ and Satan*," as Remley puts it.[4]

Materially and topically, however, *Christ and Satan* is marked as separate from its predecessors in Junius 11: it not only focuses on Christ, while the preceding poems are all based on Old Testament material, but is also written in two or three hands, while the preceding poems are written all by a single hand.[5] At its conclusion is written the phrase, "FINIT LIBER . II . AMEN," suggesting that *Christ and Satan* was considered by at least one scribe or the compiler as a unit – probably in terms of a literary work – separate from the implied Book 1, consisting of the poems on Genesis, Exodus, and Daniel, although no "LIBER I" label appears in the book as we have it. The section numbers in *Christ and Satan* underscore the break by starting anew at 1, while the section numbers of the earlier poems are continuously numbered. The distinction is even clear in broad visual terms: *Daniel* is on quite clean vellum, with blanks presumably left for the kinds of illustrations that appear in the first part of the *Genesis* poems, while *Christ and Satan* is on more worn-looking pages, without any apparent illustration blanks and with more corrections, a more aggressive-looking scribal hand (strong diagonal strokes on d and ð stand out), and more densely written text.[6]

That *Christ and Satan* is to some degree distinct, then, from the other poems in the Junius 11 manuscript is not debatable. How distinct, where all the distinctions lie, and their potential significance to an early medieval audience are less clear. The physical condition of *Christ and Satan* indicates that it was handled – in production, at the least – differently than were its companion poems. The dissimilarities of *Christ and Satan*, not least the fact that it is defined as a separate textual unit by being labelled "Liber II," seem likely to have encouraged thinking of this section of Junius 11 in terms different from those of the implied Liber I of *Genesis, Exodus,* and *Daniel*. The material distinctions reinforce the intellectual ones, and vice versa, to suggest that early readers may have understood this final section in ways other than by building overall consecutive meaning within the bounds of Junius 11, whether they encountered *Christ and Satan* as the conclusion to a salvation history or came to it on its own, outside or only within its current context.

Particularly if, before being bound into Junius 11, this copy of *Christ and Satan* circulated on its own in booklet form, as its pages suggest

4 Remley, *Old English Biblical Verse*, 23.

5 In addition to Gollancz's introduction to the facsimile, see also Muir's introductory section, "Codicology," in *Digital Facsimile of Oxford, Bodleian Library, MS. Junius 11*.

6 See also Remley's summary in *Old English Biblical Verse*, 22.

it might have, this section of the book points outward as much and perhaps more than it looks backward to its Junius 11 companions. A meaning-building context for *Christ and Satan* that is at least as compatible as that of biblical poetry can be found within the wisdom literature available in early medieval England. As with the discernment interests shared between *Daniel* and *Genesis B*, such an external affinity has been obscured, to some extent, by the fact that *Christ and Satan* survives only as the last section in a chronological series of biblical poems. These roles can, however, coexist: the emphasis on divine authority in *Christ and Satan* serves both contexts and in doing so underscores adaptability as a key component of textual culture in early medieval England.

Despite the readings of *Christ and Satan* that focus on its role as a conclusion to what *Genesis A* begins, distinctiveness from its companion pieces has long marked the reception of *Christ and Satan*, including in the predominantly negative, critical view from which the text suffered in the nineteenth and first half of the twentieth centuries. Early judgments of the poem, such as Conybeare's in 1826, condemned it as "an accumulation of detached fragments" rather "than [of] any regular design."[7] A hundred years later, Krapp comments that "one may lament the literary judgment of the person who added *Christ and Satan* to *Genesis*, *Exodus*, and *Daniel*."[8] The standard response has now swung somewhat in the other direction, with arguments focused on the poem's internal coherence and the ways in which its Gospel-based material meaningfully connects to the Old Testament–based poems that precede it in the manuscript.[9]

At issue, in part, in this reception history are the narrative units within *Christ and Satan*, which occasionally have been considered as distinct poems. The sections offer a rather homiletic overview of the actions of divine and once-divine figures at three significant moments in Christian history: first, the Fall of the Angels; then the harrowing of hell and the ensuing resurrection, ascension, and anticipated last judgment; and, finally, a chronologically out-of-place account of Christ's temptation in the wilderness. The relationships among these three pieces have been variously and extensively explained as, for instance, a rhetorical display of the "incommensurate might of God";

7 John Josias Conybeare, *Illustrations of Anglo-Saxon Poetry* (London: Harding and Lepard, 1826), 189.

8 Krapp, *Junius Manuscript*, xii.

9 See Hall, "Old English Epic of Redemption"; Finnegan, *Christ and Satan*; and Sleeth, *Studies in Christ and Satan*; as well as Garde's chapter, "The Junius Codex: A Vernacular *Heilsgeschichte*," in *Old English Poetry*, 31–4.

"a demonstrat[ion of the] various aspects of Christ's power in the context of a comparison of the forces of good and evil"; a "celebration" of "Christ's long-ago victories on the planes of heaven, hell and earth"; an exemplum-exhortation; and a comparison between Christ, who abases himself and exalts humanity, and Satan, who exalts himself and earns condemnation.[10] These readings point up not only *Christ and Satan*'s focus on Christ but also its disregard for a continuous narrative across its parts, both of which add to the dissimilarities between *Christ and Satan* and its current manuscript companions.

A common modern view of *Christ and Satan* in relation to the other poems of Junius 11 begins with Hall's arguments that the manuscript is thematically unified, and Joyce Hill deftly sums up reading *Christ and Satan*'s inclusion as structurally meaningful:

> There was at least some moment in time, in the early eleventh century, when some Anglo-Saxons read these poems as an interlocking scheme, one which could be perceived morally (tracing patterns of disobedience and obedience which shape the sequence of fall and redemption), typologically (with the Old Testament material of the first book anticipating the more directly presented redemptive patterns of the second), liturgically (in echo of Lenten, Passiontide and Easter texts), and as an epitome of Christian history, which Hall proposes as the generic model for the manuscript's compilation.[11]

Such connections, however, may reflect the interests and expectations of the manuscript's compiler – or many twentieth- and twenty-first-century readers – more than they do its early readers.[12] The idea of a broader range of categorizations, of reading and composing abilities, and of contexts for the production and reception of Old English poetry is underscored by Emily Thornbury's reading of *Christ and Satan* as the result of two significantly different poets, one with the "more or less normal experience" of a poet within a community and one who "seems

10 Huppé, *Doctrine and Poetry*, 227; Harsh, "*Christ and Satan*," 244; Garde, *Old English Poetry*, 49. See also Sleeth's chapter, "The Work and the Question of Its Unity," in *Studies in Christ and Satan*, 3–26.

11 Joyce Hill, "Confronting *Germania Latina*: Changing Responses to Old English Biblical Verse," in *Latin Culture and Medieval Germanic Europe*, ed. Richard North and Tette Hofstra, Germania Latina 1 (Groningen, The Netherlands: Egbert Forsten, 1992), 71–88; see also Phyllis Portnoy, "'Remnant' and Ritual: The Place of *Daniel* and *Christ and Satan* in the Junius Epic," *English Studies* 75 (1994): 408–22.

12 Modern response to the poems has often begun with the simple distinction of whether they deal primarily with the Old or New Testament.

to have relied mainly on written texts and his own powers of induction to create a different text out of part-salvaged and part-new verse."[13] Recognizing the intellectual unity of the manuscript, in other words, seems not to be the end of the story, for doing so does not fully address distinctions, material or literary, that define the contents of the manuscript and that separate *Christ and Satan* from the poems that precede it.

This is not to deny that *Christ and Satan* functions purposefully within Junius 11 but only to recognize that early audiences may have understood it in other ways, too, even simultaneously linking it to its Old Testament companions and distinguishing it from them, turning both backward and outward to build meaning. The concern with perception, understanding, and discernment across *Daniel* and *Genesis B* may, on the basis of a common interest, have tied those two poems together and to other poems outside this manuscript in a way beyond "salvation history" or any other unifying concern for Junius 11; and, even more so, the distinctiveness of *Christ and Satan* may have encouraged identifying it with texts outside this manuscript, something suggested from the beginning of the poem.

Reading the Text as Wisdom Literature

The opening eighteen lines, in particular, of *Christ and Satan* reveal a correspondence – one not shared by the other poems in Junius 11 – with *wisdom literature*, a popular and multi-genre category. At the same time, those opening lines pick up a frequent concern in Junius 11: divine power. Where *Genesis* asserts the sheer might of God's authority, and *Exodus* and *Daniel* offer examples of human knowledge supported by divine authority, *Christ and Satan* takes a more contemplative approach within its somewhat shrouded narrative. Its introductory passage, before locating the narrative in hell, describes divine power in terms of the physical world and ends with the question, "Hwa is þæt ðe cunne / orðonc clene nymðe ece god?" (Who possesses pure intelligence except eternal God? 17b–18).[14]

While this question answers itself, in part, for clearly God alone has "pure intelligence," the framing of the question and the more extensive answer that follows echo the kinds of questions and answers found in such works as the Old English *Solomon and Saturn*, which includes

13 Emily V. Thornbury, *Becoming a Poet in Anglo-Saxon England* (Cambridge: Cambridge University Press, 2014), 177.

14 Quotations of *Christ and Satan* are from Krapp's ASPR edition of Junius 11; translations are my own unless otherwise indicated.

questions such as, "Tell me what is God," with the answer, "I tell you he who has all things in his power is God" (*SS* 4).[15] The "pure intelligence" of God is further defined in *Christ and Satan* by enumeration of things that God "gesette" (placed) and knows:

> Seolfa he gesette sunnan and monan,
> stanas and eorðan, stream ut on sæ,
> wæter and wolcn, ðurh his wundra miht.
> Deopne ymblyt clene ymbhaldeð
> meotod on mihtum, and alne middangeard.
> He selfa mæg sæ geondwlitan,
> grundas in heofene, godes agen bearn,
> and he ariman mæg rægnas scuran,
> dropena gehwelcne. Daga enderim
> seolua he gesette þurh his soðan miht. (4–13)

> He himself placed sun and moon, stones and earth, the current outside the sea, water and cloud, by his wondrous might. God in his power encompasses the deep circuit of ocean and the whole world. He himself can look around the sea [and] the foundations in heaven, God's true Son, and He can count the drops of rain, [number] each drop. He himself appointed by his true power the number of days.[16]

The list and the human pursuit of knowledge that it indirectly advocates associate *Christ and Satan* with an intellectual "model of the universe" that Miranda Wilcox describes as a "hybrid cosmology developed by patristic exegetes who syncretised Hebraic scriptural accounts of creation with Hellenistic astronomy and physics."[17] The richly detailed opening also echoes apocryphal literature, to which the poem was some time ago connected by Clubb in the abundant notes for his edition of *Christ and Satan*.[18] In the apocryphal books of Ezra,

15 Cross and Hill, *Prose Solomon and Saturn*, 63.

16 Both "the current outside the sea" and "count the drops of rain, [number] each drop" are Thomas D. Hill's translations in "Apocryphal Cosmography and the 'stream uton sæ': A Note on *Christ and Satan*, Lines 4–12," *Philological Quarterly* 48 (1969): 550–4. Mary Clayton, ed. and trans., in *Old English Poems of Christ and His Saints*, Dumbarton Oaks Medieval Library (Cambridge, MA: Harvard University Press, 2013), translates this instead as "the current out at sea" and "count the showers of rain, every drop" (303).

17 Miranda Wilcox, "*Meotod*, the Meteorologist: Celestial Cosmography in Christ and Satan, Lines 9–12a," *Leeds Studies in English*, n.s. 39 (2008): 17.

18 Clubb, *Christ and Satan*.

Baruch, and Enoch, for instance, reference to the "number of the drops of rain" (2 Baruch 59:5) appears, like *Christ and Satan*, in the context of stressing the power of divine wisdom.[19] In the book of Ecclesiasticus, too, appears the list that opens *Christ and Satan*, but with a more riddling form that stresses the pursuit of wisdom: "harenam maris et pluviae guttas et dies saeculi quis dinumeravit altitudinem caeli et latitudinem terrae et profundum abyssi quis mensus est sapientiam Dei praecedentum omnia quis investigavit" (Who has numbered the sand of the sea, and the drops of rain, and the days of the world? Who has measured the height of heaven, and the breadth of the earth, and the depth of the abyss? Who has searched out the wisdom of God that goes before all things?, 1.2–3). Michael Stone describes the function of such lists in apocalyptic literature "as summaries of information revealed ... at the high point of visionary experiences"; as a whole, the "interrogative lists take their origin apparently in the interrogative Wisdom formulations such as Job 38," a text "designed primarily to state either things which God alone can know, or things which man cannot know" until Revelation.[20]

The emphasis on wisdom in Job includes a version of the list of revealed things found in *Christ and Satan*, with more emphasis on Revelation but with the same reference to calculations of the physical: "ipse enim fines mundi intuetur et omnia quae sub caelo sunt respicit qui fecit ventis pondus et aquas adpendit mensura quando ponebat pluviis legem et viam procellis sonantibus" (For he beholdeth the ends of the world: and looketh on all things that are under heaven. Who made a weight for the winds, and weighed the waters by measure. When he gave a law for the rain, and a way for the sounding storms, Job 28:24–6). The reference in Job, while less complete than the enumeration in Ecclesiasticus, occurs after Job's insistence on his innocence, in an explanation of how God's wisdom is the only true wisdom and exceeds in all ways human industry; it is part of the answer to the question posed in Job 28:12: "sapienta vero ubi invenitur et quis est locus intellegentiae" (where is wisdom to be found, and where is the place

19 In Baruch, the counting of raindrops is mentioned in connection with wisdom given to Moses; in 2 Enoch 60: 21–3, the numbering of raindrops appears again; see Michael E. Stone, "Lists of Revealed Things in the Apocalyptic Literature," in *Magnalia Dei: The Mighty Acts of God; Essays on the Bible and Archaeology in Memory of G. Ernest Wright*, ed. F.M. Cross et al. (Garden City, NY: Doubleday, 1976), 420, 433–4. In 2 Baruch 59, as well, appears the idea of the "measures of heaven" (Stone, "Lists of Revealed Things," 424).

20 Ibid., 435, 432.

of understanding)?[21] Remley directs attention, in addition, to "certain expanded, variant forms of the Old Latin text of Gen[esis] XXII.17, [where] the innumerability topos is made explicit: 'sicut arena maris *quae non potest dinumerari*,'" from which he suggests an example in the Old English *Exodus* may derive.[22]

The ultimate source of the list of revealed things is, unsurprisingly, obscure. Stone identifies connections in apocalyptic vision materials, in a broad selection of wisdom literature, and in hymns of praise.[23] Presumably by a variety of paths, the list becomes part of the wisdom literature that flourished in the Middle Ages. Though the Old Testament wisdom books first acquired the modern label of wisdom literature, the term, as Vivien Law neatly defines it, expanded to refer "subsequently to other ancient and medieval texts concerned with purveying moral precepts and reflections upon human existence. It is not a genre but a content-based category, a class to which texts in a large number of genres may be assigned."[24]

Law, in her study of the seventh-century Virgilius Maro Grammaticus, identifies one strand of wisdom literature as a "popular tradition which relied on an unselfconscious, though by no means unsophisticated, use of language to awaken its hearers to awareness of the wisdom permeating Creation." Within this tradition, "Riddles and enigmata heighten awareness of Creation: mundane objects or beings are invested with mystery, as the listener glimpses the elements at war within a humble cooking-pot or learns to marvel at the water-spider. The natural world plays a vital role in bringing the common man to recognise God's wisdom."[25] The list of revealed things that begins *Christ and Satan* functions in this way, as does the same list in the often apocryphal question-and-answer material of wisdom texts such as the *Joca monachorum*. The "monks' jokes" are Latin dialogue texts, a form of popular wisdom literature; they offer assortments of wisdom drawn from a range of materials, from obscure details of the Bible to secular

21 Clubb, *Christ and Satan*, cites Job 28:11, "Profunda quoque fluviorum scrutatus est," for 2. 9–10, but not 28:12 for 2. 11–13. He points instead to "general similarities" in Isa. 40:12 and Job 38:16, 36:27, 28:26 (48).

22 Remley, *Old English Biblical Verse*, 192. J.W. Bright, "On the Anglo-Saxon Poem *Exodus*," *MLN* 27 (1912): 13–19, also identifies possible biblical sources for the comments in the first section on God's extensive knowledge, among them Mark 13:31 and Luke 21:33.

23 Stone, "Lists of Revealed Things," 431.

24 Vivien Law, *Wisdom, Authority and Grammar in the Seventh Century: Decoding Virgilius Maro Grammaticus* (Cambridge: Cambridge University Press, 1995), 23.

25 Ibid., 25–6.

proverbs.[26] Two examples of *Joca*-style material include lists that are nearly identical, within a much more extensive array of partial parallels, to that at the beginning of *Christ and Satan* and, in addition, might have connections to early medieval England.

While not directly part of the group usually identified as *Joca monachorum*, the *Collectanea pseudo-Bedae* has much in common with it.[27] It includes brief wisdom pieces of the sort found in the *Joca*, as well as texts on numerology and "miscellaneous hymns and prayers."[28] The history of the *Collectanea* is uncertain, but Lapidge suggests "that the majority of its datable contents are most plausibly assigned to the middle decades of the eighth century," and "the majority of its localizable contents originated either in Ireland or England, or in an Irish foundation on the Continent."[29] Whatever the origin, the *Collectanea* includes an abundance of passages "demonstrably related to medieval dialogue-literature or riddle material."[30] "Of fifty-nine questions in the

26 The term is Walther Suchier's, taken from a title in the ninth-century MS Schlettstadt Stadtbibliothek 1073 (Suchier identifies it as "JM E"); see *Das mittellateinische Gespräch Adrian und Epictitus: Nebst verwandten Texten (Joca monachorum)* (Tübingen: Max Niemeyer Verlag, 1955), 83, 90. The editors Cross and Hill identify the OE *Prose Solomon and Saturn* as part of the *Joca monachorum* tradition; closely related is the dialogue-based *Adrian and Epictitus* group, from the names of the two speakers. Together, Martha Bayless terms the groups "trivia-dialogues" to distinguish them from the so-called more serious group of "proverb-dialogues"; see "The *Collectanea* and Medieval Dialogues and Riddles," in *Collectanea Pseudo-Bedae*, ed. Martha Bayless and Michael Lapidge et al., Scriptores Latini Hiberniae 14 (Dublin: Dublin Institute for Advanced Studies, 1998), 13. For a discussion of the tradition and antecedents of question-and-answer dialogues, see L.W. Daly and W. Suchier, *Altercatio Hadriani Augusti et Epicteti Philosophi*, Illinois Studies in Language and Literature 24, nos. 1–2 (Urbana: University of Illinois Press, 1939), 2:20–44.

27 James F. Kenney, ed., *The Sources for the Early History of Ireland: Ecclesiastical* (New York: Columbia University Press, 1920; repr., New York: Octagon Books, 1966), 680. Kenney refers to the collection simply as the *Collectanea Bedae*; the work is also referred to as *Excerptiones patrum* and *flores ex diuersis*. The Book of Cerne, an English-owned prayer book with Irish material and/or sources, includes four prayers/hymns that also occur in the *Collectanea Bedae* and includes "an apocryphal *Descenus ad inferna*" (Kenney, *Sources*, 721). Cross and Hill, *Prose Solomon and Saturn*, cite the *Collectanea* for parallels to nine questions in the OE *Prose Solomon and Saturn*.

28 Michael Lapidge, "The Origin of the Collectanea," in *Collectanea Pseudo-Bedae*, ed. Martha Bayless and Michael Lapidge et al., Scriptores Latini Hiberniae 14 (Dublin: Dublin Institute for Advanced Studies, 1998), 2–3.

29 Ibid., 12. In addition to containing five of Aldhelm's Enigmata, the *Collectanea* have close ties to Anglo-Saxon material in at least six other items, including a calf riddle, the closest parallels for which are in Eusebius and the Exeter Book; see ibid., 4, and the commentary on item 194 (243).

30 Bayless, "*Collectanea* and Medieval Dialogues," 13.

Old English *Solomon and Saturn*," by Martha Bayless's count, "thirteen are paralleled in the *Collectanea*, and of these, four are 'rare'" – that is, among a "small number ... found in very few other dialogues" and having distinctly "Insular connections."[31] One of those parallels Cross and Hill connect to *Christ and Satan*. Item 15 of the *Prose Solomon and Saturn* and item 123 of the *Collectanea* ask, in part, who "was baptized after death." The answer is Adam, whose body, Cross and Hill explain, was understood as having been baptized at the Crucifixion by the blood of Christ as it sank through the ground. The "fulwihtes bæðe" (bath of baptism, 544) in the Crucifixion account in *Christ and Satan* suggests that

> [at least] one other OE writer knew of the tradition about Adam's baptism. The poet of *Christ and Satan* certainly filled out scriptural statement with apocryphal story. ... [And] the 'baths of baptism' [there] could well be for Adam, in view of the persistent emphasis on apocryphal tradition in this poem.[32]

This yoking of the three texts, the *Collectanea*, *Prose Solomon and Saturn*, and *Christ and Satan*, is echoed in a similar link, this time in the list of revealed things, which occurs in the *Collectanea*, *Adrian and Epictitus* (like *Solomon and Saturn*, a trivia-dialogue), and *Christ and Satan*.

Item 46 in the *Collectanea* asserts that no one but God can count "the sand of the sea, the drops of rain, the days of the world, the height of heaven, the number of stars, the vastness of the earth, and the bottom of the abyss and the hairs of the head as well as the race of men and pack animals: these are to be numbered by God alone" (Arena maris, pluuiarum guttae, dies seculi, altitudo caeli, multitudo stellarum, profunditas terrae et imum abyssi et capilli capitis siue plebs hominum uel iumentorum: haec non nisi a Deo tantum numeranda sunt).[33] The Latin *Adrian and Epictitus* dialogues, which, like *Solomon and Saturn*, derive their title from the names of the voices in the dialogues, contain material probably derived from *Joca* texts. While the surviving manuscripts

31 Ibid., 20, 17.

32 Cross and Hill, *Prose Solomon and Saturn*, 76–9. The *SS* passage reads: "Saga me hwæt wæs se acenned næs and æft bebyrged was on hys moder innoðe, and æfter þam deaðe gefullod wæs. Ic þe secge, þæt was adam" (Tell me who was he who was not born and afterwards was buried in his mother's womb, and was baptized after death. I tell you, that was Adam). Cross and Hill's commentary traces the extensive tradition of this "'enigmatic question.'"

33 Bayless and Lapidge, *Collectanea Pseudo-Bedae*, 126.

are mostly from the later Middle Ages, Suchier places their origin as early as sixth-century Gaul, deriving from Greek models.[34] One version includes a nearly identical list and premise: these things "sunt difficilia, que nemo novit nisi Deus: arenam maris, pluviarum guttas, altitudinem celi, numerum stellarum, profunditatem terre, pruna abyssi" (are difficult, which no one knows except God: the sands of the sea, the drops of rain, the height of heaven, the number of stars, the vastness of the earth, the fire of the abyss).[35]

Both dialogue texts imply, by the list and their attention to the pursuit of wisdom, that to those who seek and apply what right knowledge they can, God's wisdom is made clear, although the full extent of knowledge, the actual number of raindrops and grains of sand, must wait until heavenly revelation. The currency of this kind of text in early medieval England is supported by Bayless's identification of "clear affinities" between "the trivia-dialogue sections" of the *Collectanea* and "a group of texts circulating in the early medieval period," and by the fact that among the closest-identified links among trivia-dialogues, related texts, and the *Collectanea*, "the overwhelming proportion are Insular or have Insular connections."[36]

The list of revealed things is among items in the *Collectanea* that Bayless distinguishes as "not typical *Ioca* questions" but nevertheless ones that "do find parallels in unusual *Ioca* texts."[37] A wider wisdom context, one beyond the trivia-dialogue genre, is suggested by two other occurrences of the list with Insular connections. One is in the biblical commentaries of Theodore and Hadrian; the other is in the pseudo-Isidorian *Liber de ortu et obitu patriarchum*. In the Theodore and Hadrian *Second Commentary on the Gospels* (identified as EvII by Lapidge and Bischoff), in what appears to be a preface to comment on Matthew 10:30, comes in the list in a form nearly identical to its appearance in *Adrian and Epictitus* and in the *Collectanea*, and strongly echoed in *Christ and Satan*: "Septem sunt difficilia quae nemo nouit nisi Deus: harena maris, pluuiarum guttae, altitudo caeli, numerus stellarum et profunditas terrae et ima abissi et dies saeculi" (There are seven unfathomables which no-one knows except God: sands of the sea, drops of rain, the height of heaven, the number of stars and vastness of the earth and the

34 Suchier, 101–2.

35 Ibid., 47–9; the list occurs in the version of *Adrian and Epictitus* that Suchier labels AE_1b, which begins, "Septem sunt difficilia," but only six items follow.

36 Bayless, "*Collectanea* and Medieval Dialogues," 21.

37 Ibid., 16.

depth of the abyss and the days of this world, EvII 19).[38] The substance of Matthew 10 is wisdom – specifically, the directions that Christ gives his disciples as he disperses them to teach; in verses 29–31, Christ is reiterating the extent of God's power.

Christ's power is the core of the "Christus" chapter of the *Liber de ortu et obitu patriarchum*, a collection of "[short biographical notices … on fifty-nine great heroes of the Old and New Testaments," which McNally describes as a "compact handbook valuable for Scriptural studies, especially for biblical history."[39] Like the *Collectanea*, this pseudo-Isidorian text has Irish connections. According to McNally, the *Liber de ortu et obitu* "originated about the middle of the eighth century in southeast Germany, probably in the wide circle of the Irish bishop of Salzburg, St. Virgilius."[40] Chapter 42, in itself a "tract on Christ," includes a fairly lengthy account of the extent of God's powers, including the enumeration that appears in *Christ and Satan*:

> Infernum sub terra et aquis potentia posuit et penetrat. Cardines celi ac terre terribiliter terminat. Latitudinem celi metitur palmae. … Mari mirabiliter terminum posuit. Duodecim ventos varios de suis abditis eduxit. Cursum solis et lunae et siderum sublime statuit. Arenam maris et stellas caeli, pluviae guttas et dies seculi earum numerum solus agnovit.[41]
>
> The abyss under the earth and waters His power placed and set. The center of the clouds and also of the earth He fixed, awesomely. The breadth of the clouds is measured by His hand. … He placed, marvelously, the bounds

38 Michael Lapidge and Bernhard Bischoff, *Biblical Commentaries from the Canterbury School of Theodore and Hadrian* (Cambridge: Cambridge University Press, 1994), 400–1; see also the note on 511.

39 Robert E. McNally, "'Christus' in the Pseudo-Isidorian 'Liber de ortu et obitu patriarchum,'" *Traditio* 21 (1965): 170.

40 Ibid., 168–9. If the *Liber de ortu* did come out of the circle of St. Virgilius, moreover, it may well have close connections to one more occurrence of the list of revealed things. Bischoff describes an eighth-century formulary from Salzburg in which the list is used as the opening salution of a model letter: "eine überschwengliche Freundschaftsadresse mit Bruchstücken von Hexametern aus dem Carmen paschale des Sedulius" (17). See Bernhard Bischoff, *Salzburger Formelbücher und Briefe aus Tassilonischer und Karolingischer Zeit* (Munich: Verlag der Bayerischen Akademie der Wissenschaften, 1973), 3.12. In Sedulius's Easter poem, the enumeration idea does not occur, but only reference to the fact that God "rules the universe, seas, lands, and stars"; see Sedulius, *On Christian Rulers, and the Poems*, trans. Edward Gerard Doyle, CEMERS (Binghamton: State University of New York at Binghamton, 1983), 173.

41 McNally, "'Christus,'" 178 (2.140–2). McNally edits the relevant chapter of "the oldest manuscript, Colmar (Murbach) 39 fols. 28r–37r (s. VIII–IX)" (174). A full edition of the *Liber de ortu et obitu patriarchum* appears in CCSL 108 E; see 42.6.

> of the sea. The twelve various winds he produced from their concealment. He fixed the sublime course of the sun and the moon and heaven. He alone knows the number of the sands of the sea and the stars of the sky, the drops of rain and the days of the world.

Both the *Liber de ortu et obitu patriarchum* and the biblical commentaries of Theodore and Hadrian, like the dialogue texts, suggest that the list of revealed things was found particularly effective in contemplating the bounds and extent of human and divine wisdom, and in encouraging the pursuit of wisdom.

The list of revealed things occurs not only in Latin didactic texts, where its significance is perhaps clearest, but also in vernacular poetic texts; besides appearing in *Christ and Satan*, it turns up in the Old English poems *Exodus*, *The Creed*, and *The Descent into Hell*. In the *Exodus* account of the test of Abraham's faith, lifted from the book of Genesis, the angelic voice that stops the sacrifice of Isaac goes on to describe God's wisdom in terms of the sea, stars, and the expanse of earth and heaven. The passage is a reworking of the biblical account of Abraham and Isaac, which substitutes the list of revealed things for the angel's description of how the race of Abraham will multiply: "benedicam tibit et multiplicabo semen tuum sicut stellas caeli et velut harenam quae est in litore maris" (I will bless thee, and I will multiply thy seed as the stars of heaven, and as the sand that is by the sea shore, Gen 22:17).

The Old English poem's interest in divine knowledge is introduced early, when the narrator speaks directly to the audience about Moses's history. The first time that God spoke to Moses, "He him gesægde soðwundra fela, / hu þas woruld worhte witig Drihten / eorðan ymbhwyrft ond uprodor" (he told him many marvelous truths – how the wise Lord created this world, the earth's ambit and the sky, 24–6), things that, along with the name of God, "ær ne cuðon, / frod fædera cyn, þeah hie fela wiston" (the wise race of patriarchs did not know before, though they knew much, 27b–9).[42] The story of Abraham elaborates on this idea, in a curious suspension between an account of the order of the troops marching into the Red Sea and, in part because of a lost section, the gory description of the slaughter of the Egyptians. The heavenly voice tells Abraham that

> Ne behwylfan mæg heofon and eorðe
> His wuldres word, widdra and siddra

42 All citations of *Exodus* in this section are from Lucas's edition; the translations are mine.

þonne befæðman mæge foldan sceattas,
eorðan ymbhwyrft and uprodor,
garsecges gin and þeos geomre lyft. (427–31)

Heaven and earth cannot cover over his glorious word, which is farther and wider than the surfaces of the world, the earth's circuit and the sky, the sea's great depth and this sad air can encircle.

The extent of God's knowledge thus described is then amplified by its contrast to limited human knowledge:

rim ne cunnon
yldo ofer eorðan ealle cræfte
to gesecgenne soðum wordum,
nymðe hwylc þæs snottor in sefan weorðe
þæt he ana mæge ealle geriman
stanas on eorðan, steorran on heofonum,
sæbeorga sand, sealte yða. (436b–42)

men on earth will not be able with all their skill to say in certain words the number – unless there be someone so wise of mind that he alone can count all the stones on the earth, the stars in the heavens, the sand of the sea-cliffs, the salty waves.[43]

Divine knowledge, as in *Christ and Satan,* is defined in terms of the visible, divinely ordered world and in relation to a narrative in which right and wrong knowledge play a pivotal role. While the Abraham and Isaac passage as a whole "emphasizes the renewal of the covenant between God and the Israelites," as Lucas puts it, the angel's invocation of the list of revealed things works as in the Latin examples, where reference to "the natural world plays a vital role in bringing the common man to recognise God's wisdom."[44]

In *The Descent into Hell* and *The Creed*, the object of the count varies, but a clear parallel to *Christ and Satan*'s framing list remains visible. *Christ*

43 Hall, "Old English *saebeorg*," argues for translating "sæbeorga sand" as a kenning. Lucas, *Exodus*, 130, in his notes to these lines, asserts that "these lines are an expansion of Gen. 22.17 under the influence of 13.16; cf. also Heb. 11.12." Lucas also refers to Irving's comment (in "New Notes") that the Old Latin phrasing of Gen 13:16, "si potest quis enumerare harenam maris," might have yielded "sæborga sand."

44 Lucas, *Exodus*, 124; Law, *Wisdom, Authority and Grammar*, 26.

and Satan describes God as having "gesette" the "stream uton sæ"; *The Creed* similarly asserts that God "garsecges grundas geworhtest" (created the seas' depths, 7).[45] *Christ and Satan* and *The Descent into Hell* share the subject of the harrowing of hell as well as the material example of God's expansive wisdom. In *Christ and Satan* is the assertion that "ymbhaldeð / meotod on mihtum ... alne middangeard" (God in his power encompasses ... the whole world, 7–8); in John the Baptist's perspective from hell in *The Descent* is the comparable acknowledgment that God possesses the ability to "ymbfon eal folca gesetu" (embrace all the dwellings of people, 115).[46] God, according to *Christ and Satan*, "ariman mæg rægnas scuran, / dropena gehwelcne" (may count the shower of rain, each drop, 11–12a). In *The Descent*, in a parallel cited by Clubb, God is described as able "geriman ... sæs sondgrotu" (to count the sands of the sea, 116b–17a), and *The Creed* states God's ability to count "ða menegu ... mærra tungla" (the multitudes of splendid stars, 8).[47] God's knowledge of Creation is exhaustive and exact. In both *The Descent* and *The Creed*, as in *Christ and Satan*, the enumerative passages use reference to the natural world to help characterize the supreme extent of divine wisdom – and to offer a potentially humbling glimpse of it.

We can all count drops of rain, but only the misguided or the spiritually blind will fail to see that God or Christ alone can count them all, that only the author of all Creation can reckon such multitudes. *Christ and Satan* not only invokes this wisdom with its opening use of the list of revealed things but also goes on to make it a central concern. Wehlau has argued that *Christ and Satan* makes clear both that "ultimate knowledge resides with God" and that the reader is encouraged to seek and use whatever knowledge is obtainable to fight against temptation and sin; the reader, "unlike Satan, is expected to recognize Christ's power from the beginning, as the poem's first lines make clear," and to use it to assess both Satan and Christian living, something that shared reading – whether as a listening audience or in discussion after private reading – would likely have amplified still more.[48] If the list of revealed things

45 See Hill, "Apocryphal Cosmography," for discussion of the possible meaning and source of the phrase "stream uton sæ." Quotations from *The Creed* are from Elliott Van Kirk Dobbie, ed., *The Anglo-Saxon Minor Poems*, ASPR 6 (New York: Columbia University Press, 1942).

46 Quotations from *The Descent into Hell* are taken from Krapp and Dobbie, *Exeter Book*.

47 Clubb, *Christ and Satan*, 48, note to 2. 11–13, identifies a possible source for this count in *Psalms* 146:4, "Who telleth the number of the stars, and calleth them all by their names."

48 Wehlau, "Power of Knowledge," 7.

posits a frame of mind for the reader in which an active, investigatory response is expected (from the reader or in the text), then the poem as a whole might be better understood in connection to the didacticism and the concerns of popular wisdom literature.

The recognition of divine wisdom figures prominently in *Christ and Satan*, despite Satan's attempts to obscure the truth by asserting, for instance, that he is the father of Christ. By the end of the poem, Satan's lies are fully exposed and punished, and Christ's powers are, correspondingly, made clear. Christ knows the answers to all questions, while Satan must make a futile but instructive attempt to grasp even one: Christ assigns Satan the task of measuring hell – and in a wonderful detail reminiscent of the question-and-answer minutiae (though unattested in it), he tells him to complete the task in two hours (709). Before this command, the connection of divine wisdom and revealed knowledge occurs in language that echoes the opening list at least four times, and the link is demonstrated in the stories themselves, as they recount the Fall of the Angels, the harrowing and Resurrection, and the temptation of Christ. References to right thinking and revealed knowledge are particularly thick in the middle section of the poem, that which recounts the harrowing of hell and describes the Resurrection, Ascension, and last judgment. The narrator proclaims, at the end of describing the Resurrection, that "Us is wuldres leoht / torht ontyned, þam ðe teala þenceð" (To us, those who think rightly, the brilliant radiance of heaven will be revealed, 555–6).

In the final part of the Ascension piece, the idea appears twice, first within a description of the heavenly kingdom: "Þæt is monegum cuð / þæt he ana is ealra gescefta / wyrhta and waldend þurh his wuldres cræft" (It is known to many [not all] that he alone is maker and ruler of all created things through the power of his glory, 582b–4).[49] The narrator then concludes the Ascension account by encouraging his audience, reminding them in language nearly identical to that at the end of the Resurrection piece, that "wuldres bearn ... Leaðað us þider ... þær is wuldres bled / torht ontyned" (the son of glory thither invites us ... where the glorious splendour of heaven is revealed, 588–93a). The references here correspond to a more subtly phrased reinforcement of the poem's opening passage, which occurs in the earlier Fall of the Angels section, in one of the narrator's expositions on his story: "Uton cyþan þæt! / Deman we on eorðan, ærror

49 Bredehoft, *Authors, Audiences,* identifies the phrasing here as "in the literate–formulaic mode of ... late Old English verse" (175–9).

lifigend, / onlucan mid listum locen waldendes, / ongeotan gastlice!" (Let us make it known! We must consider on earth beforehand, when living, [how to] unlock with skills the Ruler's locks [or mystery], [how to] understand spiritually!, 297b–300a).[50] The remark is perhaps the most direct encouragement of the pursuit of wisdom in the poem, but the references overall indicate the necessity of doing so even as they, and the poem's opening, emphasize the gulf between human and divine knowledge.

References to knowledge obscured rather than revealed make the same points from a different direction. That Satan has, despite his attempts, so utterly failed to unlock the Ruler's locked-up knowledge is demonstrated not just in the Fall and in hell itself but also in his companions' and his own lack of understanding. Satan's fiendish companions accuse him, "'Þu us gelærdæst ðurh lyge ðinne'"(You convinced us by your lying, 53); "'Segdest us to soðe þæt ðin sunu wære / meotod mancynnes'" (You told us as a truth that your son was the creator of mankind, 63–4a). Satan's own inability to perceive clearly is reflected in his comment, as he looks around hell, that "'Ne mæg ic þæt gehicgan hu ic in ðæm becwom, / in þis neowle genip'" (I cannot understand how I came into that, in this abysmal darkness, 178–9a).[51] All that is now clearly revealed to him is the enormity of his wrong: "'Nu is gesene þæt we syngodon / uppe on earde'" (Now it is apparent that we sinned in the dwelling above, 228–9a).

A sharp contrast to this incomprehension occurs in the striking speech by Eve, in the poem's subsequent account of the harrowing of hell. The *Christ and Satan* narrator asserts that Eve must repent aloud before Christ will free her from her hell. In doing so, she demonstrates the awareness that Satan lacks, a connection underscored by a repetition in phrasing: "'*Nu is gesene* þæt ðu eart sylfa god / and ece ordfruma ealra gesceafta'" (Now it is apparent that you are God himself and the everlasting author of all created things, 439–40; emphasis mine).

The opening "catalogue of heavenly secrets" reverberates throughout *Christ and Satan*; the idea of wisdom, which, as Stone puts it, "will be revealed eschatologically to the righteous," is never lost sight of, and the opening formulation is most pointedly reiterated in the concluding emphasis on measurement.[52] What Christ requires of Satan is that he

50 See Finnegan, *Christ and Satan*, 103–4.

51 Or "how I came to be there," as Clubb, *Christ and Satan*, 76, translates it; the reference is presumably to the *laðan ham* that Satan mentions just before (177).

52 Stone, "Lists of Revealed Things," 425.

know hell, which he himself constructed, just as thoroughly as Christ knows all Creation. Satan must reckon in numbers his punishment:

> Wite þu eac, awyrgda,   hu wid and sid
> helheoðo dreorig,   and mid hondum amet.
> Grip wið þæs grundes;   gang þonne swa
> oððæt þu þone ymbhwyrft   alne cunne,
> and ærest amet   ufan to grunde,
> and hu sid seo   se swarta eðm. (698–703)

> Know you also, cursed one, how far and wide the dreary vault of hell is, and measure it with your hands. Take hold of the abyss; go then so until that you know the whole circumference, and first measure from above to the bottom, and how wide the dark air is.

"The devils are, in a sense," as Wehlau phrases it, "constructing their own cosmos, and so Satan's measuring of hell is parallel to God's measuring out the cosmos. When Satan is told to measure hell, Christ instructs him to tell the fallen angels 'þæt ðu gemettes meotod alwihta, / cyning moncynnes' ('that you have met the measurer of all creatures, the king of mankind,' 696–7a)."[53] Satan recognizes only the vastness of the task and not the lesson in it: "þa him þuhte þæt þanon wære / to helleduru hund þusenda / mila gemearcodes" (Then it seemed to him that from there to the gate of hell was a hundred thousand miles in measure, 719–21a). Other critics have noted the appropriateness of the fact that "se mihtiga het / þæt þurh sinne cræft" – his wisdom, in other words – "susle amæte" (the Almighty through his skill commanded that, to measure misery, 721b–2). Thomas Hill has argued that the wordplay in *ametan* and *metan*, "to measure" and "to meet," adroitly emphasizes the punishment; as Satan meets Christ, he acquires the new task.[54] Wehlau suggests an accompanying wordplay in *witan* and *wite*, "to know" and "punishment," for "knowledge acquired too late is [itself] punishment"; the knowledge that Satan's action will reveal to him "is in perfect contrast to the 'unknowing' that Christ will perform on Judgment Day, when Christ will refuse to acknowledge the sinners who have previously 'forgotten' him."[55]

What the audience desiring salvation can do, according to narrator and narrative, is actively seek and see God in everything – every drop

53 Wehlau, "Power of Knowledge," 4.

54 Thomas D. Hill, "The Measure of Hell: *Christ and Satan* 695–722," *Philological Quarterly* 60 (1981): 409–14.

55 Wehlau, "Power of Knowledge," 6.

of rain, every grain of sand. Though the knowledge thus revealed will be only a fraction of what is known to God and Christ, it will serve, nevertheless, to clarify God's power and wisdom. The opening passage in *Christ and Satan* not only incorporates the list of revealed things but also, by doing so, invokes association with wisdom literature that uses the same formulation. From the start, it thus encourages the audience to be active seekers after right knowledge. They can pursue, and must, for salvation, right knowledge through the Church's wisdom, and perhaps the poet was, in a sense, advertising literary means to that end, in such texts as this poem and the *Joca monachorum* or other wisdom literature.

In its affinity with wisdom literature, as well as in its three-part structure and its focus on Christ, *Christ and Satan* moves away from the biblical paraphrase that more strongly guides the narratives preceding it in the manuscript. If Junius 11 was normally or primarily read consecutively, the "interlocking scheme" outlined by Joyce Hill would seem to have been apparent, but the literary distinctiveness of *Christ and Satan* in the manuscript heightens the possibility that readers came to the final section with a different set of expectations than for the rest of the manuscript. Despite any thematic connections the compiler may have had in mind, early medieval readers may have identified *Christ and Satan* as a revealed-wisdom poem and may, in turn, have read it not as the conclusion to the sequence begun with the *Genesis* section, but more loosely related or even on its own and for reasons lying largely outside Junius 11. How carefully or frequently any of this book's poems was read is, of course, impossible to discern with certainty, but the manuscript itself presents some intriguing material clues that underscore the likelihood that an audience knew *Christ and Satan* outside Junius 11 and that, even within Junius 11, readers may have approached this last section with a different eye than the one they turned to the preceding poems – if, indeed, these readers did not restrict their reading of Junius 11 to *Christ and Satan*. The material distinctions of "LIBER II" reinforce its intellectual distinctions, and, in doing so, they stress that Junius 11 is a complex collection in production and reception, one for which readers need not necessarily take the autonomous authority of the book itself as the central or most necessary building block for constructing meaning.

Reading the Material "Liber II"

In visual terms, the pages of *Christ and Satan* appear rather splotchy, stained and worn, with margins of varying sizes; while the two or three hands are still beautiful, none of the scribes is the single scribe of the preceding poems, and the text in this last section of the manuscript has been corrected or revised.[56] The addition of one more line of text per page – twenty-seven, in comparison to the preceding standard of twenty-six – adds, too, to a sense of a more cramped page, as do the slightly smaller letters of the first hand and, most noticeably, the increasingly cramped letters of the second hand. The status of the Junius 11 manuscript as a whole seems to have declined during its production.[57] Not only are the illustrations limited to *Genesis*, with blanks for full- and half-page illustrations continuing through *Exodus* and *Daniel*, but also *Christ and Satan*, at a glance, looks the least prestigious of its contents.[58] Krapp, in his edition of the Junius 11 poems, hypothesizes that

> interest in the manuscript as a piece of fine bookmaking had fallen off after the completion of *Daniel*. ... [Or] perhaps a fully thought out plan was never formed for the whole manuscript. ... Certainly even the plan as first made was not carried out with rigorous oversight, since after p. 96 there are many blank spaces left for illustrations and some for capitals that were never inserted.[59]

Lucas has argued that *Christ and Satan* shows evidence of having circulated independently before being bound into Junius 11, and his claims would explain the wear in this section without reference to the other poems in the manuscript. Raw, however, counters this claim with a close examination of the stitching and binding of the manuscript, which leads her to conclude that *Christ and Satan* was "a fairly early afterthought" in the construction of the manuscript and, as such, was copied expressly for Junius 11 rather than being incorporated as an existing unit. The "extraordinarily dirty and crumpled state of the last

---

56 In a note, Raw, "Construction," 189n7, suggests that only two hands are at work in *Christ and Satan*.

57 The manuscript now has 116 vellum leaves, numbered pages 1–229 by a modern hand. (The frontispiece, a blank at what would be p. 116, and an unnumbered blank p. 230, the verso of 229, are unnumbered.) As Raw has demonstrated, it quite quickly lost leaves, perhaps a victim of vellum swiped for a more pressing project; see ibid., especially 191*ff*. The full manuscript can be viewed, page by page, through the Bodleian Library's Early Manuscripts website.

58 The illustrations in Junius 11 appear to be the work of three artists. The first illustrator runs from p. 1 to p. 62 and is responsible for thirty-eight drawings; the second illustrator contributes ten drawings, pp. 73–88. The third artist pops up briefly on p. 96 with an unfinished drawing, and scattered throughout the manuscript are also several drypoint or metalpoint doodles or partial illustrations. Raw, "Construction," 203, argues that spaces for continuing the program of illustration once existed in *Christ and Satan*.

59 Krapp, *Junius Manuscript*, xi–xii.

gathering" – that containing *Christ and Satan* – Raw attributes to the thirteenth-century devaluation of earlier medieval books. She offers no explanation for the clear crease in this gathering, although she dates the damage to the first half of the twelfth century or slightly earlier, to "the time of the re-sewing of the manuscript."[60]

Raw's arguments regarding the stitching and binding are strong, but that one gathering could have been so "seriously mistreated" (Raw's assessment) while the poem immediately preceding it, and, indeed, all the poems that precede it, look quite clean is baffling, particularly since the damage occurs not just on the outer pages of the gathering but also throughout it. Simple neglect seems an insufficient explanation for the physical condition of *Christ and Satan*. Particularly in its visual contrast to the relatively clean vellum containing *Daniel*, the condition of the pages containing *Christ and Satan* might instead be read as signs of use, before or after binding, if indeed the damage occurred after the vellum was written on, as seems to be the case.[61]

The most prominent visual aspect of the pages containing *Christ and Satan* is the horizontal fold that led Lucas to propose that the inner part of this final quire was once a folded booklet. Striking, too, is the increase in the quantity of ink on the page, largely the result of corrections done in one or more hands other than the scribes'.[62] The *Genesis* and *Christ*

---

60 Raw, "Construction," 203, 202, where she argues that the book has been bound only twice, once initially, around 1000, and then again between 1100 and 1250, although she suggests that the likely date is in the latter part of this range. Lucas argued for dating the binding to "the latter part of the first half of the eleventh-century; see "MS Junius 11 and Malmesbury," 198–9.

61 Disagreement exists about whether the fold happened before or after the writing. Raw, "Construction," 202, e.g., argued that the folding occurred when the manuscript was re-sewn, as did Clubb, *Christ and Satan*, xv, although for different reasons; Finnegan, *Christ and Satan*, 10, like Gollancz, *Cædmon MS*, describes it as having happened before the copying. The ink does seem to be more worn at the fold, and this supports the idea that the fold occurred after copying. Regarding the idea that the ink is so worn in places as to suggest multiple folding and refolding, see also Peter J. Lucas, "On the Incomplete Ending of *Daniel* and the Addition of *Christ and Satan* to MS Junius 11," *Anglia* 97 (1979): 49.

62 The purpose of the accents in the manuscript, many of which are now so faded as to be hardly discernable, remains unclear. G.C. Thornley suggested more than fifty years ago that the accents, though perhaps inserted by different hands, might have been added for a single, "liturgical recitative" purpose – that is, "to assist a lector who was intoning the poems"; see "Accents and Points of MS Junius 11," *Transactions of the Philological Society* (1954): 183. No more persuasive explanation has since been offered. One difficulty with such a claim, however, is the uneven distribution of accents. The final pages containing *Daniel* (210 and 212), e.g., have only seven and eleven accents, respectively, while the first page of *Christ and Satan*

and Satan sections are the most heavily corrected; Krapp describes "the number of corrections in *Exodus* and *Daniel*" as "very small, and practically all of them were made by the scribe of Liber I in correction of obvious errors as he wrote."[63] The corrector's goal in *Christ and Satan* was both simple correction of errors and "normalization" of the poem's Anglian exemplar "into late West Saxon," according to Sleeth.[64] The corrector's work varies, as Clubb notes, becoming less plentiful "after line 125, where the second scribe, who did most of the normalizing himself, begins to write," and it is not limited to changes in word forms; the corrector also attempts to clarify passages, with rewriting or explanation, sometimes following on erasures. Clubb deems some of this work of "questionable value" and asserts that "most of his changes are unnecessary," but they reflect active interest in the text.[65]

Clubb, like Gollancz, finds a few corrections that appear to be the work of a second corrector, in addition to the distinct hand usually identified as that of the annotator.[66] The work, even if done immediately

---

has fifty-nine accents in what might be two (or more) hands – the ink colour and shapes of the marks vary. This pace is not maintained; p. 225 of *Christ and Satan* has only three accents, showing how marked are the variations in this poem, in particular. At least two shapes of accent mark appear; these Krapp describes in his edition of the *Vercelli Book* as "a long slanting accent which is found throughout Liber I and not at all in Liber II, and a shorter and less slanting accent, which in Liber I is found only in the first thousand lines of Genesis but which occurs regularly throughout Liber II" (liv). In both accents and points, the colour of ink is distinct from that of the text in *Christ and Satan*, and Thornley suggests that the notations here may have been added in two stages, with dots being first added, then changed to various kinds of punctuation (189). The dots in *Christ and Satan* may be "the remains of metrical punctuation," and, Thornley argues, although the pointing, like the accents, is incomplete, the marks above the dots look like various punctuation marks: "This evidence makes it likely that the text of at least one poem in the MS. was prepared, or was in the process of being prepared, for use with the liturgical recitative, or for reading aloud according to the rules of the Church" (185–9). On the pointing in the manuscript, see John Lawrence, *Chapters on Alliterative Verse* (London: Henry Frowde, 1893), 14; and Clubb, *Christ and Satan*, xiv.

63 Krapp, *Junius Manuscript*, xiii. See also Doane, *Genesis A*, 14–16. Doane suggests that the corrections in *Genesis A* by a hand other than the scribe's might have been in preparation for recopying the manuscript (14n24); this may also be true of the heavier corrections in *Christ and Satan*.

64 Sleeth, *Christ and Satan*, 34; he provides a detailed analysis of the corrections, drawing on the dialect work of Friedrich Groschopp, "Das ags Gedicht 'Crist und Satan,'" *Anglia* 6 (1883): 248–76; and Theodor Frings, "*Christ und Satan*," *Zeitschrift für deutsche Philologie* 45 (1913): 216–36.

65 Clubb, *Christ and Satan*, xvi–xvii.

66 Ibid., xvi.n17; Gollancz, *Cædmon Manuscript*, xxix. Finnegan, *Christ and Satan*, 5, identifies only a Corrector and an Annotator.

after the scribe's work, surely indicates some expectation or evidence of ongoing use. This is borne out in the only written evidence of ongoing readership of the whole manuscript, what Raw identifies as "two marginal notes in hands of the twelfth century," one on the last page of *Daniel* (page 212), which is in the same gathering as *Christ and Satan*, and one in *Christ and Satan* (page 219).[67] If this final section of the manuscript attracted separate attention or, at least, was judged in need of comment in the twelfth century, it may have done so in the eleventh as well. Certainly, in the eleventh century, it was already visually distinct from the preceding poems.

The multiple hands in this section, none of which appear in the book's first three sections, and the folded pages contribute most forcefully to the sense that the inner pages (213 to 28) of Quire 17, those containing *Christ and Satan*, were treated differently than preceding pages. The smaller marks and the impression of wear heighten that sense. *Daniel*, in sharpest contrast and closest proximity, did not require the corrections deemed necessary for *Christ and Satan*, and its pages show not only few extraneous marks but also little of the blurring and staining that has affected the pages of *Christ and Satan*.[68] Raw's codicological assessments tie the last quire to the rest of the manuscript, but, still, *Christ and Satan* does not look like the implied "LIBER I," and not all of its condition can be attributed to the time of the rebinding.[69] *Christ and Satan*, then, shows material evidence of being both part of and distinct from the rest of the manuscript.

67 Raw, "Construction," 204; on the date, too, of the corrections/annotations, see Clubb, *Christ and Satan*, xvi. Finnegan, *Christ and Satan*, 5, ascribes the p. 219 "omnis homo primum bonum" to the *Christ and Satan* annotator. Raw ("Construction," 204) continues that there are, as well, "two twelfth-century drawings. The first of these (p. 31) is not related to the text but that on p. 96 shows the messenger telling Abraham about the capture of Lot, an incident described on p. 94 of the manuscript (*Genesis A* 2018–23). The drawing dates from the second half of the twelfth century and shows that the text was still considered to be of interest at that date."

68 In the forty pages, including blanks, that contain *Daniel*, very few extraneous marks appear: *xb* (crossed *b*) appears on p. 183 and on p. 190; on p. 181 is a pair of double horizontal lines in the margin (slightly longer than those that turn up earlier in the MS), and, on p. 185, the letter *f* is rewritten in the margin, where it is blurred on the line. The word *innan* turns up as the sole inhabitant of p. 211 (besides a slash just before it). The discolourations are also minor, including only such things as some stains along the outer edges of pages and two small drops of red as well as three smudges that just might be the faint residue of diagonally placed fingertips on p. 191. It is impossible, of course, to date any of these marks.

69 Remley, *Old English Biblical Verse*, 22–3n34, offers a useful summary of the evidence usually brought to bear in arguments about the status of the *Christ and Satan* pages.

If *Christ and Satan* was understood by an audience in pre-Conquest England as a poem of a different nature than its predecessors in the manuscript, readers may have approached and used it separately from its companions before it was bound into the manuscript, just as they might any text in the other surviving collections of Old English verse. Such a possibility addresses both the distinct visual condition of the poem and one of its literary categories, and that does not conflict with Raw's careful examination of the lining of the pages and the sewing of the manuscript. Raw notes that, because it shares stitch marks with the rest of the manuscript, *Christ and Satan* "had already been added to the rest of the manuscript by the time that it was first sewn and that if this text had an earlier, independent existence, as Lucas has claimed, it was used unstitched."[70]

Yet if *Christ and Satan* circulated separately, the crease might be the result of folding that would make stitching largely unnecessary. The fold itself would hold the pages together in a compact, portable unit; unfolded, stitching held these pages together by binding them into the larger collection. Ælfric's letter to the monks of Eynsham in CCCC MS 265 (ecclesiastical handbook from Worcester) appears to have been used in just this way. As Budny describes it, "The first recto and last verso of Quire 17 (pp. 253 and 268), which contains the second and final quire of Ælfric's abridgement of the *Regularis Concordia*, are darkened and stained, probably from exposure while a separate unit."[71] While CCCC 265, as a "miscellaneous collection of canonical, liturgical, legal, and other texts," is more diverse in character from the biblically based poems of Junius 11, it does provide roughly contemporary evidence of a manuscript "made in stages" but with some continuity of design and construction: the Ælfric section, section 3, like the texts before and after

70 Raw, "Construction," 189; see also Alessandra Molinari, "A Crease in Gathering 17 of Bodleian MS. Junius 11," *Linguæ & – Revista di lingue e culture moderne* 14 (2015): 55–85. Lucas, "On the Incomplete Ending of *Daniel*," 46–59, argues that *Christ and Satan* was created independently and circulated as a folded booklet. In Robinson's terms, this means "a small but structurally independent production containing a single work or a number of short works," and he describes a number that were folded ("Self-Contained Units," 231–2). See also Bernhard Bischoff, "Über gefaltete Handschriften, vornehmlich hagiographischen Inhalts," *Mittelalterliche Studien* 1 (Stuttgart: Hiersemann, 1966–7), 93–100.

71 Mildred Budny, *Insular, Anglo-Saxon, and Early Anglo-Norman Manuscript Art at Corpus Christi College, Cambridge* (Kalamazoo, MI: Medieval Institute Publications, 1997), 1:605. See also M.R. James's description of the manuscript in *A Descriptive Catalogue of the Manuscripts in the Library of Corpus Christi College Cambridge* (Cambridge: Cambridge University Press, 1911), 14–21.

it, is "laid out in single columns of twenty-six lines."[72] Copies of the Gospels may have been actually designed to be used separately before binding, even when clearly designed as a unit and actually written by a single scribe, as in Oxford, Bodleian Library MS Bodley 441. Not only does each Gospel begin on a new page, but the last leaves of Mark, Luke, and John are also lost, suggesting that the four gospels were read separately for some time.[73]

Raw argues that *Christ and Satan* was an early addition to the manuscript, yet, even so, Junius 11 shows signs of some degree of assemblage in stages.[74] Its illustration cycle, by two artists, remains unfinished, and one might wonder whether binding was held off until it became clear that the spaces left for illustrations were unlikely to be completed. The shift in hands in *Christ and Satan*, likewise, might be read as evidence of production in stages, with the single hand of the first part working at one time and the hands of *Christ and Satan* working at another.[75] While Raw's arguments are strongly against a wholly independent existence of the *Christ and Satan* section of Junius 11, the manuscript does appear to have been written in stages, and *Christ and Satan* did generate some different early responses than did its companion poems. The material and the literary evidence suggest that *Christ and Satan* could have been both "added before the manuscript as a whole had been sewn" and used separately before the manuscript had been sewn. Readers may first have read the text with an interest in it as wisdom literature or for some other interest independent of its role as the culmination of a coherent sequence or thematically unified collection.[76]

---

72 Budny, *Insular, Anglo-Saxon, and Early Anglo-Norman Manuscript Art*, 1:599, 602.

73 R.M. Liuzza, ed., *The Old English Version of the Gospels*, EETS 304 (Oxford: Oxford University Press, 1994), 1:xx–xxi.

74 Raw, "Construction," 203. In describing gathering 17, Raw (200) suggests that even it might have been completed in two stages: "The real division is between the outer three bifolia (pp. 211–16 and 225–9) and the inner sheets (pp. 217–24). The three outer bifolia were pricked in both margins like those in the rest of the manuscript; the central bifolium (pp. 219–22), on the other hand, is pricked in the outer margins only."

75 Finnegan, *Christ and Satan*, 4, notes, "Though the styles of the scribes differ, they do not do so in any degree that would allow us to suppose that a significant interval separated their work." Scribal similarities lead Clubb, *Christ and Satan*, xii, to assert that all three worked within the span of no more than a single generation.

76 Raw, "Construction," 203. Clubb, *Christ and Satan*, xv, argues that by the late eleventh century, at least, the collection existed as a unit, based on his belief that "there are traces in the *Genesis* of the hand of the Late West Saxon Corrector who was so active in *Christ and Satan*," a claim that Gollancz, *Cædmon Manuscript*, xxix, found unsupportable but Krapp, *Junius Manuscript*, xiv–xv, developed.

Both the enumerative opening and the larger narrative concerns of *Christ and Satan* connect it to the variable-genre, "content-based" category of wisdom literature and, more specifically, to an assortment of similar or identical revealed-wisdom material that appears in both Latin and vernacular texts that were associated with early medieval England.[77] The physical appearance of the poem, particularly in contrast with the poem that precedes it, *Daniel*, indicates, at worst, wear associated with devaluation and, at best, an audience interested in updating, improving, and reading *Christ and Satan*. Together, the material and literary distinctions of the poem suggest that while the compiler of Junius 11 may well have had a plan, the book's earliest readers or audiences may – like many a modern reader of collections – have made their own, non-sequential choices; in the case of *Christ and Satan*, a choice might well have been made to read the wisdom poem at the end of the collection without reading the biblical poems that precede it.

The final section of Junius 11 demonstrates exceptionally well that perceived coherence as well as categorization rested with the reader and more than likely varied among readers as well as between readers and the compiler. Depending upon how readers perceived the book that we know as Junius 11, or any section of the book, they may have read from page to page, expecting and finding unity and coherence, or they may have treated the book's contents as aggregative rather than linear or interlocked. *Christ and Satan* is both the end of the book and the last section of the collection, and while those roles may overlap, no necessity of connection restricts readers' understanding of the text.

77 Law, *Wisdom, Authoity and Grammar*, 23.

Chapter 5

The Book in the Library

Saga me hwæt bockinna and hu fela syndon[1]

How early medieval readers perceived the book we know as Junius 11 must have rested, in large part, on their experience with text, in both material and intellectual terms. If we could connect Junius 11 with a particular library or owner, we would presumably know much more about both its perceived purpose and the ways in which it might have been read. Yet neither the planned purpose nor the specific provenance of the Junius 11 manuscript is known, and long debates concerning its history reveal just how difficult making definite claims about the manuscript and, in turn, its earliest readers, can be. The date of the compilation is traditionally placed at ca. 1000, depending upon which aspect of the manuscript is under discussion. Lockett's thorough investigation of the features of the manuscript led her to convincingly date the compilation to ca. 960–990, but where the compilation took place and for whom remains more debatable.[2] Gollancz and Krapp tentatively linked Junius 11 to the New Minster at Winchester, an attribution subsequently supported by Ohlgren, among others, while James, Ker, Wormald, Raw, and Doane find Christ Church, Canterbury the likely origin.[3] Both placements determine a monastic origin for this book of illustrated

1 "Tell me what kinds of books and how many there are": Cross and Hill, *Prose Solomon and Saturn*, 59.1, 34.

2 Lockett, "Integrated Re-examination."

3 Gollancz, *Cædmon Manuscript*, xviii; Krapp, *Junius Manuscript*, x–xi; Thomas H. Ohlgren, "Some New Light on the Old English *Cædmonian Genesis*," *Studies in Iconography* 1 (1975): 63–4; M.R. James, *The Ancient Libraries of Canterbury and Dover: The Catalogues of the Libraries of Christ Church Priory and St. Augustine's Abbey at Canterbury, and of St. Martin's Priory at Dover* (Cambridge, 1903); Ker, *CMCAS*; Francis

Old English poetry, as do arguments that have posited Junius 11 as a production of Malmesbury or Glastonbury, and a monastic production does not conflict with the possibility of a lay patron.[4]

The manuscript's initial audience, or planned audience, at least, may well have been secular. Heslop, for instance, argues in favour of secular environments for vernacular manuscripts as richly or extensively illustrated as Junius 11, particularly if it had been completed, and Raw proposes that "the density of illustration in Junius 11 implies that it," like London, BL, Claudius B.iv, the Old English Hexateuch, "was intended for some purpose other than private reading within the monastery," such as use by "educated laymen."[5] Anlezark further refines the field to "a politically powerful lay reader who moved in royal circles," more specifically positing the ealdorman Æthelweard, whom Ælfric identifies as reader of his Genesis translation and other works.[6] While such scholarship is increasingly persuasive about the patron and intended initial audience for the book, monastic production remains highly probable. The overlap between monastic and political spheres in the tenth and eleventh centuries is such that Æthelweard or any lay patron of literature would probably have developed a close relationship with one or more scriptoria; as Anlezark explains, Æthelwold's son Æthelmær shifted back and forth from public to monastic life.[7]

Whether produced for a lay or a monastic readership, Junius 11 is almost certainly a monastic production and would have been shaped, to some extent, by a particular foundation.[8] We have the benefit of

---

Wormald, *English Drawings of the Tenth and Eleventh Centuries* (London: Faber and Faber, 1952); Raw, "Construction"; Doane, *Saxon Genesis*.

4 Lucas, "MS Junius 11 and Malmesbury"; Karkov, *Text and Picture*, 35; and John Higgitt, "Glastonbury, Dunstan, Monasticism and Manuscripts," *Art History* 2, no. 3 (1979): 282–3.

5 T.A. Heslop, "The Production of *De Luxe* Manuscripts and the Patronage of King Cnut and Queen Emma," *ASE* 19 (1990): 151–90; Barbara Raw, "The Probable Derivation of Most of the Illustrations in Junius II from an Illustrated Old Saxon Genesis," *ASE* 5 (1976): 135.

6 Anlezark, "Lay Reading, Patronage, and Power," 76, 79.

7 Ibid., 79.

8 See Lucas, "MS Junius 11 and Malmesbury," 211–2, for one review – and rejection – of the lay audience proposal. For information on "The Physical Arrangement of Anglo-Saxon Libraries," see Lapidge, *Anglo-Saxon Library*, 60–2, where he offers a striking image: "The sum of this evidence perhaps suggests that Anglo-Saxon libraries were normally housed in book-chests, and that when an Anglo-Saxon scholar wished to consult a book, he got down on his hands and knees and rummaged around in the chest until he came upon the book he required. It needs hardly to be said that such an arrangement could scarcely accommodate a very large library."

knowing at least something, then, about the other books that might have influenced the construction and even perhaps shared a shelf or a book-chest with Junius 11. Surviving volumes from monastic libraries in early medieval England offer a glimpse, albeit limited, of what a particular house had and read, what volumes and texts were available individually, in other collections, or in an existing compilation of *Genesis, Exodus*, and *Daniel*, and, thus, they offer a context for attempting to understand what kind of book Junius 11 was to its makers and first readers and how it might have reflected discernable distinctions of place at the time of its compilation and shortly afterwards.

The two most frequently named probable homes or production sites for Junius 11 remain Christ Church, Canterbury and the New Minster, Winchester, despite Lucas's detailed arguments for Malmesbury. For Christ Church, in particular, the attribution might reflect a general gravitational pull; John Higgitt's assessment of the situation still applies: "More of Canterbury's than of Glastonbury's pre-Conquest books survive and so related books of uncertain provenance tend to get associated with Canterbury."[9] Prior Henry of Eastry's list of books at Christ Church ca. 1330 does include, in its section on earlier books, a "genesis anglice depicta" that may be what is now known as MS Junius 11, but, as James admits, St. Augustine's at Canterbury also possessed an English version of Genesis (BL, Claudius B.iv).[10] The poems in Junius 11 appear to have been written at different times and, at least to some extent, in different places (*Genesis B*'s Saxon connections being the most obvious example), and so other houses, too, may well have had illustrated versions of Genesis. While the surviving collections, so far as others have defined them, of Christ Church, the New Minster, Winchester, and Malmesbury might have been among such sites, the remnants of these libraries' pre-Conquest books show that the greatest affinities occur between Junius 11 and the New Minster books.

As a physical object, Junius 11 has yielded no definitively localized features. The pattern of page arrangement – within each quire, hair sides facing hair sides and flesh sides facing flesh sides – might be a particular feature of manuscripts produced in southern England in the tenth century, according to David Dumville, but neither this nor other codicological aspects appear to be distinctive to any single southern foundation.[11] The current binding of the manuscript, though clearly

9 Higgitt, "Glastonbury, Dunstan, Monasticism and Manuscripts," 282.

10 James, *Ancient Libraries*, xxv–xxvi.

11 David N. Dumville, "English Square Minuscule Script: The Mid-Century Phases," *ASE* 23 (1994): 142.

early, Raw dates to between 1100 and 1250, and, despite the common practice of reusing binding boards, even its boards are apparently not pre-1100. "Perhaps," as Raw suggests, "the old boards were too damaged to be re-used, or possibly the manuscript was bound originally in limp covers (*in pargameno*) instead of in boards (*in asseribus*) as was the case with many of the manuscripts listed in the fragmentary late-twelfth-century catalogue of Christ Church, Canterbury."[12]

The catalogue to which Raw refers offers a more hopeful route for trying to define Junius 11's early companion books. Written on the flyleaf of CUL Ii.3.12, the partial catalogue reveals that, by the second half of the twelfth century, around 1170, Christ Church owned more than 223 volumes. Yet the list, as James long ago pointed out, leaves out volumes that presumably were, in fact, owned and used at Christ Church, such as Bibles and Gospel books, and the extent and full range of contents of Christ Church's book collection 150 to 200 years before the catalogue was drawn up remain more elusive, just as they do for the New Minster, Winchester, and even more so for Malmesbury.[13] Even surviving books themselves firmly identified as from a particular monastic centre can paint a misleading picture of the monastery's textual holdings by reflecting preservation interests rather than a broader range of library possessions. Dumville reminds us that "a high proportion of our surviving manuscript volumes comprises gospel-books, miscellaneous books of the bible, legendaries and passionals, and more strictly liturgical books."[14]

In addition, many surviving manuscripts have a disputed or very brief connection to a particular place. The York Gospels, for instance, may have been produced at Christ Church, or may have been there briefly for one of Christ Church's scribes to complete a single page, or may never have been at Christ Church at all. Gneuss and Lapidge's *Handlist* gives the book's tenth- or early eleventh-century location as Christ Church with a question mark, then notes that its provenance was York by about 1020. Heslop more firmly assigns the York Gospels' place of production to Canterbury, although he acknowledges the possibility, put forward by McGurk, that the single page, f. 23v, thought to be in the hand of famed Christ Church scribe Eadui Basan was completed by bringing the scribe to the book rather than the book to the scribe.[15]

12 Raw, "Construction," 265, 263, 266.

13 James, *Ancient Libraries*, xxv, xxviii–xxix, and the reproduction of the list at 3–12.

14 David N. Dumville, "English Libraries before 1066: Use and Abuse of the Manuscript Evidence," in *Anglo-Saxon Manuscripts: Basic Readings*, ed. Mary P. Richards (New York: Garland, 1994), 189.

15 Heslop, "Production of *De Luxe* Manuscripts," 155.

So while the York Gospels *might* have been written at Christ Church, no firm evidence fixes its production there, and, indeed, a reasonable explanation for the manuscript's single page with connection to Christ Church exists without the manuscript having been produced at Christ Church or even having ever been brought there.

Ker, in *Medieval Libraries of Great Britain*, noted that "about five hundred medieval libraries are represented by one book or more." The full contents of any medieval English library, however, remain difficult to assess, and Ker's summary of the situation with which he was familiar makes plain the problems:

> By the fallacious test of surviving books fourteen libraries appear vastly more important than all the others. They are the libraries of the great Benedictine houses at Bury, Christ Church and St Augustine's at Canterbury, Durham, Norwich, Reading, Rochester, St Albans, and Worcester, of the secular cathedrals of Exeter, Hereford, Lincoln, and Salisbury, and of the comparatively unimportant Augustinian priory of Lanthony in the suburbs of Gloucester. We have over five hundred and fifty extant books from Durham, over three hundred and fifty from Worcester, about three hundred from Christ Church, Canterbury, about two hundred and fifty from Bury and St Augustine's, over two hundred from Salisbury, and over one hundred from each of the other seven libraries. On the other hand there are over four hundred libraries from which we have only between one and ten identifiable books.[16]

For pre-Conquest libraries, the difficulties are even greater, as Lapidge has shown in the *Anglo-Saxon Library*. The tenth-century reforms certainly led to increases in monastic library holdings, but determining which books were where is often out of reach. Despite the number of surviving manuscripts from this period, Lapidge points out that "it is possible only in certain cases to assign them to particular centres, and thus to evaluate overall holdings." He refers to Dumville's work in identifying pre-1100 manuscript homes for the examples of "monastic libraries such as Glastonbury, Abingdon, and Peterborough, which from the 940s onwards were undoubtedly the most productive centres of scholarship in the country, [yet] no more than a handful of manuscripts in each case can be identified as having belonged to the monastic library."[17] And while Lapidge strongly cautions about using quotations

16 N.R. Ker, *Medieval Libraries of Great Britain: A List of Surviving Books*, 2nd ed. (London, Offices of the Royal Historical Society, 1964), xi.

17 Lapidge, *Anglo-Saxon Library*, 50–1.

or references to authors or works as a reliable means of knowing what books a collection had, he provides examples of where it has been possible to work backwards to add a book to the known contents of an early library, as in the case of "a contemporary of Byrhtferth, the anonymous Winchester poet who produced a metrical Life of the Breton saint Iudoc" and, by so doing, to find some surprises. The poet included an

> unusual, indeed unique, hexameter cadence *concorditer ambo,* [which] occurs in only one poet previous to the tenth century: Q. Ennius, who in book i of his *Annales* ... had written the hexameter "aeternum seritote diem concorditer ambo" ("join harmoniously together the eternal day"). One would be staggered to think that there was a copy of Ennius' *Annales* at Winchester in the late tenth century; and the more likely explanation is that the Winchester poet remembered the Ennian cadence from having read it in the grammarian Charisius, who alone of the Latin grammarians preserves this line. But at least we now know that a copy of Charisius was available at Winchester in the late tenth century: a not unimportant fact, given that no copy of Charisius is found among surviving Anglo-Saxon manuscripts.[18]

A more thorough accounting of the books in pre-Conquest collections emerges as such connections are pursued, but for now the most reliable indicator, flawed though it clearly is, remains surviving books.

For Christ Church, Canterbury, a relatively large number of manuscripts associated with its collection or with production there survive to provide a picture of the monastery's books at the time in which Junius 11 might have been a new book. Nicholas Brooks in his *Early History of the Church of Canterbury* lists sixty-eight manuscripts probably at Christ Church from about the second half of the tenth century to the turn to the eleventh. He divides these into six groups: twenty-one books from the late tenth century, thirteen from the late tenth to early eleventh, four from the early eleventh, sixteen from the first half of the eleventh, eight from the mid-eleventh, and then six books "which, though written elsewhere and often very much earlier, passed to Christ Church (in some cases certainly, in others probably) between 989 and 1066."[19] With re-evaluation drawing on subsequent work, the list expands to eighty-eight books with certain or tentative Christ Church provenance from the mid-tenth to the mid-eleventh century.

---

18 Ibid., 98–9.

19 Nicholas Brooks, *The Early History of the Church of Canterbury: Christ Church from 597 to 1066* (Leicester: Leicester University Press, 1984), 267–70.

A counter-example to such a list is what we know for Malmesbury. Rodney Thomson confidently identifies only two surviving books that were among the pre-Conquest holdings at Malmesbury Abbey: CCCC 23, which includes an illustrated Prudentius's *Psychomachia* as well as other works; and Oxford, Bodleian Library, Marshall 19, *Liber interpretationes Hebraicorum nominum* by Jerome.[20] With less confidence, the subsequent *Handlist* identifies four more books with possible Malmesbury provenance in the mid-tenth to mid-eleventh century:

CCCC 304
  s. viii[1], Italy, prov. s. ix ex. or x in. England (Canterbury CC? Malmesbury?)
  Contents: Isidore, *Versus in bibliotheca* [*CPL* 1212; SK 15860: excerpts]; Iuvencus, *Euangelia* [*CPL* 1385]
CCCC 330 pt. ii.
  s. ix ex., France, prov. England s. x, (prov. Malmesbury)
  Contents: "Dunchad" (Martin of Laon?), Commentary on Martianus Capella; *glossae collectae*
CCCC 361
  s. xi med. or xi[2], England? Malmesbury?, (prov. Malmesbury)
  Contents: Gregory, *Regula pastoralis* [*CPL* 1712]; *Passio S. Mauritii* (f; s. xi/xii; a version of *BHL* 5746)
London, BL, Cotton Otho C.i, vol. I (with London, BL, Cotton Otho B.x, fol. 51)
  s. xi[1] and xi med., prov. Malmesbury?
  Contents: gospels* (incomplete) (s. xi[1]), bull of Pope Sergius* (s. xi med.)[21]

Regarding CCCC 361, Thomson weakens the case for an early Malmesbury provenance, asserting that the book "certainly did not arrive in England or at Malmesbury before [William of Malmesbury's] time,"

---

20 Rodney M. Thomson, "Identifiable Books from the Pre-Conquest Library of Malmesbury Abbey," *ASE* 10 (1981): 16. The *Handlist* dates and places the manuscripts similarly: CCCC 23: "prov. Malmesbury prob. by s. xi[1]"; Oxford, Bodleian Library, Marshall 19: "prov. Malmesbury s. x[2] or x ex."

21 The manuscript summaries here and throughout this chapter are quoted from Gneuss and Lapidge's *Handlist*, which provides a full key to abbreviations as well as a complete bibliography. I have provided a key to the most frequent abbreviations at the front of the book. See also Ker, *Medieval Libraries of Great Britain*, 128–9; and Dumville, "English Libraries before 1066." Note that Ker's list of New Minster, Winchester books appears under "Hyde" (103–4).

given that "a *Passio S. Mauricii* has been added to the last verso in a continental (probably Norman) hand of c. 1100."[22]

Malmesbury undoubtedly had a far more extensive collection of books than the evidence now reveals, particularly during Aldhelm's time, but too little remains to give much of a picture of its contents in the hundred years before the Conquest.[23] In between the Christ Church and Malmesbury survivals lies New Minster, Winchester, with at least fourteen manuscripts that with varying degrees of certitude can be placed there, and substantially more that are connected to Winchester generally, without a particular house having been identified, and so worth some consideration in any attempt to understand the book environment at the New Minster. Necessarily leaving aside the meagre remnants of Malmesbury and focusing on the two most often proposed homes for Junius 11, we can identify tendencies and interests suggested by the surviving books that point to the New Minster library as the more companionable and more purposeful home, or at least birthplace, for Junius 11. New Minster was perhaps even a place to which a politically active lay patron would purposefully have turned for such a book.

The sheer number of books that have been connected to pre-Conquest Christ Church makes it a tempting provenance for Junius 11. Gneuss and Lapidge uncertainly favour Christ Church, following Wormald's tentative assignment of the manuscript to Canterbury – "Origin uncertain, but it probably belonged to Christ Church, Canterbury"[24] – and Ker's even more tentative placement, "Possibly identical with the 'Genesis anglice depicta' in the early-fourteenth-century catalogue of Christ Church, Canterbury."[25] If the surviving Christ Church books provide any sense at all of the dominant contents of the library from ca. 950 to 1050, however, the Junius 11 manuscript would have stood out as quite different. The *Handlist* suggests, marked by varying degrees of

22 Rodney M. Thomson, *William of Malmesbury*, rev. ed. (Woodbridge, UK: Boydell Press, 2003), 78–9.

23 None of the books that Aldhelm appears to have known at Malmesbury survives: "Thomson suggested that one such book, a copy of Junillus, *Instituta regularia diuinae legis*, written in Anglo-Saxon miniscule dating from *c.* 700 and now preserved as a mere fragment in the Cottonian collection in the British Library, might have been available to Aldhelm at Malmesbury. In favour of Thomson's conjectural identification are the facts that the *Instituta* of Junillus are an exceptionally rare text, and that Aldhelm quotes from them at several points (unfortunately, his quotations do not overlap with text preserved on the extant fragment). Beyond this one possible exception, however, Aldhelm's library at Malmesbury has completely vanished" (Lapidge, *Anglo-Saxon Library*, 34).

24 Wormald, *English Drawings*, 76.

25 Ker, *CMCAS*, 408.

confidence, that the following books or at least one element of their contents were at Christ Church during the period from the mid-ninth to the mid-tenth centuries. In an attempt to provide a clearer sense of the kinds of books that the surviving evidence indicates that Christ Church had, each summary of manuscript dates, places, and contents listed below is quoted directly from the *Handlist*. But instead of following Gneuss and Lapidge's alphabetical and numbered organization of manuscripts by current location, I have re-arranged the manuscripts in terms of content; as a result, occasional problems arise in placing a book with diverse contents. I have also supplied a preceding question mark to indicate at a glance which books have more questionable attribution to Christ Church:[26]

Bible:

London, BL, Royal 1.E.vii + 1.E.viii
s. x/xi, prov. Canterbury CC
Contents: Bible (pandect)

Gospels:

? Cambridge, Trinity College, B. 10. 4 (215)
s. xi$^{1/4}$, Canterbury CC? Peterborough?
Contents: gospels, gospel list[27]

26 Not included in this list are manuscripts that the *Handlist* identifies as connected to post-Conquest Christ Church but for which it does not claim a pre-Conquest provenance, including CCCC 272, a Psalterium Gallicanum; Canterbury, Cathedral Library and Archives, Add.25, a fragment of Gregory's *Dialogi*; London, BL, Cotton Vespasian D.xiv, fols. 170–224, which includes Isidore's *Synonyma*; Oxford, Bodleian Library, Bodley 97, Aldhelm's *De uirginitate* (prose); and Oxford, St. John's College, 194, the gospels and short texts. The *Handlist*, 8, explains the notation system as follows:

(no symbol)	text in Latin
*	text in OE
**	text in OE alliterative verse
(*)	text partly in OE
+*	text in Latin, accompanied by a prose version in OE; or a Latin–OE glossary
°	Latin text with continuous OE interlinear gloss, or having substantial sections, or a fairly large number of words, glossed in OE
(f)	only minor fragments of text are preserved

27 Heslop, "Production of *De Luxe* Manuscripts," 154n10, argues that the attribution to Christ Church "is at best insubstantial." In Simon Keynes, ed., *Anglo-Saxon Manuscripts and Other Items of Related Interest in the Library of Trinity College, Cambridge*, OEN Subsidia 18 (Kalamazoo, MI: Medieval Institute Publications,

London, BL, Add. 34890 (the "Grimbald Gospels")
  s. xi$^{1/4}$, Canterbury CC, prov. Winchester NM; s. xi ex., Winchester NM
  Contents: gospels and gospel list (s. xi$^{1/4}$); Letter by Fulk of Rheims to King Alfred (s. xi ex., Winchester NM)[28]

London, BL, Cotton Tiberius A.ii (with London, BL, Cotton Claudius A.iii, fols. 2–7 and 9* + Faustina B.vi, vol. i, fols. 95 and 98–100)
  s. ix/x or x in., Lobbes, prov. England (royal court) before 939, prov. Canterbury CC s. x^{1}
  Contents: gospels, gospel list; dedication poem praising King Æthelstan [SK 14294] and prose dedication (929 × 939); records(*) (s. xi^{1} – xii in.) … ; spurious letter by Pope Boniface IV [N.R. Ker (1957) pp. 472–3] and two letters by Pope Sergius (c. 1070) …

London, BL, Royal 1.D.ix.
  s. xi in., Canterbury CC (or Peterborough?), prov. s. xi (prob. by 1018) Canterbury CC
  Contents: gospels, gospel list; records* (not after 1020): notice of confraternity, writ [Sawyer (1968) no. 985]

? London, BL, Loan 11 (the "Kidderminster Gospels")
  c. 1020, Canterbury CC or Peterborough?, (prov. Windsor, St. George's Chapel) [owner: Langley Marish Parish Church, Buckinghamshire]
  Contents: gospels, gospel list (f)

London, Lambeth Palace Library, 1370 (with London, BL, Cotton Tiberius B.iv, fol. 87) (the "Macdurnan Gospels")
  s. ix^{2}, Ireland (prob. Armagh), prov. Canterbury CC by 924 × 939
  Contents: gospels; records* and writs* (s. xi^{1})

1992), Keynes notes that the B.10.4 scribe also wrote the Copenhagen Gospels, the Missal or Sacramentary of Robert of Jumièges, the gospel book of BL Royal 1.D.ix, and the Kedderminster or Langley Marish Gospels, plus "the surviving fragments of two other gospel books," and he "was probably active *c.* 1020" (32–3).

28 Dumville clarifies the travels of the manuscript: "As T.A.M. Bishop (1971:22) has observed, it was written by Eadwig Basan (cf. Dumville 1992*a*) who by *ca* 1020 was a monk of Christ Church, Canterbury. In due course it migrated to the New Minster, Winchester, for there a known scribe added on fos 158r–160v a copy of a letter from Fulk, archbishop of Rheims, to King Alfred, recommending to Grimbald (who was later culted as a patron of the New Minster)." Despite published attributions to varying dates, he asserts, "There need be no confusion: the addition can be placed at the New Minster, probably after 1087/8. The manuscript had migrated from its place of origin to Winchester … by that date." See David N. Dumville, "On the Dating of Some Late Anglo-Saxon Liturgical Manuscripts," *Transactions of the Cambridge Bibliographical Society* 10 (1991): 44–5.

? Salisbury, Cathedral Library, Portfolio 4/1
s. xi in., Canterbury CC?, Peterborough?
Contents: gospels (f)
? York, Minster Library, Add. 1, fols. 10–161
s. x ex.–xi in., prob. Canterbury CC, prov. York (by 1020–3)
Contents: gospels; additions: records (surveys of archiepiscopal land), three short sermons or tracts*, writ or letter of King Cnut* (all s. xi^1); inventory of liturgical books and church goods* (s. xi med.); prayers* (s. xi^1); list of sureties (s. xi^2)[29]
Hannover, Kestner-Museum, W.M.XXIa, 36
c. 1020, Canterbury CC, prov. Germany by s. xi, (Hersfeld?, later prov. Lüneburg, abbey of St Michael)
Contents: gospels, gospel list; verse colophon
? New York, Pierpont Morgan Library, M 869 (the "Arenberg Gospels")
s. x ex., prob. Canterbury CC, (prov. Köln, St Severin, by s. xii, or s. xi?)
Contents: gospels
Stockholm, Kungliga Biblioteket, A.135 (the "Codex aureus")
s. viii med., Kent (Minster-in-Thanet or Canterbury?), prov. Canterbury CC
Contents: gospels; donation inscription* (added s. ix med.)

Psalters:

? CCCC 411
s. x^2, Canterbury (CC?), or s. x^1, W France (Loire valley: Tours?)?, prov. Abingdon?, (prov. Canterbury)
Contents: Mass chants (s. xi/xii or xii); Psalterium Gallicanum, with scholia; canticles; two litanies (one added s. x/xi); prayers; seven gospel pericopes (add. s. xii)[30]
? London, BL, Add. 37517 (the "Bosworth psalter")
s. $x^{3/4}$, x/xi, and xi in.; whole MS Canterbury (CC?)

29 "'Eadwig' presumably finished his small contribution to York, Minster Library, Add. 1, before the death in 1023 of Wulfstan, archbishop of York, to whom it belonged": Rebecca Rushforth, "The Prodigal Fragment: Cambridge, Gonville and Caius College 734/782a," *ASE* 30 (2001): 139.

30 Brooks does not include CCCC 411 in his list, but Budny, in her description of the manuscript (no. 22 in her list), supports Canterbury, "perhaps Christ Church," as the origin and provenance of the manuscript; see *Insular, Anglo-Saxon, and Early Anglo-Norman Manuscript Art*, 254.

Contents: liturgical calendar: s. x/xi; Psalterium Romanum° with extensive Latin commentary, Ps. CLI; canticles°: $x^{3/4}$; litany: s. x/xi or xi in.; prayers, hymnal, Monastic canticles: $x^{3/4}$; OE glosses: s. xi in.; Ordinary and canon of the Mass, Mass of the Holy Trinity, part of Office of the Dead: s. x/xi[31]

London, BL, Arundel 155, fols. 1–135 and 171–91

1012 × 1023, Canterbury CC, with additions ibid. s. xi^2 (OE gloss, *Gloria*, Creeds, *Pater noster*); further insertions ibid. s. xii^1

Contents: liturgical calendar; computus material; Psalterium Romanum (extensively corrected to Gallicanum, s. x^2); canticles [insertions of xii^1: canticles (continued), litany Mass prayers, hymnal, Monastic canticles, Office of the Dead]; and prayers°; add. s. xi^2: *Gloria*, creeds, *Pater noster*

? London, BL, Cotton Vespasian A.i. (the "Vespasian Psalter")

s. $viii^{2/4}$, prob. Canterbury StA, with later additions: s.ix, prob. ix med. (OE gloss), s. xi^1 (*Te Deum*°, *Quicumque uult*°, prayers), Canterbury (CC?), (prov. Whole MS Canterbury StA)[32]

Contents: introductory texts to the psalms (including SK 10728, 12730); interpretations of *Alleluia, Gloria* and Hebrew letters (in Psalm CXVIII); Psalterium Romanum°; excerpts from Cassiodorus, *Expositio psalmorum* [*CPL* 900]; canticles°; three hymns° [SK 15627, 3544, 14234] from the Old Hymnal; *Te Deum*°, *Quicumque uult*° (Athanasium Creed), prayers [added s. xi^1]

31 "The body of the manuscript ... may be attributed to the last third of the tenth century and located at Christ Church, Canterbury, or at Westminster," according to Dumville, "On the Dating," 45. See also P.M. Korhammer, "The Origin of the Bosworth Psalter," *ASE* 2 (1973): 173–87. Korhammer concludes "that the manuscript was originally produced in Christ Church, Canterbury, or possibly Westminster Abbey. The calendar, as we have seen, gives us no reason to suppose that B had moved by the time that this addition was made between 988 and 1008. None of the material which was added around or slightly later than the turn of the century provides any evidence for the subsequent history of the book" (187).

32 See R.W. Pfaff, "Eadui Basan: Sciptorum Princeps?," in *England in the Eleventh Century: Proceedings of the 1990 Harlaxton Symposium*, ed. Carola Hicks (Stamford, UK: Paul Watkins, 1992), 267–84. The Vespasian Psalter, according to Pfaff, "was kept at St Augustine's in the fifteenth century, and there is no reason to think that it was not there in the eleventh," although Eadui's work is evident in the manuscript on 155r–160r. Pfaff, 277, proposes "that the Vespasian psalter was for some reason loaned to Christ Church and that while it was there something – spillage, rats, a small fire – ruined the final gathering: whereupon the monks not of St Augustine but of Christ Church naturally turned to their eminent master-scribe Eadui Basan to supply the damaged material. This is far-fetched, perhaps, but it does fit the facts of the existing situation" (276).

London, BL, Harley 603 (the "Harley Psalter")
s. x/xi or xi^{1}, Canterbury CC
Contents: Psalterium Romanum [but Ps. C–CV.25 are Gallicanum], incomplete (ends in Ps. CXLIII.11)

? London, BL, Royal 2.B.v. (the "Royal Psalter")
s. x med., prov. Winchester, prov. Canterbury CC s. xi; with additions s. x ex.– xi^{1}, xi in., xi med. or xi^{2}
Contents: Psalterium Romanum° with commentary; canticles°: s. x med., prov. Winchester, prov. Canterbury CC s. xi. Additions: encyclopedic notes ... on Christ's Incarnation, the Ages of the World (followed here by Bede, *De temporibus* ch. xvi), the Ages of Man, the numbers of bones, veins and teeth in humans, the Dimensions of the World, the Temple of Solomon, the Tabernacle, St. Peter's in Rome, Noah's Ark; the numbers of books in the Old and New Testament, the number of verses in the Psalms, units for measuring distances; thunder prognostics; prayers*; note on Friday fasts*; s. x ex. or xi^{1}; prayer: s. xi in., Winchester; Office of the Virgin: s. xi med. or xi^{2}, Winchester Nun.? proverbs+*, prayer*: s. xi med.[33]

? [Rome], Città del Vaticano, Biblioteca Apostolica Vaticana, Reg. lat. 12
s. xi$^{2/4}$, prob. Canterbury CC, prov. Bury St. Edmunds, (prov. Jouarre s. xii)
Contents: liturgical calendar; computus material; Psalterium Gallicanum; Ps. CLI; canticles; litany; prayers (*orationes post psalterium*)

Utrecht, Universiteitsbibliotheek, 32 (Script. eccl. 484), fols. 1–91 (the "Utrecht psalter")
s. ix^{1} (c. 816 × c. 840), Hautvillers or Rheims, prov. Canterbury CC by s. x ex. or xi in.
Contents: Psalterium Gallicanum; canticles

Benedictionals, Pontificals, Other Liturgical:

? CCCC 44
s. x$^{2/4}$ or xi med. or xi$^{3/4}$, Canterbury (StA or CC?), (prov. Ely)
Contents: excerpt from Amalarius, *Liber officialis* III.i*; pontifical (including litanies and second English coronation *ordo*)[34]

---

33 Phillip Pulsiano, ed., *Psalters I*, ASMMF 2 (Tempe, AZ: ACMRS, 1994), 57: "Almost certainly written at Winchester in 10c, with additions in 11c. Associated with Canterbury 12c and later."

34 Although no clear association with Christ Church before the Conquest has been identified, another surviving Amalarius (in Latin) manuscript, CCCC 192, might have been at Christ Church before 1050 as its 10th-century provenance is uncertain, and Gneuss and Lapidge indicate that the manuscript was likely to have been

Cambridge, Gonville and Caius College 734/782a
s. xi[1], Canterbury CC
Contents: mass lectionary (f)
? London, BL, Add. 57337 (the "Anderson Pontifical")
s. x/xi (or 1020s?), Canterbury CC (or Winchester OM?)
Contents: pontifical (including litany and second English Coronation *ordo*); benedictional (incomplete)
London, BL, Burney 277, fols. 69–72 (with London, BL, Stowe 1061, fol. 125)
s. xi in. or xi[1], Canterbury CC (Exeter?)
Contents: antiphoner (f)
? London, BL, Cotton Claudius A.iii, fols. 9–18 and 87–105
s. xi$^{2/4}$ or xi med., prob. Canterbury CC
Contents: pontifical (including litany and second English Coronation *ordo*) (incomplete)
London, BL, Cotton Vespasian D.xii
s. xi med., Canterbury CC
Contents: introductory note (from Isidore *De ecclesiasticis officiis* I.vi and *Etymologiae* VI.xix.17); poem [SK Suppl. 7969a]; hymnal with supplement (s. xi[2]–xii/xiii); *Expositio hymnorum*°; Monastic canticles; Monastic canticles (with rearranged word-order)°
London, BL, Harley 2892, fols. 17–214 (the "Canterbury Benedictional")
s. xi$^{2/4}$, Canterbury CC (or Winchester, for use at Canterbury?)
Contents: benedictional
London, Collection of R.A. Linenthal Esq., s.n.
s. x ex., Christ Church, Canterbury
Contents: versary (f)
Oxford, Bodleian Library, Lat. liturg. d.3 (S.C. 31378), fols. 4–5
s. xi[1], Canterbury CC
Contents: missal (f)
? Florence, Biblioteca Medicea Laurenziana, Plut. xvii.20
s. xi$^{2/4}$, Canterbury CC?, prov. Continent s. xi
Contents: gospel lectionary
? Paris, Bibliothèque nationale de France, lat. 943
s. x$^{3/4}$ [after 959], prob. Canterbury CC, with additions s. x/xi–xi[1], Sherborne; prov. whole MS Sherborne by s. x/xi, France s. xi[2]
Contents: Letter (spurious?) from Pope John XII to Dunstan; pontifical (including litanies and second English Coronation *ordo*);

at Christ Church after the Conquest: "s. x med. (prob. 952), Landévennec, prov. England (Canterbury StA?) s. x[2], (prov. prob. Canterbury CC)."

benedictional; prologue to *Poenitentiale Egberti* [*CPL* 1887]; First Capitulary of Gerbald of Liège; forms of absolution. Additions (s. x/xi–xi¹): list of bishops of Sherborne; letter to Bishop Wulfsige III of Sherborne; two homilies for the Dedication of a church* (one by Ælfric); rules of confraternity* and formula-letter announcing the death of a monk; part of Mass of the Dead; two penitential letters; writ by Bishop Æthelric of Sherborne*

? Paris, Bibliothèque nationale de France, lat. 987
s. x²ᐟ³, Winchester OM [fols. 1–84]; s. xi²ᐟ⁴, or xi³ᐟ⁴, Canterbury CC [fols. 85–111]; (prov. France before late s. xvi?)
Contents: benedictional; Sanctorale et Commune sanctorum added on fols. 85–111

? Rouen, Bibliothèque municipale, 274 (Y.6) (the "Sacramentary of Robert of Jumièges")
1014 × 1023, prov. (and origin?) Canterbury CC?, prov. Jumièges s. xi med.
Contents: liturgical calendar; computus material; sacramentary (including litany)[35]

Calendars/Computistica:

? London, BL, Cotton Julius A.vi
s. xi in.; s. xi¹ or xi med.; additions s. xi ex.; all parts prob. Canterbury CC, (prov. Durham)
Contents: metrical calendar and computus material (s. xi in.); *Expositio hymnorum*° and Monastic canticles° (s. xi¹ or xi med.); Latin hymn by Peter Damian [*AH* XLVIII.52] and Latin poem on the liberal arts [SK 188]

? London, BL, Cotton Tiberius B.v, fols. 2–73, 77–88
s. xi²ᐟ⁴, Canterbury CC? Winchester?, (prov. Battle)
Contents: computus material ("Leofric-Tiberius Computus"); metrical calendar ("of Hampson"); Bede, *De temporibus* ch. xiv; lists of: popes, the seventy-two disciples of Christ (erased), Roman emperors, high priests of Jerusalem, bishops of Jersualem, Alexandria and Antioch, nineteen lists of bishops of Anglo-Saxon dioceses;

35 The manuscript appears in Brooks's list, but Gneuss and Lapidge offer only weak support for a Christ Church origin, and it may have been at Christ Church for just a short while in the first half of the eleventh century. See Robert, *The Missal of Robert of Jumièges*, ed. H.A. Wilson, HBS 11 (London: Henry Bradshaw Society, 1896), in which Wilson viewed the book as the "work of a scribe of the Winchester school," with its contents suggesting the "New Minster, rather than the Old," as the house in which it was written (xxxix).

royal genealogies of Anglo-Saxon kingdoms(*) in sixteen lists; list of the abbots of Glastonbury; Archbishop Sigeric's journey to Rome; Ælfric, *De temporibus anni**; astronomical texts; Cicero, *Aratea* with scholia by Hyginus; excerpts from: Pliny (*Naturalis historia*), Macrobius (*Comm. in Somnium Scipionis*), Martianus Capella (*De nuptiis Philologiae et Mercurii* VI.595–8, VIII.860); map of the world; Priscian, *Periegesis; Vita, Miracula, Translatio S. Nicolai* (in verse; SK 7869); "Marvels of the East" (*Mirabilia orientis*)+*; *Jamnes and Mambres*+*

Paris, Bibliothèque nationale de France, lat. 10062, fols. 162–3
s. xi in., Canterbury CC, (prov. Saint-Évroult)
Contents: liturgical calendar (f)

Saints' Lives:

London, BL, Harley 3020, fols. 36–94
s. x/xi, Canterbury CC, (prov. Glastonbury)
Contents: eight *passiones martyrum:* Pope Callistus I [*BHL* 1523], Pope Stephen I [*BHL* 7845], SS. Abdon and Sennen [*BHL* 6], St Felicity and her seven children [*BHL* 2853], SS. Simplicius, Faustinus and Beatrix [*BHL* 7790], Pope Felix II [*BHL* 2857], St Agapitus [*BHL* 125], Pope Cornelius [*BHL* 1958]; sequence (f) [SK 10021] and responsory (s. xi^1)

Rules, Canon Law, Penitentials:

London, BL, Cotton Faustina B.iii, fols. 158–98 (with London, BL, Tiberius A.iii, fols. 174–7)
s.xi med., Canterbury CC
Contents: list of Roman emperors (added s. xi/xii or xii^1); *Regularis concordia*, chs. xiv–xix*; *Regularis concordia*; three formula-letters announcing the death of a monk with antiphon and verse

London, BL, Cotton Tiberius A.iii, fols. 2–173
s. xi med., Canterbury CC[36]
Contents: *Regula S. Benedicti*° [*CPL* 1852]; Ambrosius Autpertus (pseudo-Fulgentius), *Admonitio*°; *Memoriale qualiter*, chs. x–xix°; "De festiuitatibus anni" (Ansegisus, *Capitularium Collectio* II.33); *Capitulare monasticum; Regularis concordia*°; *Somniale Danielis*°; prognostics° (including two dream *lunaria*); prognostics(*); notes on Adam*, Noah, and Old Testament figures*, on the Ages of

36 James, *Ancient Libraries*, xxviii, 50, identifies this manuscript as No. 296 in Eastry's catalogue.

the World, on Friday fasts*, on the age of the Virgin*; prayers(*); Handbook for a confessor*; Office of All Saints (Vespers, Lauds); Ælfric, *Colloquium*°; Ælfric, *De temporibus anni** (part); encyclopedic notes* on the dimensions of Noah's Ark, of St. Peter's in Rome, of the Temple of Solomon; the names of thieves hanged with Christ; Life of St. Margaret*; Ælfric, *Catholic Homily* .Hom. XIV*; Sunday Letter*; the Devil's account of the next world*; homiletic pieces*; examination of a bishop (extract from pontifical); *Monasteria indicia* (treatise on monastic sign language)*; lapidary*; excerpt from Isidore, *Synonyma* [*CPL* 1203] (chs. 88–96)*; *Regula S. Benedicti*, ch. iv+*; Alcuin, *De uirtutibus et uitiis*, chs. xiv and xxvi*; charm*; Ælfric, Pastoral Letter III*; Office of the Virgin (including litany)

? Oxford, Bodleian Library, Bodley 718 (S.C. 2632)

s. x^2 or x ex., S England (Canterbury CC? Exeter? Sherborne?), prov. Exeter s. xi^2

Contents: a list of chs. i–xx to *Poenitentiale Egberti* [*CPL* 1887], Prologue; First Capitulary of Gerbald of Liège; *Poenitentiale Egberti*, chs. i–xviii; two orders of confession, one with litany; *Quadripartitus* [collection of patristic excerpts and canons], bks. II–IV; excerpts from councils [add. s. xi^2, xi ex.]; prayer [s. xi/xii]; Letter of Pope Leo IX to Edward the Confessor [s. $xi^{3/4}$]

Oxford, Bodleian Library, Hatton 42 (S.C. 4117)

s. $ix^{1/3}$, Brittany [fols. 1–142]; s. ix^1, N France? [fols. 142–88]; s. ix med., France [fols. 189–204]; whole MS s. x in. England, prov. Glastonbury?, prov. Canterbury CC s. x/xi, prov. Worcester by s. xi in.

Contents: fols. 1–142: *Collectio canonum Hibernensis* (recension B) [*CPL* 1794; *BCLL* 613]; *Canones Wallici* [*CPL* 1880; *BCLL* 995]; *Canones Adamnani* [*CPL* 1792; *BCLL* 609]; incipits of Mass texts (added s. xi at Worcester); Gaius, *Institutiones*, bk. I; tables of affinity of kinship; notes on weights and measures

fols. 142–88: *Collectio canonum Dionysio-Hadriana*

fols. 189–204: Ansegisus, *Capitularium collectio*, bk. I

Herbal:

? London, BL, Cotton Vitellius C.iii, fols. 11–85

s. xi^1 or xi med., Canterbury CC?[37]

37 Linda E. Voigts suggests that the MS is in a Rochester script or has a connection, because of the St. Bertin style of illustrations, with a foundation in the fenlands; see "A New Look at a Manuscript Containing the Old English Translation of the

Contents: Enlarged *Herbarius** (Antonius Musa, *De herba uettonica;* pseudo-Apuleius, *Herbarius;* herbs from pseudo-Dioscorides, *Liber medicinae ex herbis femininis* and *Curae herbarum*); *Medicina de quadrupedibus** (*De taxone liber;* treatise on mulberry tree; Sextus Placitus, *Liber mediciniae ex animalibus*); medical recipes(*) (s. xi med.–xi/xii)

Glossary:

? London, BL, Cotton Otho E.i.
s. x/xi, prob. Canterbury StA, prov. Canterbury CC?
Contents: glossary+*

Alcuin:

? London, BL, Cotton Tiberius A.xv, fols. 1–173
s. xi in., prob. Canterbury CC
Contents: Alcuin, a selection of his letters; a collection of letters and poems mainly to tenth-century archbishops of Canterbury [including SK 1384, 4087, 7503, 9863, 10852, 11705, 13764, 15719, 17394]

Aldhelm:

CCCC 326
s. x/xi, Canterbury CC
Contents: *Aldhelm*** (OE poem); Aldhelm, *De uirginitate*° (prose) [*CPL* 1332]; Abbo of Saint-Germain-des-Prés, *Bella Parisiacae urbis* III.1–17, with Latin gloss; glosses; *sententiae;* On Adam's creation: Latin poem (by Alcuin?) [SK 10046]; *De ebrietate* [extract from a florilegium]; three Latin notes, one on grammar; rota poem [SK 11297]; runic colophon (?)

London, BL, Cotton Domitian ix. fols. 2–7
s. x in. or x[1], Canterbury CC
Contents: Aldhelm, *Epistola ad Heahfridum* [*CPL* 1334]

London, BL, Royal 5.E.xi
s. x/xi, OE glosses s. xi in., xi med.; all Canterbury CC
Contents: Aldhelm, *De uirginitate* (prose)° [*CPL* 1332]

Herbarium Apulei," *Manuscripta* 20 (1976): 44n16, 56. George T. Flom, "On the Old English Herbal of Apelius, Vitellius C. III," *JEGP* 40 (1941): 37, dates the MS to c. 1040–1050, from Canterbury or Rochester.

London, BL, Royal 6.A.vi
s. x ex., Canterbury CC
Contents: Aldhelm, *Epistola ad Heahfridum* [*CPL* 1334], *De uirginitate* (prose)° [*CPL* 1332]; colophon [SK 16451 and 13375]
Oxford, Bodleian Library, Bodley 577 (S.C. 27645)
s. x/xi, Canterbury CC
Contents: Aldhelm, *Carmen de uirginitate* [*CPL* 1333]
? Salisbury, Cathedral Library, 38
s. x ex, Canterbury (CC or StA?)
Contents: Aldhelm, *Epistola ad Heahfridum* [*CPL* 1334] (incomplete), *De uirginitate* (prose)° [*CPL* 1332]

Arator:

Cambridge, Trinity College, B. 14. 3 (289)
s. x/xi, Canterbury CC
Contents: Arator, *Historia apostolica* [*CPL* 1504] with scholia (by "Anonymous X"); Dunstan, (part of) acrostic poem [SK 10972]

Augustine:

? Cambridge, Pembroke College, 41
s. xi in. or xi$^{1/4}$, Canterbury CC?, (prov. Bury St Edmunds)
Contents: Augustine, *Enchiridion* [*CPL* 295]
? Cambridge, Trinity College, B. 3. 25 (104)
s. xi ex. (1080s),[38] Canterbury CC
Contents: Augustine, *Confessiones* [*CPL* 251], *Retractationes* [*CPL* 250] II.vi, *De haeresibus* [*CPL* 314]

Ælfric:

? Cambridge, Trinity College, B. 15. 34 (369)
s. xi med., prob. Canterbury CC
Contents: Ælfric, Homilies*
? Durham, Cathedral Library, B.III.32

38 While the *Handlist*'s date for this manuscript is later than my stated parameters of this list, Brooks, *Early History*, 269, includes it with books dated to "s. xi (i)" rather than even under the subsequent heading of "Books of saec. xi med." Keynes, *Anglo-Saxon Manuscripts*, 33–4, dates it similarly: "written by a single scribe in Anglo-Caroline minuscule some time during the first half of the eleventh century."

s. xi^{1}–xi med.; Canterbury, prob. CC (StA?)
Contents: Hymnal$^{\circ}$, Monastic canticles$^{\circ}$: s. xi$^{2/4}$; proverbs^{+*}: s. xi med; Ælfric, *Grammar*$^{+*}$: s. xi^{1} or xi med.

Bede:

? London, BL, Harley 1117
s. x/xi, prob. Canterbury CC[39]
Contents: verses on the Translation of St Edward, king and martyr (inc. "Omnibus est recolenda dies qua maximus Anglum"; not in SK or SK Suppl.); Bede, *Vitae S. Cudbercti* (prose) [*CPL* 1379; *BHL* 2019]; excerpts from Bede, *Historia ecclesiastica* (IV.xxix–xxx) [on St Cuthbert]; Office of St Cuthbert; Bede, *Vita s. Cudbercti* (verse) [*CPL* 1380; *BHL* 2020]; poem on Abbot Wigbeorht [inc. "Iusserat ecclesiae Wigbeorhtus scribere nabla hoc"; not in SK or SK Suppl.]; Offices of St Benedict and St Guthlac

Worcester, Cathedral Library, Q.5
s. x ex., Canterbury CC, (prov. Worcester)
Contents: Bede, *De arte metrica* [*CPL* 1565]; inscription [SK 1479]; Bede, *De schematibus et tropis* [*CPL* 1567]; Priscian, *Institutio de nomine, pronomine et uerbo* [*CPL* 1550]; parsing grammar "Anima quae pars"; grammatical notes; explanations of technical terms and Greek words; two glossarial poems on Greek medical terminology [SK 13822 and 3618; 11969]; Israel the Grammarian, *De arte metrica* [SK 14392]; verses by Alcuin (from *Carm.* lxxx) [SK 11084]; "*Pauca de philosophiae partibus*"; table of metrical feet; charm$^{(*)}$ (added s. xi med.)

? [Rome], Città del Vaticano, Biblioteca Apostolica Vaticana, Reg. lat. 204
s. xi in., Canterbury StA (CC?), (prov. Bonneval by s. xiv)
Contents: Office of St Cuthbert (f); Bede, *Vita S. Cudbercti* (verse) [*CPL* 1380; *BHL* 2020], with glosses; note on the Six Ages of Man

Boethius:

CCCC 260
s. x^{2} or x ex., Canterbury CC
Contents: Boethius, *De institutione musica* [*CPL* 880] V.16–18, serving as introduction to *Musica Enchiriadis; Scholica Enchiriadis de musica; Commemoratio breuis de tonis*

39 Ker, *CMCAS*, 307, in describing the OE glosses, says, "written in England, s. xi^{1}, to the order of an abbot Wigbeorht, according to the verses on f. 62v," and he notes that the glosses, both in OE and in Latin, are contemporary with the text.

Oxford, Bodleian Library, Auctarium F.1.15 (S.C. 2455), fols. 1–77
s. x^2, Canterbury St.A, prov. Canterbury CC s. x/xi, prov. Exeter s. xi^2
Contents: *Vita III Boethii; accessus* to *De consolatione Philosophiae;* Lupus of Ferrières, *De metris Boethii;* Boethius, *De consolatione Philosophiae* [*CPL* 878], with commentary by Remigius; donation inscription+* (s. $xi^{3/4}$)
Paris, Bibliothèque nationale de France, lat. 6401A
s. x ex. or x/xi, Canterbury CC, prov. France (Saint-Vaast, Arras?) s. xi (or later?)
Contents: Boethius, *De consolatione Philosphiae* [*CPL* 878], with glosses and commentary by Remigius [redaction BN]
Paris, Bibliothèque nationale de France, lat. 14380, fols. 1–65
s. x ex., Canterbury CC, (prov. Paris, Saint-Victor, Augustinian canons)
Contents: Boethius, *De consolatione Philosophiae* [*CPL* 878], with *accessus* and commentary by Remigius
? Paris, Bibliothèque nationale de France, lat. 17814
s. x ex., prob. Canterbury CC
Contents: Boethius, *De consolatione Philosophiae* [*CPL* 878], with *accessus* and commentary by Remigius

Byrhtferth:

? Oxford, Bodleian Library, Ashmole 328 (S.C. 6882 and 7420)
s. xi med., Canterbury CC?
Contents: Byrhtferth, *Enchiridion*+*; homiletic piece [*Ammonitio amici*]*; *Alleluia* verse [prayer to St Dunstan] (s. xi^2)

Defensor of Ligugé:

? London, BL, Royal 7 C.iv
s. xi^1, Canterbury CC?, (prov. ibid.); OE gloss s. xi med.
Contents: Defensor of Ligugé, *Liber scintillarum*° [*CPL* 1302]; *Pauca de uitiis et peccatis*° [extracts from Ecclesiasticus and Isidore, *Sententiae* (*CPL* 1199)]

Eugenius of Toledo:

? Grand Haven, Michigan, The Scriptorium, VK 861
s. x/xi, Canterbury CC?, prov. N. France s. xi (doubtful) [a flyleaf]
Contents: three verse riddles [the third of which is listed SK and SK Suppl. 3618]; Eugenius of Toledo (?), *Heptametron de primordio mundi*

[SK 12551]; encyclopedic note on the languages of the world; note on loan of books (s. xi/xii)

Frithegod:

? London, BL, Cotton Claudius A.i, fols. 5–36
s. x med., Canterbury CC? glosses s. x^2, (prov. Glastonbury?)
Contents: Fredegaud/Frithegod of Canterbury and Brioude, *Breuiloquium Vitae Wilfridi*, glossed
? St. Petersburg, Russian National Library, O.v.XIV.1
s. x med., prob. Canterbury CC, (prov. Corbie)
Contents: Fredegaud/Frithegod of Canterbury and Brioude, *Breuiloquium Vitae Wilfridi* [*BHL* 8891; SK 8137] (incomplete: lines 1–1218 only)
[originally formed one volume with St Petersburg, Russian National Library, O.v.XVI.1 and Paris, BNF, lat. 14088, fols. 99–119]
? Paris, Bibliothèque nationale de France, lat. 8431, fols. 21–48
948 × 958, Canterbury CC, prov. France (s. x^2?)
Contents: Fredegaud/Frithegod of Canterbury and Brioude, prefatory *Epistola, Breuiloquium Vitae Wilfridi* [SK 8137], with commentary

Gregory:

? London, Lambeth Palace Library, 204
s. xi^1, Canterbury CC?, (prov. Ely)
Contents: Gregory, *Dialogi*[40] [*CPL* 1713]; Ephraem Syrus, *De compunctione cordis* (in Latin translation); Rota poem [SK 11297]
Oxford, Bodleian Library, Bodley 708 (S.C. 2609)
s. x ex., Canterbury CC, prov. Exeter
Contents: Gregory, *Regula pastoralis* [*CPL* 1712]; donation inscription[+*] [add. s. $xi^{3/4}$)
? Rouen, Bibliothèque municipale, 506 (A.337)
s. x ex., prob. Canterbury CC, prov. Jumièges by s. xi^2 or xii
Contents: Gregory, *Dialogi* [*CPL* 1713] (part)

40 The *Dialogues* include "four Old English glosses, eleventh century. The first two lines of the second portion of the manuscript *Liber beati Efrem*, have an interlinear Old English translation"; see Herbert Dean Meritt, *Old English Glosses* (New York: Modern Language Association, 1945), xiii.

Isidore:

Cambridge, Trinity College, B. 4. 27 (141)
s. x ex., Canterbury CC
Contents: Isidore, *Mysticorum expositiones sacramentorum seu Quaestiones in Vetus Testamentum* [*CPL* 1195]; Adalbert of Metz, *Speculum Gregorii* (epitome of *Moralia*); Augustine, *In Ioannis epistulam ad Parthos tractatus .x.* [*CPL* 279]

Julian of Toledo:

London, BL, Royal 12.C.xxiii
s. x^2, or x/xi, Canterbury CC
Contents: Iulianus Toletanus, *Prognosticon futuri saeculi* [*CPL* 1258], with glosses; *Enigmata* of Aldhelm, Symposius, Eusebius, Tatwine (all with glosses and scholia); pseudo-Smaragdus, *Opus monitorium*; pseudo-Smaragdus, monitory poems [SK 7810, 10988]; *Versus cuiusdam Scotti de alphabeto* [SK 12594]

Juvencus:

? CCCC 304
s. viii[1], Italy, prov. s. ix ex. or x in. England (Canterbury CC? Malmesbury?)
Contents: Isidore, *Versus in bibliotheca* [*CPL* 1212; SK 15860: excerpts]; Iuvencus, *Euangelia* [*CPL* 1385]

? Paris, Bibliothèque Sainte-Geneviève 2410 (with Paris, Bibliothèque de l'Arsenal 903, fols. 1–52)
s. x ex.–xi in., Canterbury, prob. StA
Contents: Iuvencus, *Euangelia* [*CPL* 1385]; commentary on the gospel of Matthew (incomplete; related to *BCLL* 341); Greek litany and *Sanctus*; Eugenius of Toledo (?), *Heptametron de primordio mundi* [SK 12551]; Israel the Grammarian, *De arte metrica* [SK 14932]; *Rubisca* [*BCLL* 314; SK 11608]; metrical versions of *Pater noster* and creed [SK 10905; 15347 (from Iuvencus, *Euangelia* I.589–603)]; 2593; Greek numbers in Latin letters; poem *De quattuor clavibus sapientaie* [SK Suppl. 3716a]; two distichs from Ovid (*Amores* iii.8.3.–4 [SK 8093] and *Ars amatoria* ii.279–80 [SK 8353]); verses by Alcuin (from *Carm.* lxxx.1 [SK 11084]); Sedulius, Letter I to Macedonius, *Carmen paschale* [*CPL* 1447] (glossed), *Hymnus* I [*CPL* 1449; SK 33]; poems on Sedulius [SK 14842, 14841]; excerpt from Aldhelm, *Epistola ad Acircium* [*CPL* 1335]; Odo of Cluny, *Occupatio* (bks I and II are glossed)

Persius:

? Oxford, Bodleian Library, Auctarium F.1.15 (S.C. 2455), fols. 78–93
s. x^2, Canterbury St.A, prov. Canterbury CC by s. x ex.?, prov. Exeter s. xi^2
Contents: donation inscription+* (s. $xi^{3/4}$); Persius, *Satirae*, with gloss

Prosper:

Cambridge, Trinity College, O.2.31 (1135)
s. x/xi, Canterbury CC[41]
Contents: Prosper, *Epigrammata ex sententiis S. Augustini* [*CPL* 526] and *Versus ad coniugem* [*CPL* 531; SK 458] with gloss; *Disticha Catonis*, with gloss;[42] Bede, *Versus de die iudicii* [*CPL* 1370]; Prudentius, *Dittochaeon* [*CPL* 1444] (all except Prosper incomplete); responsory from Office for St Æthelthryth (f; s. xi^2)
London, BL, Harley 110
s. x ex., Canterbury CC
Contents: Prosper, *Epigrammata ex sententiis S. Augustini* [*CPL* 526] and *Versus ad coniugem* [*CPL* 531; SK 458]; Isidore, *Synonyma de lamentatione animae peccatricis* [*CPL* 1203]; all glossed

Prudentius:

London, BL, Cotton Cleopatra C.viii, fols. 4–37
s. x/xi, Canterbury CC
Contents: Prudentius, *Psychomachia* [*CPL* 1441]; pseudo-Columbanus (pseudo-Alcuin), *Praecepta uiuendi* [SK 5960] (f)

---

41 Keynes, *Anglo-Saxon Manuscripts*, 27, agrees that the manuscript may be a Christ Church product, particularly because of its scribal similarities to Cambridge, Trinity College, B. 4.27 and B. 14.3, although he remarks that Susan Rankin "expresses some surprise" at the fact that the "Insular text-hand" also wrote "what are plainly French neumes" in the St. Æthelthryth chant. K.D. Hartzell, *Catalogue of Manuscripts Written or Owned in England up to 1200 Containing Music* (Woodbridge, UK: Boydell Press, 2006), says the responsory was "written in England, perhaps at Ely Abbey" (129).

42 Both the *Epigrammata* and the *Distichs* include glosses in Old English, in ink and scratched. See Michael Wright and Stephanie Hollis's *Manuscripts of Trinity College, Cambridge*, in *Anglo-Saxon Manuscripts in Microfiche Facsimile*, vol. 12 (Tempe, AZ: ACMRS, 2004), 66; and R.I. Page, "New Work on Old English Scratched Glosses," in *Studies in English Language and Early Literature in Honour of Paul Christophersen*, ed. P.M. Tilling, Occasional Papers in Linguistics and Language Teaching 8 (Coleraine: New University of Ulster, 1981), 105–15.

Oxford, Oriel College, 3
s. x ex., Canterbury CC
Contents: Prudentius, *Praefatio operum* [*CPL* 1437], *Cathemerinon* [*CPL* 1438], *Peristephanon* [*CPL* 1443]; epigrams for the basilica of St Agnes by Constantina [SK 2659] and Damasus [SK 4939]; Prudentius, *Dittochaeon* [*CPL* 1444], *Contra Symmachum* [*CPL* 1442]

Boulogne-sur-Mer, Bibliothèque municipale, 189
s. x/xi, Canterbury CC; s. xi in., xi^1 (addition of OE glosses)
Contents: Sibylline prophecies [SK 8495]; verses excerpted from Optatianus Porphyrius Optatianus, *Carm.* xxv [SK 1005]; prefatory letter to Fredegaud/Frithegod, *Breuiloquium Vitae Wilfridi* [*BHL* 8891]; collection of drinking verses [SK 4819]; Prudentius, *Praefatio operum*° [*CPL* 1437], *Cathemerinon*° [*CPL* 1438], *Peristephanon*° [*CPL* 1443], *Contra Symmachum*° [*CPL* 1442], *Epilogus*° [*CPL* 1445]

? Christchurch, New Zealand, private collector, s.n.
s. x/xi, Canterbury, prob. CC
Contents: Prudentius, *Contra Symmachum* [*CPL* 1442], with gloss (f)

Sedulius:

CCCC 173, fols. 57–83[43]
s. viii^2, S England, prob. Kent, prov. Winchester from s. ix ex. or x in.?, prov. Canterbury CC
Contents: Sedulius, Letters I and II to Macedonius (s. ix), *Carmen paschale*° [*CPL* 1447], two hymns° [*CPL* 1449]; epigram by Damasus on St Paul [SK 7486]; excerpts from Augustine, *De ciuitate Dei* [*CPL* 313], XVIII.23, with three versions of Sibylline prophecies

London, BL, Royal 15.B.xix, fols. 1–35
s. x^2 or x ex., Canterbury CC
Contents: Sedulius, *Carmen paschale*[44] [*CPL* 1447], hymn [*CPL* 1449; SK 1904]; two poems on Sedulius [SK 14842, 14841]

Smaragdus:

CUL, Ff.4.43
s. $x^{4/4}$, Canterbury CC
Contents: Smaragdus of Saint-Mihiel, *Diadema monachorum*

43 The first part of the manuscript, fols. 1–56, was also at Christ Church before the Conquest, but probably not until the end of the eleventh century, according to the *Handlist* entry (52): "s. ix/x, Wessex, perh. Winchester, prov. Winchester by s. x med., prov. Canterbury CC s. xi ex. or xii in."

44 The *Carmen* has "a few Old English glosses in several different hands," which Meritt, *Old English Glosses*, xv, dates to the tenth century.

Sulpicius Severus:

London, BL, Add. 40074
  s. x/xi, Canterbury (CC or StA?)
  Contents: "Martinellus": Sulpicius Severus, *Vita S. Martini* [*CPL* 475], *Epistolae* [*CPL* 476], *Dialogi* [*CPL* 477]; pseudo-Sulpicius, *Tituli metrici de S. Martino* [*CPL* 478; SK 17053]; note on the basilica at Tours; *Symbolum "Clemens trinitas"* (the "Confessio S. Martini") [*CPL* 1748a]
[Rome], Città del Vaticano, Biblioteca Apostolica Vaticana, Reg. lat. 489, fols. 61–124
  s. xi[1] or earlier, Canterbury CC
  Contents: a "Martinellus": Sulpicius Severus, *Vita S. Martini* [*CPL* 475; *BHL* 5610], *Epistulae* [*CPL* 476], *Dialogi* [*CPL* 477]; Gregory of Tours, extracts from *Historia Francorum* [*CPL* 1023], *De uirtutibus S. Martini* [*CPL* 1024; cf. *BHL* 5618d], and *Vita S. Bricii* [*BHL* 1452, from *Historia Francorum* II.1]

Many of these books are distinguished by their ornament, particularly the eleven gospel books, most of which are lavishly decorated, among them the Trinity, Grimbald, Cnut, MacDurnan, and Eadwig Gospels. Such books align well with the group of eight Christ Church psalters, which include the beautifully illustrated examples of the Vespasian, Bury, and Utrecht Psalters. Other liturgical material – pontificals, benedictionals, lectionaries, missals, hymnals – makes up another sizeable group of at least thirteen books.[45] Such works, about forty percent of the collection, presumably attest not just to use and reading interests but also to production interests at Christ Church. The books as a group provide a sense of what readers at Christ Church at this time might have seen and understood of the meaning of the word *boc*, which is clearly tied to church ritual and display. In Brooks's summation, the collection shows "overriding emphasis on the gospels and to a lesser extent upon the psalms and hymns – the cornerstones of the monastic liturgical régime."[46]

Also among these Christ Church books, however, appears substantial emphasis on literary texts, including Latin poetry. Brooks

45 Sorting books with multiple contents into one area has challenges, as in the case of Durham, Cathedral Library, B.III.32, which includes poetic proverbs, monastic canticles, and Ælfric's *Grammar*; it has been categorized here under the latter.
46 Brooks, *Early History of the Church of Canterbury*, 275.

characterizes this aspect of the collection as "dominated by works in hexameters, but ... largely limited to the Christian poets – Juvencus, Sedulius, Prudentius, Prosper, Arator – and the *Disticha Catonis*. No trace of Vergil here, let alone of Horace, Ovid, Statius, [or] Terence." Instead, "perhaps the outstanding feature of this list is the proportion of books intended to inculcate Christian moral teaching and the values of the monastery."[47] These books as a group look different from the rich productions of the gospels and liturgical books. They instead appear to be what Brooks describes as "well-written texts of the basic books that formed the 'Anglo-Saxon curriculum,' that is the works that served for the instruction and regular annual reading of English monks. They are in fact library-books, not altar books."[48]

The manuscripts containing Sedulius's *Carmen paschale* provide clear support for this view, often showing signs of heavy use. Budny characterizes CCCC 173, for instance, as "extensively used and abused as a 'classbook,' and restored as a valued text," in the "late ninth or early tenth century."[49] At the same time, many of these schoolbooks do include decoration, not always of the same type but often of similar extent or relation to the text. Both Royal 15.B.xix and the Corpus Sedulius have elaborately decorated initials,[50] as does Sainte-Geneviève 2410, including one that begins the Sedulius piece.[51] Even more visually striking, the Arator text in Cambridge, Trinity College B. 14. 3 begins with a gorgeous zoomorphic Q. Similarly, of the six Christ Church–linked manuscripts containing any substantial piece of Aldhelm's writings, two, Royal 5.E.xi and Bodley 577, offer full-figure images of Aldhelm, and at least three of the others have coloured, decorated

47 Ibid., 276. While the Christ Church attribution is questionable, Sainte-Geneviève 2410 does include a little Ovid.

48 Ibid., 267.

49 Budny, *Insular, Anglo-Saxon, and Early Anglo-Norman Manuscript Art*, 78, 80. BL Royal 15.B.xix(i), fols. 1–35 and the Corpus Sedulius (CCCC 173, fols. 57–83) also show glossing in OE and what may be markers to assist reading sequence. The Corpus Sedulius may have originated at Winchester before being brought to Christ Church.

50 Such as a large – although now damaged – *P* in the former and a wealth of "Insular Display Capitals, sometimes decorated with interlace, spiral, subfoliate, and zoomorphic ornament" in the latter; see ibid., 78.

51 This is the third section of Sainte-Geneviève 2410, which begins, says Lapidge, with a "decorated initial in a recognizable style that is associated with Canterbury" – although he prefers St. Augustine's to Christ Church as the home within Canterbury. See Michael Lapidge, "Israel the Grammarian in ASE," in *Anglo-Latin Literature, 900–1066*, ed. Michael Lapidge (London: Hambledon Press, 1993), 95.

initials.[52] These books of Latin poetry were mostly constructed with attractive decorative detail, at the least, even when the pages then appear to have endured everyday, often rather hard, use. As a result, the books carry a degree of visual harmony with each other in addition to their similarities in content, and they suggest a place or at least an origin in a well-established and wealthy foundation with a tradition in manuscript production.[53]

The surviving and so far identified pre-1100 Christ Church group of books overall, and unsurprisingly, offers more in Latin than in Old English. R.W. Southern, in outlining the monastic community at Christ Church before the Norman Conquest, found the presence of Old English among surviving Christ Church books remarkable: "The most significant thing about them is the extent to which they are written in the vernacular: sixteen of the thirty-seven volumes [identified by Ker] are either in Old English or have Old English glosses to a Latin text."[54] In the enlarged list of eighty-eight, however, thirty-two books are identified in the *Handlist* as including some Old English, although sometimes only small amounts. If the businesslike additions of records and donation inscriptions are excluded, the number shrinks to twenty-five or -six. If we then separate the texts interwoven with or paired on the page with Latin, such as interlinear glosses and the glossary in Cotton Otho E.i., the number of books presenting Old English text (those marked with an asterisk in the *Handlist*) shrinks to about twenty – the number is complicated by such instances as the grammar in Durham, Cathedral Library, B.III.32, which might belong in the Latin–OE group, though the forty-six proverbs that accompany it include some that "echo lines from early Old English poetry."[55] Indeed, only a very small number of books out of the whole list of eighty-eight have substantial, primary contents in Old English unaccompanied by Latin, a fact that

52 CCCC 326 includes "numerous lively and intricately decorated initials" (Budny, *Insular, Anglo-Saxon, and Early Anglo-Norman Manuscript Art*, 246), Royal 6.A.vi has red and green decorated initials, and Royal 12.C.xxiii (which includes a text of Aldhelm's riddles) uses interlace as well as red and green initials. Only two of the Aldhelm texts are plainer: the five folios of BL Cotton Domitian ix, which contain the *Epistola ad Heahfrid*, and Bodley 97, with a version of the prose *De virginitate*.

53 Brooks, *Early History of the Church of Canterbury*, 273–4.

54 R.W. Southern explains the prevalence of Old English as being "as much a result of the low standard of Latin scholarship as of a marked insularity of taste and feeling, for the Latin texts are often deplorably inaccurate" in *Saint Anselm and His Biographer* (Cambridge: Cambridge University Press, 1966), 243.

55 Thijs Porck, "Treasures in a Sooty Bag? A Note on *Durham Proverb* 7," *Notes and Queries* 62 (2015): 203.

may be simply the result of survival tendencies but one that is nevertheless difficult to ignore. The collection of Ælfric's homilies in Trinity College B.15.34 and the *Herbarius* in Cotton Vitellius C.iii, a book that may instead have come from Rochester, are the two clearest cases of books dominated by Old English; the assortment of texts in Cotton Tiberius A.iii, fols. 2–173, also includes many in Old English.

Other Old English texts in this group include prayers as well as Ælfric's *De temporibus anni* (Cotton Tiberius B.v), short tracts by Wulfstan (in the York Gospels), homilies for the dedication of a church (BN, lat. 943), an excerpt from Amalarius (CCCC 44), excerpts from the *Regularis Concordia* (Cotton Faustina B.iii), and an *Aldhelm* poem (CCCC 326). The "Leofric-Tiberius Computus" (Cotton Tib. B.v, fols. 2–73 and 77–88) includes one of the most interesting arrays of Old English, with its various notes, confessor's guide, part of Ælfric's *De temporibus anni*, a Life of St. Margaret, a monastic sign language treatise, and homiletic pieces.

A collection consisting exclusively of Old English verse, even if illustrated, is not particularly similar to any of these surviving Christ Church books. The unfinished state of Junius 11 hinders confident association of it with more ceremonial texts such as the Christ Church psalters and gospels, or with the most familiar texts of the monastic liturgy, although its texts may well have had a role in relation to the liturgical calendar. To some extent, the Junius 11 poems echo earlier biblical epics such as Juvencus' *Evangelia*, a nearly 3200-line Latin poem that harmonizes the Gospels, but Junius 11 is not a schoolbook with some fine, decorated initials or a drawing or two, and the works of Juvencus, Sedulius, and Arator certainly were not exclusively available at Christ Church. The illustrations and initials in Junius 11 do bear resemblance to some surviving Christ Church productions and, in particular, to those with the Prudentius *Psychomachia* in CCCC 23, which has been tentatively attributed to Christ Church.

That the same artist worked on both manuscripts has long been established, and both might most easily be understood as library books, but placing the Corpus Prudentius at Christ Church around the year 1000 simply has not been given firm support. The *Handlist*'s summary of scholarship offers only "S[outhern] England," then the tentative "(Canterbury? SW England?)" for its production in the second half of the tenth century or beginning of the eleventh and identifies its provenance as Malmesbury "probably by [the first half of the eleventh century]." Other arguments based on artistic connections have also not proved definitive regarding the location of the manuscript's production. Doane, for instance, asserts that "the Junius illustrator turned to a tradition of genealogy illustration current in Canterbury," while Ohlgren argues against similarity to Canterbury styles. Although Doane, for one, argues that "the Junius [book] resembles known New Minster manuscripts even less" than it does Canterbury manuscripts, his assertion, like Wormald's, focuses on ornament and illustration.[56]

Junius 11 as a whole resonates well neither with the surviving Christ Church manuscripts of Latin poetry, with which it might have some literary affinity, nor with the Christ Church manuscripts of religious material, with which it may have had some functional affinity. Were it included among these survivals, Junius 11 would be quite distinctive in its combination of vernacular language and poetic form, if not perhaps in what Lockett identifies as its "peculiar constellation of letter forms." In those letter forms, Lockett sees a connection between Junius 11 and three Trinity College, Cambridge manuscripts, B.11.2, O.2.30, fols. 129–72, and O.4.10, identified in the *Handlist* (by T.A.M. Bishop) as products of a single scribe at St. Augustine's, Canterbury. The similarities may support a Canterbury production location for all four manuscripts, but Lockett carefully notes that "Junius 11 is clearly a less formal script" than these Trinity manuscripts and "We need not assume that Junius 11 came from the same scriptorium as the Trinity College manuscripts, because scribes and books travelled, and a writing master could have used as his teaching exemplar a high-grade manuscript from another house."[57]

In content and language, surviving Winchester books have at least slightly more in common with Junius 11 than do Christ Church, Canterbury books, although the picture from the books alone may be skewed simply by the relatively small number of survivals that can be linked to New Minster, in particular. Despite the richness of building at early medieval Winchester, and "although Winchester was clearly a major literary centre," as Malcolm Godden puts it, "few late Old English manuscripts can be assigned to it."[58] Mechthild Gretsch, in advocating New Minster as the home of the Junius Psalter, characterizes the kind of literary centre the New Minster, in particular, might have been in the tenth century:

> The number of manuscripts probably written at Winchester (the Junius Psalter among them) is especially noteworthy, given the fact that, for whatever reasons, Winchester manuscripts appear to have a rather low survival rate. The evidence of the surviving Winchester psalters might therefore suggest that, by the eleventh century at the latest, Winchester had developed into some sort of headquarters for the production of

56 Doane, *Genesis A*, 32; Ohlgren, "Some New Light," 63.

57 Lockett, "Integrated Re-examination," 163, 167.

58 Malcom Godden, "Old English Composite Homilies from Winchester," *ASE* 4 (1975): 57.

> glossed psalters, catering for the needs of monasteries and minsters in other parts of the country.[59]

Ker assigns New Minster, or Hyde, as the abbey later became known, to the group of medieval libraries (including post-Conquest) from which "between twenty-one and forty" books survive.[60] The survivals that have been linked to pre-Conquest New Minster are still fewer, and a substantial number of these are dated just a little too late to be counted as initial companions for Junius 11 – if Junius 11, as we have it, was completed within a fairly short span of time. The *Handlist* connects, with varying degrees of confidence, fifteen surviving books specifically to the New Minster, as opposed to Winchester more generally, from the mid-tenth century to the mid-eleventh; as above, the dates, locations, and contents of each manuscript here are quoted from the *Handlist*:

Gospels:

? Besançon, Bibliothèque Municipale, 14
 s. x ex (c. 980–90), or xi in.? Winchester NM?, (prov. Abbey of Saint-Claude, Jura, by s. xii ex.)
 Contents: gospels[61]

? Copenhagen, Kongelige Bibliotek, G.K.S.10 (2°)
 s. x ex or xi in.? Winchester NM? or Peterborough?, prov. s. xi Peterborough or Canterbury, (prov.: had left England by s. xii ex.?)
 Contents: gospels

Psalters:

? London, BL, Cotton Galba A.xviii (with Oxford, Bodleian Library, Rawlinson B. 484, fol. 85 [S.C. 11831]) (the "Æthelstan Psalter")
 s. ix^{1}, NE France (Liège area or Rheims area?); with additions of s. ix^{2}, France and s. x in., England and s. ix$^{2/4}$ England; MS in Italy s.

59 Mechthild Gretsch, "The Junius Psalter Gloss: Its Historical and Cultural Context," *ASE* 29 (2000): 88.

60 Ker, *Medieval Libraries of Great Britain*, xi.

61 Heslop, "Production of *De Luxe* Manuscripts," provides arguments in favour of New Minster, noting, "It seems quite probable that the Besançon Gospels was produced at Winchester. In so far as 'art' is any guide to place of origin, the best comparisons for the evangelist drawing and the canon table heads in Besançon are to be found in New Minster books of the 1020s and 1030s. As far as the capital letters are concerned, they are very closely related to those in the Benedictional of Archbishop Robert, a book containing benedictions for SS Grimbald and Judoc, both of whom are buried at the New Minster" (171).

ix^{2}? In England from s. ix^{2} or x in., prov. royal court or a Winchester minster

Contents: Psalterium Gallicanum and canticles (s. ix^{1}) with additions: prayers (s. ix^{2}, France); PS CLI; metrical calendar, computus material (s. x in., England); psalter collects; litany, *Pater noster*, creed, and *Sanctus* (all in Greek, added s. x$^{2/4}$, England)[62]

London, BL, Cotton Vitellius E.xviii

s. xi med. or xi$^{3/4}$, Winchester NM, (prov. Winchester OM)

Contents: liturgical calendar; computus material$^{(*)}$ ("Winchester Computus," fragmentary); prognostics* (including *lunaria*); charms*; two veterinary recipes*; prayers; explanations of cryptogrammatic writing^{+*}; Psalterium Gallicanum° with "argumenta"; Ps. CLI; canticles° (incomplete)

? London, BL, Stowe 2

s. xi med. or xi$^{3/4}$, SW England, prob. Winchester NM

Contents: Psalterium Gallicanum°, with psalter collects; canticles°

Liturgical:

? Oxford, Bodleian Library, Bodley 572 (S. C. 2026), fols. 1–50

s. x in. or x med., Cornwall [fols. 1–25]; s. x, Cornwall, with additions of s. x/xi and xi med. [fols 26–40]; s. x, prob. Wales, with additions of s. x/xi and xi/xii [fols. 41–50]; prov. all parts Wales, s. x ex. England (Glastonbury?), s. xi prob. Winchester NM, s. xi ex. Canterbury StA

Contents [fols. 1–25]: Mass of St. Germanus; *Expositio missae* (inc. "Dominus uobiscum"); Biblical book of Tobias; [fols. 26–40]: Augustine, *Epist.* cxxx ("De orando Deo"); Caesarius of Arles, *Sermo* clxxix; antiphons (s. xi/xii); benedictions (s. x ex.); cryptograms* (s. xi med.); paschal table (s. x/xi); [fols. 41–50]: *De raris fabulis* (scholastic *colloquium* or Latin conversation manual); chants for a burial office (s. x/xi), other chants, sequence (s. xi/xii)

62 Robert Deshman finds that this psalter has "clear stylistic links to the Winchester fresco fragment, which antedates 903"; see "The Galba Psalter: Pictures, Texts and Context in an Early Medieval Prayerbook," *ASE* 26 (1997): 137; see also M. Biddle and B. Kjølbye-Biddle, "The Dating of the New Minster Wall Painting," in *Early Medieval Wall Painting and Painted Sculpture in England*, ed. S. Cather, D. Park, and P. Williamson, BAR Brit. Ser. 216 (Oxford, BAR Publishing, 1990), 45–63. Gretsch suggests that Galba A.xviii "may have been one" of the "books and texts [Grimbald of Saint-Bertin brought] to England" when he came, "at King Alfred's invitation in 886 or 887 to help in the king's programme of intellectual reform" ("Junius Psalter Gloss," 113).

?[63] Le Havre, Bibliothèque municipale, 330
s. xi$^{3/4}$ or xi^{2} (or xi^{1}?), Winchester NM, (prov. Saint-Wandrille before s. xviii?)
Contents: missal (incomplete)

Rouen, Bibliothèque municipale, 369 (Y. 7) (the "Benedictional of Archbishop Robert")
s. x$^{4/4}$ (s. xi$^{2/4}$?), Winchester NM (for Selsey?), (prov. Rouen cathedral from s. xii^{1})[64]
Contents: benedictional; pontifical (including litanies and Second English Coronation *ordo*)

Charters, History:

London, BL, Cotton Vespasian A.viii, fols. 1–33 (the "New Minster Charter")
966, Winchester OM, prov. Winchester NM
Contents: Latin distich (inc. "Sic celso residet": SK Suppl. 15252a); New Minster foundation charter

London, BL, Stowe 944, fols. 6–61
A.D. 1031[65] and additions, Winchester NM
Contents: account of the history of New Minster, Winchester; *Liber uitae* of New Minster; will of King Alfred*; tracts on: the Six Ages of the World*, royal Kentish saints*, "Resting-places of English saints"*; West-Saxon regnal list*; gospel lectionary (incomplete); benedictions; lists of relics; pseudo-Damasus and pseudo-Jerome, Colloquy on celebrating Mass+*; *Gloria, Pater noster*, creeds; encyclopedic note on the languages of the world

---

63 The question mark here refers not to the New Minster attribution but to the date at which it might have been there since Gneuss and Lapidge in the *Handlist* acknowledge the possibility of an earlier eleventh-century date.

64 See also the note on Rouen, Bibliothèque municipale, 274 (Y. 6), listed above among the possible Christ Church manuscripts, for the comments by Wilson, ed. of Robert, *Missal of Robert of Jumièges*, xxxix, regarding that manuscript's connection to New Minster.

65 As Simon Keynes points out, "There is reason to believe that some of the main elements of the New Minster's 'Liber Vitae' may have originated in the 980s, during the reign of King Æthelred and under the regime of Bishop Æthelgar"; see Keynes, ed., *The Liber Vitae of the New Minster and Hyde Abbey, Winchester: British Library Stowe 944; Together with Leaves from British Library Cotton Vespasian A. VIII and British Library Cotton Titus D. XXVII* (Copenhagen: Rosenkilde and Bagger, 1996), 31.

Calendar/Computus:

London, BL, Cotton Titus D.xxvi + xxvii
1023 × 1031, Winchester NM
Contents: *lunaria*; prognostics; liturgical calendar with necrology; computus material ("Winchester Computus"); Ælfric, *De temporibus anni**; alphabet with OE sentences*; The Passion according to St. John (Euangelium Iohannis XVIII–XIX); devotions to the Holy Cross; Offices of the Trinity, the Holy Cross, the Virgin; private prayers; directions for private devotions*; note in cryptography; notes on the names of the Seven Sleepers, on the age of the Virgin*, the Ages of the World, the length of Christ's body, on the rainbow; *Somniale Danielis*; medical recipe*; rules of confraternity*; collectar; litany; Euangelium Iohannis I.1–14[66]

Abbo of Fleury:

Cambridge, Trinity College, R.15.32 (945)
s. xi in. [pp. i–ii, 1–12, 37–218]; s. xi[1] (1035/6) [pp. 13–36]; whole MS Winchester NM, prov. by s. xi ex. Canterbury StA
Contents [pp. i–ii, 1–12, 37–218]: *Inuolutio sphaerae* (excerpt from Aratus, *Phainomena*, in Latin translation); Abbo of Fleury, *De differentia circuli et sphaerae* and *De duplici signorum ortu uel occasu*; *Dies Aegyptiaci*; Hyginus, *Astronomica*; Martianus Capella, *De nuptiis Philologiae et Mercurii*, bk. VIII (part with gloss); Helperic, *De computo*; Abbo of Fleury, *De figuratione signorum* (based on Hyginus); prayers; tract on the stars; Cicero, *Aratea* (incomplete)
Contents [pp. 13–36]: liturgical calendar; *computistica* ["Winchester Computus"]

Augustine:

? CUL Kk.5.34
s. x ex., prob. Winchester OM or NM, (prov. Glastonbury)
Contents: Augustine, *Quaestiones Euangeliorum* [*CPL* 275] [excerpt, text altered]; Ausonius, *Ephemeris* iii [SK 11338], *Technopaegnion* vi–xiv; three Anglo-Latin poems from Winchester [SK 15226, 5533, 3197]; Remigius Favius (?), *Carmen de ponderibus et mensuris* [SK 12104]; pseudo-Vergil, *Culex*, *Aetna*

66 For another useful account of the manuscript's contents, see R.M. Liuzza, "Anglo-Saxon Prognostics in Context: A Survey and Handlist of Manuscripts," *ASE* 30 (2001): 198–200.

Ælfric:

CUL Ii.4.6
s. xi med., Winchester NM, (prov. Tavistock)
Contents: thirty-six Homilies[*] (mostly by Ælfric)

Wulfstan:

? CCCC 201, pp. 8–160, 167–76
s. xi^{1} or xi med., Winchester NM?
Contents: On the Seven Ages of the World[+*]; Homilies[(*)] (twenty by Wulfstan); Ælfric, Pastoral Letter II (revised version)[*]; a collection of Anglo-Saxon Laws[*]; Wulfstan, *Institutes of Polity*[*], "*Canons of Edgar*"[*]; *De ecclesiasticis gradibus*[*]; "Benedictine Office"[+*] (with excerpts from Hrabanus Maurus, *De clericorum institutione* II.1–10); Handbook for a confessor[*]; *Apollonius of Tyre*[*]; Kentish royal saints[*], Resting-places of English saints[*]; Genesis[*] (part, from OE Hexateuch); *Lord's Prayer II*[**] and *Gloria I*[**]; forms of absolution and confession

So small a set of survivors rules out determining any "overriding emphasis," such as Brooks identifies in the Christ Church collection, and a substantial portion of this New Minster list corresponds to the holdings at Christ Church or is likely to have been in any monastic collection, including works or excerpts by Augustine, homilies, prayers, gospels, psalters, benedictionals, calendars and computistical texts, and charters. Included here, too, is the collection of Latin verses that endorse learning what constitutes good poetry (see chapter 3 above), encouraging us to imagine the pleasure that a reader like, or well trained by, Winchester's Bishop Æthelwold might find in *Exodus.* But Old English texts, as distinct from Old English glosses on Latin texts, make a strong showing among the New Minster survivals, limited though the view is.

While both foundations have among their later books more in Old English, as would be expected, the tenth- to early eleventh-century New Minster books include laws in Old English, two collections of homilies (twenty by Wulfstan in one collection and most by Ælfric in the other), and narrative texts (*Apollonius of Tyre* and part of Genesis from the Hexateuch in CCCC 201) as well as verse (also in CCCC 201). Also in Old English are much of the slightly later Ælfwine's Prayerbook and *Liber Vitae* manuscripts (Cotton Titus D.xxvi + xxvii and Stowe 944). In total, of the fifteen New Minster–linked books listed here, at least seven include Old English, and in only one of those instances is the Old English restricted to interlinear glossing (Stowe 2). With the exception of the cryptogram in Bodley 572, the Old English in these books is in general substantial and varied, and presented as more independent of Latin, something that may reflect a particular interest of the community or just the kind of unstable conclusion that Southern drew about Christ Church from a smaller set of identified pre-Conquest survivals than we now have (see p. 174 above, on the significance of vernacular/Latin proportions).

Parkes offers an excuse for also at least considering here manuscripts attributed to Winchester generally rather than to New Minster specifically. In his work on the second booklet of the Parker Chronicle, Parkes notes that the manuscript might come from any of the three scriptoria at Winchester: Old Minster, New Minster, or Nunnaminster. But he surmises that "the 'library' (if such an institution can be said to have existed) [at Winchester in the tenth century] consisted of a number of books which were passed from hand to hand when anybody required them."[67] Such practice might explain the lack of surviving schoolbooks from the New Minster and might have allowed for New Minster to develop quite specific areas in its collection.

One item questionable in its Winchester affiliation but still an intriguing possible addition to the New Minster books listed here is the saint's life in the Texts for Feasts of Saint Judoc, now in BL, Royal 8.B.xiv, folios 118–44 (the *Handlist* places the book "s.xi^{1}, France (Saint-Josse, Brittany?); s. xi^{2}, England; both parts in England (Winchester?) by s. xi ex."). A remark by Simon Keynes in his introduction to the facsimile of the New Minster Liber Vitae suggests the connection. Keynes points out that the New Minster had a flourishing cult of Saint Judoc, and "someone working apparently at Winchester in the late tenth century produced a versification of the *Vita prima S. Iudoci*, asserting that the relics lay in Winchester [because in 977 was the 'supposed discovery of St Judoc's relics … at their original resting-place at Saint-Josse-sur-Mer']."[68] If the saint's life in the Royal 8.B.xiv manuscript, or some other lost book, was produced at the New Minster, the work would reflect the community's late tenth-century interest in itself and in immediately relevant historical texts, particularly ones that might validate its status and place in Christian history.

The possibility of such an interest is strengthened in conjunction with another link to Saint Judoc in Rouen, Bibliothèque Municipale 369, known as the Benedictional of Archbishop Robert (of Jumièges) and

67 M.B. Parkes, "The Paleography of the Parker Manuscript of the *Chronicle*, Laws, and Sedulius, and Historiography at Winchester in the Late Ninth and Tenth Centuries," *ASE* 5 (1976): 170.

68 Keynes, *Liber Vitae*, 29.

among the New Minster books I have listed above. Though its date is not certain, and Dumville argues for post-1020, Keynes favours an earlier date and a New Minster origin:

> The manuscript is presumed, on the basis of its script and decoration, to have been produced at Winchester in the last quarter of the tenth century; and, since it contains benedictions for festivals of St Grimbald and St Judoc, the manuscript is presumed furthermore to have originated at the New Minster. If so, it would be difficult indeed to resist the supposition that the book was produced for Æthelgar himself in the 980s, taking advantage of his position at the New Minster to commission a book which he would be able to use in his capacity as a bishop.[69]

The book, then, would function as an individualized and locally contextualized version of public offices. Its deluxe production entails the use of gold and included at least five miniatures with elaborate borders, though only three survive. H.A. Wilson describes one aspect of its production that interestingly, if loosely, echoes Junius 11 in "a distinction between the two parts [the benedictional itself and a pontifical], so far as the decoration is concerned: the ornamental borders and full-page miniatures are confined to the Benedictional proper: and at the end of this part, and at the beginning of the Pontifical portion, some leaves seem to have been left blank, as though it might have been intended to bind the two portions separately."[70] The disjunction between plan and execution, suggestive of either an inability to carry out this particular grand-scale production or a shift in interest, brings to mind the illustration blanks and later addition of *Christ and Satan* in Junius 11, which may have suffered from a similar lapse at about the same time.

A more visually suggestive connection between the New Minster books and Junius 11 can be found in one of the listed manuscripts of probably a slightly later date, "Ælfwine's prayerbook" (Cotton Titus D.xxvi + xxvii), dated to between 1023 and 1031. While Doane's argument against any similarity between Junius 11 and the New Minster books includes citation of this book as evidence, the small prayerbook includes not only texts in Old English but also an illustration on folio 75v of a hellmouth that looks remarkably like that on pages 3 and 16 in Junius 11. The prayerbook image includes a bound Satan at the top of a hellmouth, with Christ above him and centrally placed. Wormald notes

69 Ibid., 31.

70 Robert, *The Benedictional of Archbishop Robert*, ed. H.A. Wilson, HBS 24 (London: Henry Bradshaw Society, 1903), xi.

that the style of the prayerbook illustrations "strongly resembles that of the drawings in the New Minster Register, [BL] Stowe MS 944, and is a development of the 'Utrecht' style," and, indeed, another very similar drawing of the hellmouth shows up on folio 7r in Stowe 944, the New Minster *Liber Vitae* manuscript that is dated to 1031.[71]

The similarity of this image in these three manuscripts has been repeatedly remarked upon, including by William Noel in his work on the *Harley Psalter* and Beate Günzel, in her work on Ælfwine's Prayerbook, and Günzel stresses that "the influence of the Utrecht Psalter – usually pointed to as influencing Junius 11 illustration – was also felt in Winchester, where the outline drawings replaced the rich paintings of the Winchester School."[72] The possibility exists of close influence from Junius 11 on these other images in New Minster books with Old English or of a shared local definition of the image. In this sense, at least, Junius 11 does look like some known New Minster books.

The intellectual emphasis in the New Minster books may provide the best reason for associating Junius 11 with that community. Parkes traces to Grimbald of Saint-Bertin a distinct Winchester interest in history – the New Minster list includes several items with substantial historical and sometimes localized interests – and such an interest might well have informed the production of Junius 11, which reconstructs Christian history in Old English. A remark by Southern about what he perceived as a certain fixedness among the Christ Church survivals offers a point of contrast: "Some of the gaps must be due to chance, but there is no mistaking the general character of the interests which these volumes display. … The hand of the past lies heavily on the collection as a whole. Except for glosses, and perhaps some of the prayers, there is no sign of original composition by any member of the community in the generation before the Conquest."[73] Even in decoration, New Minster may have

71 Wormald, *English Drawings*, 69. Gary D. Schmidt also identifies the hellmouth in the Tiberius Psalter, Winchester c. 1050 (London, BL Cotton Tiberius C.6) as having similarities to the two other Winchester images, although there the hellmouth is in an illustration of the harrowing; see *The Iconography of the Mouth of Hell* (Selinsgrove, PA: Susquehanna University Press, 1995), 72–9.

72 Beate Günzel, *Ælfwine's Prayerbook*, HBS 108 (London: Boydell Press, 1993), 14. William Noel explains, "This type of Hell Mouth was a common image by the first half of the eleventh century; it is also found in the 'Quinity' of Winchester (on fol. 75v of BL Cotton Ms. Titus D.xxvii), on pages 3 and 16 of the Cædmon Genesis (Oxford, Bodleian Library, Ms. Junius 11), and on fol. 7r of BL Stowe Ms. 944"; see Noel, *The Harley Psalter* (Cambridge: Cambridge University Press, 1995), 170n50. See also Dimitri Tselos, "English Manuscript Illumination," *Art Bulletin* 41 (1959): 149.

73 Southern, *Saint Anselm*, 243–4.

sought to define itself in terms of both history and distinctiveness, as Gretsch has suggested in relation to the Junius Psalter (Oxford, Bodleian Library, Junius 27):

> If we now ask who may have been responsible for preserving Grimbald's legacy and for having the calendar copied into a lavishly decorated manuscript, in a new type of script, and together with a glossed psalter whose vernacular gloss very possibly reflects the new political order, we inevitably meet with Frithestan, bishop of Winchester (909–31), who is commemorated in the New Minster tradition for having established good relationships between the two minsters, and who seems to have established equally good relationships between leading ecclesiastical quarters and the royal family. ... By the same token, Frithestan is likely to have been somehow involved in the production of two other earlier-tenth-century manuscripts, which probably originated at the same scriptorium, written, perhaps, by the same scribe as the Junius Psalter, and also containing vernacular texts: the Parker Chronicle and the Lauderdale Orosius.[74]

The narrative within "Edgar's Privilege," a text also known as the New Minster Charter, although it is much longer than most Anglo-Saxon charters (the manuscript is BL, Cotton Vespasian A.viii, folios 2v–33r), provides more specific support for such a local-interest connection between Junius 11 and the books more definitely attributed to New Minster. The Fall of the Angels in *Genesis A* fits particularly well, as chapter 1 in this study has pointed out, into the perspectives evident in "Edgar's Privilege" as well as the Anglo-Latin charter for Burton Abbey (Aberystwyth, National Library of Wales, Peniarth 390, ff. 178v–179r). As Johnson notes, these versions of the story differ "from other Anglo-Latin and Old English accounts of the fall ... [in their] shared cosmographical perspective. ... In *Genesis A* and the two charters, creation – or at least the creation of the earth – is the direct consequence of the fall of Lucifer."[75] Adam and Eve and their offspring will then fill the resulting vacancy in heaven. Johnson cites six specific overlaps among these three texts, and both "Edgar's Privilege" and the Burton Abbey charter were produced at Winchester in the second half of the tenth century.[76] He concludes that all three seem to have had some

74 Gretsch, "Junius Psalter Gloss," 119.

75 Johnson, "Fall of Lucifer," 516.

76 The manuscript in which the Burton Abbey charter survives is late thirteenth century. See S 863 in Peter Sawyer, *Anglo-Saxon Charters* (London: Royal Historical Society, 1968); or the online version *The Electronic Sawyer: Online Catalogue of*

now lost common source, whether an actual text or something more "textually amorphous" such "as an Anglo-Saxon preaching tradition." Between "Edgar's Privilege" and *Genesis A* exists especially close connection. Johnson notes, for example, that, in both texts, "God is moved by the fact that the thrones which the fallen angels once occupied were empty … and *therefore* determined to create a new heaven and earth. The crucial terms here – *sede*/ *setl*, and *cultor*/ *buend* – parallel each other exactly."[77]

"Edgar's Privilege" documents the founding of the New Minster, and, as Johnson points out, its reference to "the fall of the angels and the prelapsarian glory of Adam are immediately relevant to the foundation and ordering of the monastery. The terrestrial paradise is thus a 'type' of the spiritually ordered Christian life, perfectly realized under reformed Benedictine monasticism." Or, as Alexander Rumble puts it, "Explicit parallels are intended to be drawn between the ejection of the secular canons [at the reform] and firstly the Fall of Lucifer and his Angels and secondly the Fall of Adam and his ejection from Paradise."[78] The Fall of the Angels story occurs three times across the poems of Junius 11, as well as being twice illustrated, and both Johnson and Rumble identify a historical and political value for the story that was particularly strong at the late tenth-century New Minster. Junius 11, like other early medieval books and markedly distinct from the uniformity of modern publishing, is locally produced and may well have been locally inflected. Whether its contents were read sequentially or selectively, the Fall of the Angels repetitions might well be explained and understood as a purposeful reflection of the local interests of the New Minster.

Junius 11 as a whole, as a major, illustrated book of Old English verse, calls attention to its moment of production. It is the product of a community in ca. 1000 England that highly valued the vernacular and possessed the wealth needed to undertake an ambitious schedule of illustration. Given the resources required for such a book, it seems safe to say that the community that produced it also possessed a strong desire to retell Christian history in more familiar terms, including, but not limited to, the Old English language itself, quite possibly as part of a program to put the stamp of the community on Christian history. The New Minster in the late 900s seems to have been just such a place.

Anglo-Saxon Charters (esawyer.lib.cam.ac.uk), overseen by the Centre for Computing in the Humanities at King's College London and developed by Susan Kelly, Rebecca Rushforth, and others.

77 Johnson, "Fall of Lucifer," 526, 518–19.

78 Ibid., 520; Alexander Rumble, *Property and Piety*, 67–8.

Where the book might have gone from there, to what medieval readers, remains unknown. If it stayed at Winchester, Junius 11 might easily have been among the books that John Leland collected in the sixteenth century on one of his multiple post-Dissolution visits there, passing it, with others, through a chain of antiquaries and readers up to Ussher and Junius, and on to us.[79]

79 See James P. Carley's edition of Leland's *De viris illustribus* for an overview of Leland's visits to Winchester: Carley, ed. and trans., *John Leland: de uiris illustribus* (Toronto: Pontifical Institute of Mediaeval Studies. 2010), lxv.

Closing the Book

þonne befealdaþ þes heofon togædere, swylce man ane boc betine[1]

A striking simile in an anonymous Old English homily links the closing of a book to the end of the world. When Doomsday arrives, according to this homily, which borrows from the Apocalypse of Thomas, the stars will fall from heaven, the sun will disappear, the moon will turn to blood, and, just after the angels sound the trumpets, heaven will fold like a book: "þonne befealdaþ þes heofon togædere, swylce man ane boc betine." Joyce Bazire and James Cross describe the homilist's primary interest as presenting a "visualization of the physical terrors of the Last Days and, especially, of Doomsday (lines 35–120) and of the sensual delights in the Heavenly City (121–41). Even simple reasoning and explanation were overwhelmed by exhortation through these fearful and enticing mental pictures. ... His aim was to arouse, not inform, and he gathers and adapts to this end."[2] The book simile, then, must be understood as distinctly more than mild. The end of the world is terrifying, so if it is at all like the closing of a book, then that action – cutting humanity off from God – is an imagistic choice for terror. In addition to its visual power for anyone familiar with books, the simile speaks to the central significance of books in Christian understanding and the need to, in effect, engage with books while they are open, to live among them and pursue the wisdom they carry. For audiences in early medieval

1 "Then this heaven will fold together, just as a person closes a book" (ll. 77–8) in a Rogationtide homily identified as Bazire-Cross 3; see Joyce Bazire and James E. Cross, *Eleven Old English Rogationtide Homilies* (Toronto: University of Toronto Press, 1982), 42.

2 Ibid., 41.

England, books provided a means by which they might better understand what flows from God, beginning, as *Genesis A* does, with why "us is right micel" to praise God and all that God created and ending with the heavens closing up and closing off the pursuit of knowledge.

In the introductory chapter of this book, I used the metaphor of a house to describe the various access points by which a reader in tenth- or eleventh-century England might have approached the contents of Junius 11, suggesting that the front door – page 1 and *Genesis A* – served as only one entry point to the book's contents for its earliest readers and that readers might have entered the book at other places and for purposes other than those the compiler might have had in mind. The kinds of reading explored in the chapters that followed suggest, however, that, for early medieval readers, a book was not just a house to enter but also one in which to live and one with which a reader will be truly finished only at Doomsday.

In a culture in which books were not duplicated and were relatively rare, each book was an investment, by its makers as well as from its readers. Through extended access and through memory, and often because of a limited library from which to draw books for study, readers must, in general, have engaged with fewer books and more deeply than the mass availability of books encourages us to do. In the case of Junius 11, most readers in late tenth-century England would have come to its pages already familiar with the stories of Genesis, Exodus, and Daniel as well as stories, biblical and otherwise, about Christ's temptations and his power over Satan. They would have heard these stories in Latin or English, seen them in various kinds of art, and perhaps read them in other books. From the start, then, the poems in this manuscript would have been received with some understanding already attached to them. The readers' tasks involved building on whatever understanding they already possessed.

What we know of monastic education in early medieval England suggests reading practices tied explicitly to understanding and contemplating a text from multiple perspectives: linguistic, narrative and stylistic, moral, philosophical, and religious. Such work might well require multiple readings of a single text or book. A layperson might be similarly trained, or might focus more narrowly on narrative, but, for any reader, every book was a unique container of knowledge to be explored and studied. Reading, as Ælfric explains it in an Easter homily, is fundamental to Christian life: "þæt us is twyfeald neod on boclicum gewritum. Anfeald neod us is þæt we ða boclican lare mid carfullum mode smeagan, oðer þæt we hi to weorcum awendon" (that for us [there] is a two-fold need in the writings of books. One need for us is that we consider with attentive mind the teachings of books, the other is that we turn it to works).[3] As a writer anxious about audience understanding – famously expressed, among other places, in his *Preface to Genesis*, where he worries about readers misunderstanding the text he is translating – Ælfric provides tools for improving reading. His *Grammar* explains grammatical concepts not just for those learning Latin but also for those reading English, as Melinda Menzer argues: when Ælfric states in the preface to the *Grammar* that "grammar is the key that unlocks the meaning of those books," he is asserting that "his grammar will help people read his English-language translations" and engage in literary interpretation of them.[4]

Meaning-making from books in early medieval England was, however, as I have tried to show in *Reading Old English Biblical Poetry*, neither necessarily uniform in its approach nor limited by the sequence of pages and content in any given book. Nancy Thompson, in writing about Old English homilies, points out that seemingly "muddled texts were copied and recopied" and appear to have been valued in early medieval England, although how and why they were valued sometimes remains difficult for us to perceive. Indeed, "many homilies seem [to modern readers] confused, repetitive, even self-contradictory. They wander from one topic to another. Frequently it seems as though the only thing holding them together is the compiler's piety; there is no other clear organizing principle." One example she gives is Blickling Homily 4, a sermon, copied more than once, that "combines a tithing sermon of Caesarius of Arles, miscellaneous material, and an excerpt drawn from the *Visio Pauli*. ... It begins with an exhortation to tithing, shifts rather abruptly to pastoral care and godly behavior, then turns back to tithing again."[5] Thompson's overall point is that "homilists wished only to bring out the truths embodied in their texts," and their means of doing so subordinated what we might perceive as coherence. Audiences, whether lay or religious and whether skilled or novice readers, who were familiar with such sermons and such approaches to building meaning, would hardly have found the repetitions and disjunctions across the contents of Junius 11 in conflict with understanding. Coherence can be, and apparently was, constructed from more than one method of reading.

3 Ælfric, *Alius sermo de die Paschae*, in Ælfric, *Ælfric's Catholic Homilies: The Second Series*, ed. Malcolm Godden, EETS, s.s. 5 (London: Oxford University Press, 1979), 162.

4 Melinda Menzer, "Ælfric's English 'Grammar,'" *JEGP* 103 (2004): 123–4.

5 Nancy M. Thompson, "Hit segð on halgum bocum: The Logic of Composite Old English Homilies," *Philological Quarterly* 81, no. 4 (2002), 383*ff.*

Writers' ongoing engagement with what they read neatly comes across in the conventional comparative assertion of "as books say," a formulaic phrase that both reflects and contributes to the authoritative status of books in early medieval England and the adaptive roles of texts. Ælfric's homily on the Assumption of the Virgin, for instance, rests on material "swa swa we on bocum rædað" (just as we read in books) – the verb is in the present tense; reading is ongoing work – and, in his homily on the octave of Pentecost, Ælfric's information is "swa swa we leorniað on bocum" (just as we learn in books).[6] The habit of such reference is not one limited to Ælfric's lifetime or to homilies but extends across the corpus. Bede includes the same kind of phrasing in the *Ecclesiastical History*, with reference to the life of St. Fursey, which he tells "swa swa seo boc sagað" (just as books say), and such testimonials also appear in Old English poetry.[7] In *Elene*, for example, Elene speaks of what she has learned "þurg witgena wordgeryno / on godes bocum" (through the obscure sayings of the prophets in the books of God, 289–90a), and the narrator, or Cynewulf himself, grounds in his reading the whole story of the finding of the cross: it is "swa ic on bocum fand" (as I found in books, 1254b).

The authority of books is, too, repeatedly cited in *Genesis A*. In the land encircled by one of the four rivers that flow from Paradise, the Phison, people can find great wealth, "gold and gymcynn. … ða selestan þæs þe us secgað bec" (gold and kinds of gems … the best, as books say to us, 226–7), and the story of Cain and Abel is delivered as "us cyðað bec" (books declare to us, 969b); variations on the phrase appear three further times in the poem. Such references concentrated in *Genesis* emphasize the biblical foundation of the narrative being presented and, in turn, the textual foundation of Christianity more generally. They allow the narrator of *Genesis A* to acknowledge this textual foundation while also acknowledging the (written) poem itself as a vernacular step in the documentation of Christian history and authority. As a broader convention in Old English texts, "as books say" references allow writers to call attention to what they have written and to what they have read, and they demonstrate the general value and practice of reading, by which one text informs another and enriches understanding. Indeed, the references encourage readers to make cross-textual and therefore non-sequential connections,

6 Ælfric, *Catholic Homilies* 1, 435; Ælfric, *Homilies of Ælfric: A Supplementary Collection*, ed. John C. Pope, EETS (Oxford: Oxford University Press, 1967–8), 424; the same homily repeatedly also uses the phrase "swa swa us secgað bec" (426, 427).

7 Bede, *Old English Version of Bede's EH*, 212.

something surely made easier with repeated returns to a single text. This is the context in which Junius 11 was produced and which guided its early readers, whether they read all or only part of the book.

Books in early medieval England were repositories of wisdom to be used according to each individual reader's context and interests, which might have varied more widely than we have imagined or can recover, and within a reading culture that clearly valued non-linear connections and contextualization. Precisely because the Junius 11 manuscript so clearly possesses larger unities – because it presents poems that share a biblical foundation and thematic concerns, poems that follow Christian chronology and offer interrelated narratives – this particular book simultaneously calls attention to distinctions within it. Particularly for those with reading experience, the repetitions, juxtapositions, and disjunctions in Junius 11 invite readers, then and now, to seek meaning in difference and to participate in an intellectual conversation by way of reading any one or all of the texts, in their existing presentation sequence or not, between the book's outer boards.

Bibliography

Primary Sources

Ælfric. *Ælfric's Catholic Homilies: The First Series; Text.* Edited by Peter Clemoes. EETS, s.s. 17. London: Oxford University Press, 1997.

– *Ælfric's Catholic Homilies: The Second Series.* Edited by Malcolm Godden. EETS, s.s. 5. London: Oxford University Press, 1979.

– *Ælfric's Homilies on Judith, Esther, and The Maccabees.* Edited by Stuart D. Lee. 1999. http://users.ox.ac.uk/~stuart/kings.

– *Homilies of Ælfric: A Supplementary Collection.* Edited by John C. Pope. EETS, 259–60. Oxford: Oxford University Press, 1967–8.

– *The Old English Version of the Heptateuch: Ælfric's Treatise on the Old and New Testament and His Preface to Genesis.* Edited by S.J. Crawford. EETS, o.s. 160. London: Oxford University Press, 1922.

Alcuin. "Alcuini Epistolae." In *Monumenta Germaniae Historica.* Vol. 4, *Epistolae Karolini aevi II,* edited by Ernst Dümmler. Berlin: Weidmann, 1895.

Ambrose. *Hexameron, Paradise, Cain and Abel.* Translated by John J. Savage. Fathers of the Church 42. New York: Fathers of the Church, 1961.

– *Hexameron: Sancti Ambrosii Opera.* Part 1, *Exameron, De Paradiso, De Cain et Abel, De Noe, De Abraham, De Isaac, De bono mortis.* CSEL 32. Edited by Carolus Schenkl. Vienna: F. Tempsky, 1896.

Athanasius. *The Life of Antony and the Letter to Marcellinus.* Translated by Robert C. Gregg. New York: Paulist Press, 1980.

– *Vita Antonii.* Edited by J.P. Migne. *PG* 26. Paris, 1857.

Augustine. *Augustine: Confessions.* Edited and translated by James J. O'Donnell. 3 vols. Oxford: Clarendon Press, 1992.

– *De Genesi ad litteram.* CSEL 28. Edited by Joseph Zycha. Vienna: F. Tempsky, 1894.

– *King Alfred's Version of St. Augustine's Soliloquies.* Edited by Thomas A. Carnicelli. Cambridge, MA: Harvard University Press, 1969.

– *Saint Augustine: Confessions.* Edited and translated by Henry Chadwick. New York: Oxford University Press, 1991.

– *Sancti Aurelii Augustini De ciuitate Dei XXII.* Edited by Bernhard Dombart and Alfonsus Kalb. 2 vols. CCSL 47–8. Turnhout, Belgium: Brepols, 1955.

– *St. Augustine: The Literal Meaning of Genesis.* Translated by John Hammond Taylor. Ancient Christian Writers 42. New York: Newman Press, 1982.

Bazire, Joyce, and James E. Cross. *Eleven Old English Rogationtide Homilies.* Toronto: University of Toronto Press, 1982.

Bede. *Bede's Ecclesiastical History of the English People.* Edited by Bertram Colgrave and R.A.B. Mynors. Oxford Medieval Texts. Oxford: Clarendon Press, 1969.

– *The Old English Version of Bede's Ecclesiastical History of the English People.* Edited by Thomas Miller. EETS, o.s. 95, 96, 110, 111. London, 1890–8. Reprint, London: Oxford University Press, 1959.

Blackburn, Francis A., ed. *Exodus and Daniel: Two Old English Poems.* Boston: D.C. Heath, 1907.

Bradley, S.A.J., ed. and trans. *Anglo-Saxon Poetry.* London: Everyman, 1982.

Cassian, John. *Conférences.* Edited by E. Pichery. Sources Chrétiennes 42. Paris: Éditions du Cerf, 1955.

– *Conferences.* Translated by Colm Luibhéid. New York: Paulist Press, 1985.

Challoner, Richard, ed. *Holy Bible: Douay-Rheims Version.* Rockford, IL: Tan Books, 2000.

Clayton, Mary, ed. and trans. *Old English Poems of Christ and His Saints.* Dumbarton Oaks Medieval Library. Cambridge, MA: Harvard University Press, 2013.

Clubb, Merrel Dare, ed. *Christ and Satan.* New Haven, CT: Yale University Press, 1925.

Conybeare, John Josias. *Illustrations of Anglo-Saxon Poetry.* London: Harding and Lepard, 1826.

Daly, L.W., and W. Suchier. *Altercatio Hadriani Augusti et Epicteti Philosophi.* Illinois Studies in Language and Literature, vol. 24, nos. 1–2. Urbana: University of Illinois Press, 1939.

Davril, Anselme, ed. *Consuetudines Floriacenses Saeculi Tertii Decimi.* Corpus Consuetudinum Monasticarum 9. Siegburg, Germany: Franz Schmitt, 1976.

Doane, A.N., ed. *Genesis A: A New Edition, Revised.* Medieval and Renaissance Texts and Studies 435. Tempe, AZ: ACMRS, 2013.

– *The Saxon Genesis.* Madison: University of Wisconsin Press, 1991.

Dobbie, Elliott Van Kirk, ed. *The Anglo-Saxon Minor Poems.* ASPR 6. New York: Columbia University Press, 1942.

Farrell, R.T., ed. *Daniel and Azarias.* London: Methuen, 1974.

Finnegan, Robert Emmett, ed. *Christ and Satan: A Critical Edition.* Waterloo, ON: Wilfrid Laurier University Press, 1977.

Gollancz, Israel, ed. *The Cædmon MS of Anglo-Saxon Biblical Poetry: Junius XI; In the Bodleian Library*. London: Oxford University Press, 1927.

Gordon, R.K., trans. *Anglo-Saxon Poetry*. New York: E.P. Dutton, 1926.

Grant, Raymond S. *The B Text of the Old English Bede*. Atlanta, GA: Rodopi, 1989.

Greene, David, and Fergus Kelly, eds. and trans. *The Irish Adam and Eve Story from Saltair na Rann*. Vol. 1, *Text and Translation*. Dublin: Dublin Institute for Advanced Studies, 1976.

Gregory. *King Alfred's West-Saxon Version of Gregory's Pastoral Care*. Edited by Henry Sweet. EETS, o.s. 45, 50. London, 1871–2. Reprinted with corrections by N.R. Ker, London: Oxford University Press, 1958.

– *Morals on the Book of Job*. 3 vols. Library of Fathers 18. Oxford: J.H. Parker, 1844.

– *S. Gregorii Magni: Moralia in Iob*. Edited by Marc Adriaen. 3 vols. CCSL 143, 143a, 143b. Turnholt, Belgium: Brepols, 1979.

Irenaeus. *Epideixis: Patrologia Orientalis*. Vol. 12, no. 5. Edited and translated by Karapet ter Mekerttschian and S.G. Wilson. Paris: Firmin-Didot, 1919.

– *Irenaeus: Proof of the Apostolic Preaching*. Translated by Joseph P. Smith. Ancient Christian Writers 16. Westminster, MD: Newman Press, 1952.

Irving, Edward Burroughs, ed. *The Old English Exodus*. New Haven, CT: Yale University Press, 1953.

Isidore. *The Etymologies of Isidore of Seville*. Edited and translated by Stephen A. Barney, W.J. Lewis, J.A. Beach, and Oliver Berghof. Cambridge: Cambridge University Press, 2006.

Kenney, James F., ed. *The Sources for the Early History of Ireland: Ecclesiastical*. New York: Columbia University Press, 1920. Reprint, New York: Octagon Books, 1966.

Krapp, George Philip, ed. *The Junius Manuscript*. ASPR 1. New York: Columbia University Press, 1931.

–, ed. *The Paris Psalter and the Meters of Boethius*. ASPR 5. New York: Columbia University Press, 1932.

–, ed. *The Vercelli Book*. ASPR 2. New York: Columbia University Press, 1932.

Krapp, George Philip, and Elliot Van Kirk Dobbie, eds. *The Exeter Book*. ASPR 3. New York: Columbia University Press, 1936.

Liuzza, R.M., ed. and trans. *Old English Poetry: An Anthology*. Peterborough, ON: Broadview Press, 2014.

–, ed. *The Old English Version of the Gospels*. Vol. 1. EETS 304. Oxford: Oxford University Press, 1994.

Lucas, Peter J., ed. *Exodus*. Exeter: University of Exeter Press, 1994.

– *Franciscus Junius: Caedmonis monachi paraphrasis poetica Genesios ac praecipuarum sacrae paginate historiarum, etc.* Early Studies in Germanic Philology. Atlanta, GA: Rodopi, 2000.

MacLean, George E., ed. "Ælfric's Version of *Alcuini Interrogationes Sigeuulfi in Genesin*." PhD diss., University of Leipzig. Halle: E. Karras, 1883.

Menner, Robert J., ed. *The Poetical Dialogues of Solomon and Saturn*. New York: Modern Language Association, 1941.

Muir, Bernard J., ed. *A Digital Facsimile of Oxford, Bodleian Library, MS. Junius 11*. CD-ROM. Software by Nick Kennedy. Oxford: Bodleian Library, University of Oxford, 2004.

Origen. *Homélies sur l'Exode*. Edited by Marcel Borret. Sources Chrétiennes 321. Paris: Éditions du Cerf, 1985.

– *Origen: Homilies on Genesis and Exodus*. Translated by Ronald E. Heine. Fathers of the Church 71. Washington, DC: Catholic University Press, 1982.

Pitman, James H., ed. *The Riddles of Aldhelm*. Yale Studies in English 67. New Haven, CT: Yale University Press, 1925. Reprint, Hamdon, CT: Archon Books, 1970.

Pulsiano, Phillip, ed. *Psalters I*. ASMMF 2. Tempe, AZ: ACMRS, 1994.

Robert. *The Benedictional of Archbishop Robert*. Edited by H.A. Wilson. HBS 24. London: Henry Bradshaw Society, 1903.

– *The Missal of Robert of Jumièges*. Edited by H.A. Wilson. HBS 11. London: Henry Bradshaw Society, 1896.

Scragg, D.G., ed. *The Vercelli Homilies and Related Texts*. EETS 300. Oxford: Oxford University Press, 1992.

Sedgefield, W.J., ed. *An Anglo-Saxon Verse Book*. Manchester: Manchester University Press, 1922.

Sedulius. *On Christian Rulers, and the Poems*. Translated by Edward Gerard Doyle. CEMERS. Binghamton: State University of New York at Binghamton, 1983.

Sévère, Sulpice. *Vie de Saint Martin*. Edited and translated by Jacques Fontaine. 3 vols. Sources Chrétiennes 133–5. Paris: Éditions du Cerf, 1967–9.

Sleeth, Charles R. *Studies in Christ and Satan*. Toronto: Toronto University Press, 1982.

Suchier, Walther, ed. *Das mittellateinische Gespräch Adrian und Epictitus: Nebst verwandten Texten (Joca monachorum)*. Tübingen: Max Niemeyer Verlag, 1955.

Tatwine. *Tatuini Opera omnia*. Edited by Maria De Marco and F. Glorie. CCSL 133. Turnhout, Belgium: Brepols, 1968.

Timmer, B.J., ed. *The Later Genesis*. Oxford: Scrivener, 1948.

"Vita Adae et Evae." In *The Apocrypha and Pseudepigrapha of the Old Testament*. Vol. 2 of *Pseudepigrapha*, edited by R.H. Charles. Oxford University Press, 1913.

Weber, Robert, ed. *Biblia Sacra Iuxta Vulgatam Versionem*. Stuttgart: Deutsche Bibelgesellschaft, 1969.

Whitelock, Dorothy, ed. *English Historical Documents*. Vol. 1, *c.500–1042*. 2nd ed. New York: Oxford University Press, 1979.

Secondary Sources

Abbetmeyer, C. *Old English Poetical Motives Derived from the Doctrine of Sin*. PhD diss., University of Minnesota. Minneapolis: H.W. Wilson, 1903.

Anlezark, Daniel. "The Fall of the Angels in *Solomon and Saturn II*." In *Apocryphal Texts and Traditions in Anglo-Saxon England*, edited by Kathryn Powell and Donald Scragg, 121–33. Cambridge: D.S. Brewer, 2003.

– "Lay Reading, Patronage, and Power in Bodleian Library, Junius 11." In *Ambition and Anxiety: Courts and Courtly Discourse c. 700–1600*, edited by Giles E.M. Gasper and John McKinnell, 76–97. Durham Medieval and Renaissance Monographs and Essays 3. Toronto: Pontifical Institute of Medieval Studies, 2014.

– "The Old English *Genesis B* and Irenaeus of Lyon." *Medium Ævum* 86 (2017): 1–21.

Bakka, Egil. "The Alfred Jewel and Sight." *Antiquaries Journal* 46 (1966): 277–82.

Bately, Janet. "Those Books That Are Most Necessary for All Men to Know: The Classic and Late Ninth-Century England; A Reappraisal." In *The Classics in the Middle Ages: Papers of the Twentieth Conference of the Center for Medieval and Early Renaissance Studies*, edited by Aldo S. Bernardo and Saul Levin, 45–78. Binghamton, NY: CEMERS, 1990.

Bayless, Martha. "The *Collectanea* and Medieval Dialogues and Riddles." In *Collectanea Pseudo-Bedae*, edited by Martha Bayless and Michael Lapidge et al., 13–24. Scriptores Latini Hiberniae 14. Dublin: Dublin Institute for Advanced Studies, 1998.

Bayless, Martha, and Michael Lapidge et al., eds. *Collectanea Pseudo-Bedae*. Scriptores Latini Hiberniae 14. Dublin: Dublin Institute for Advanced Studies, 1998.

Belanoff, Patricia A. "Women's Songs, Women's Language." In *New Readings on Women in Old English Literature*, edited by H. Damico and A.H. Olsen, 193–203. Bloomington: Indiana University Press, 1990.

Benskin, Michael, and Brian Murdoch. "The Literary Tradition of Genesis." *NM* 76 (1975): 389–403.

Biddle, M., and B. Kjølbye-Biddle. "The Dating of the New Minster Wall Painting." In *Early Medieval Wall Painting and Painted Sculpture in England*, edited by S. Cather, D. Park, and P. Williamson, 45–63. BAR Brit. Ser. 216. Oxford, BAR Publishing, 1990.

Bischoff, Bernhard. *Salzburger Formelbücher und Briefe aus Tassilonischer und Karolingischer Zeit*. Munich: Verlag der Bayerischen Akademie der Wissenschaften, 1973.

– "Über gefaltete Handschriften, vornehmlich hagiographischen Inhalts." *Mittelalterliche Studien* 1, 93–100. Stuttgart: Hiersemann, 1966–7.

Bredehoft, Thomas. *Authors, Audiences, and Old English Verse.* Toronto: University of Toronto Press, 2009.

– *Textual Histories: Readings in the Anglo-Saxon Chronicle.* Toronto: Toronto University Press, 2001.

Bright, J.W. "On the Anglo-Saxon Poem *Exodus.*" *MLN* 27 (1912): 13–19.

Brooks, Nicholas. *The Early History of the Church of Canterbury: Christ Church from 597 to 1066.* Leicester: Leicester University Press, 1984.

– "A New Charter of King Edgar." In *Anglo-Saxon Myths: State and Church, 400–1066*, 217–37. Rio Grande, OH: Hambledon Press, 2000.

Brown, George Hardin. "The Dynamics of Literacy in Anglo-Saxon England." *Bulletin of the John Rylands Library* 77, no. 1 (1995): 109–42.

Brown, Katherine DeVane. "Antifeminism or Exegesis? Reinterpreting Eve's *wacgeþoht* in *Genesis B.*" *JEGP* 115 (2016): 141–66.

Budny, Mildred. *Insular, Anglo-Saxon, and Early Anglo-Norman Manuscript Art at Corpus Christi College, Cambridge.* 2 vols. Kalamazoo, MI: Medieval Institute Publications, 1997.

Burchard, Rachel. "Angel or Devil? Visionary Dilemmas in the Egyptian Desert." *Essays in History* 32 (1989): 69–84.

Burchmore, Susan. "Traditional Exegesis and the Question of Guilt in the Old English 'Genesis B.'" *Traditio* 41 (1985): 117–44.

Butler, Emily. "The Role of Compiler in the Paris Psalter." *English Studies* 98 (2017): 26–34.

Calder, D.G., and M.J.B. Allen. *Sources and Analogues of Old English Poetry: The Major Latin Texts in Translation.* Cambridge: D.S. Brewer, 1976.

Carley, James P., ed. and trans. *John Leland: De uiris illustribus.* Toronto: Pontifical Institute of Mediaeval Studies, 2010.

Chaganti, Seeta. "Vestigial Signs: Inscription, Performance, and *The Dream of the Rood.*" *PMLA* 125 (2010): 48–72.

Clark Hall, J.R. *A Concise Anglo-Saxon Dictionary.* 4th ed. Medieval Academy Reprints for Teaching 14. Toronto: University of Toronto Press, 1960.

Clayton, Mary. "Homiliaries and Preaching in Anglo-Saxon England." In *Old English Prose: Basic Readings*, ed. Paul Szarmach, 151–98. New York: Garland, 2000. Reprinted from *Peritia* 4 (1985): 207–42.

Clemoes, Peter. "The Production of an Illustrated Version." In *The Old English Illustrated Hexateuch*, edited by C.R. Dodwell and Peter Clemoes. EEMF 18. Copenhagen: Rosenkilde & Bagger, 1974.

Conner, Patrick W. "The Structure of the Exeter Book Codex (Exeter, Cathedral Library, MS 3501)." *Scriptorium* 40, no. 2 (1986): 233–42.

Creed, Robert P. "The Art of the Singer: Three Old English Tellings of the Offering of Isaac." In *Old English Poetry: Fifteen Essays*, edited by Robert P. Creed, 69–82. Providence, RI: Brown University Press, 1967.

Crehan, J.H. "Devil." In *A Catholic Dictionary of Theology.* 2 vols. New York: Nelson, 1962–7.

Cross, James E., and Thomas D. Hill. *The Prose Solomon and Saturn and Adrian and Ritheus.* Toronto: University of Toronto Press, 1982.

Cross, J.E., and S.I. Tucker. "Allegorical Tradition and the Old English *Exodus.*" *Neophilologus* 44 (1960): 122–7.

DeAngelo, Jeremy. "*Discretio spirituum* and *The Whale.*" *ASE* 42 (2013): 271–89.

Dekkers, E., and A. Gaar, eds. *Clavis Patrum Latinorum.* 3rd ed., revised. Turnhout, Belgium: Brepols, 1995.

Dendle, Peter. *Satan Unbound: The Devil in Old English Narrative Literature.* Toronto: University of Toronto Press, 2001.

Deshman, Robert. "The Galba Psalter: Pictures, Texts and Context in an Early Medieval Prayerbook." *ASE* 26 (1997): 109–38.

DiNapoli, Robert. "The Heart of Visionary Experience: *The Order of the World* and Its Place in the Old English Canon." *English Studies* 79 (1998): 97–108.

Dockray-Miller, Mary. "Female Devotion and the Vercelli Book." *Philological Quarterly* 83, no. 4 (2004): 337–54.

Dumville, David N. "English Libraries before 1066: Use and Abuse of the Manuscript Evidence." In *Anglo-Saxon Manuscripts: Basic Readings,* edited by Mary P. Richards, 169–219. New York: Garland, 1994. First published 1981 in *Insular Latin Studies: Papers on Latin Texts and Manuscripts of the British Isles; 550–1066,* edited by Michael W. Herren, 153–78, Papers in Medieval Studies 1, Toronto: Pontifical Institute.

– "English Square Minuscule Script: The Mid-Century Phases." *ASE* 23 (1994): 133–64.

– "On the Dating of Some Late Anglo-Saxon Liturgical Manuscripts." *Transactions of the Cambridge Bibliographical Society* 10 (1991): 40–57.

Earl, James W. "Maxims I, Part I." *Neophilologus* 67 (1983): 277–83.

Electronic Sawyer: Online Catalogue of Anglo-Saxon Charters. Developed by Susan Kelly, Rebecca Rushforth, et al. London: Centre for Computing in the Humanities, King's College.

Ericksen, Janet Schrunk. "Legalizing the Fall of Man." *Medium Ævum* 74, no. 2 (2005): 205–20.

Evans, J.M. *Paradise Lost and the Genesis Tradition.* Oxford: Clarendon Press, 1968.

Finnegan, Robert Emmett. "Eve and 'Vincible Ignorance' in *Genesis B.*" *Texas Studies in Literature and Language* 18 (1976): 329–39.

Flom, George T. "On the Old English Herbal of Apelius, Vitellius C. III." *JEGP* 40 (1941): 29–37.

Fox, Michael. "Ælfric on the Creation and Fall of the Angels." *ASE* 31 (2002): 175–200.

Frank, Roberta. "Did Anglo-Saxon Audiences Have a Skaldic Tooth?" *Scandinavian Studies* 59 (1987): 338–55.

– "What Kind of Poetry Is *Exodus*?" In *Germania: Comparative Studies in the Old Germanic Languages and Literatures*, edited by Daniel G. Calder and T. Craig Christy, 191–205. Woodbridge, UK: D.S. Brewer, 1988.

Frings, Theodor. "*Christ und Satan*." *Zeitschrift für deutsche Philologie* 45 (1913): 216–36.

Fulk, R.D. *A History of Old English Meter*. Philadelphia: University of Pennsylvania Press, 1992.

Gameson, Richard, ed. *The Cambridge History of the Book in Britain*. Vol. 1, *c.400–1100*. Cambridge: Cambridge University Press, 2012.

– "The Origin of the Exeter Book of Old English Poetry." *ASE* 25 (1996): 135–85.

Gannon, Anna. "The Five Senses and Anglo-Saxon Coinage." *Anglo-Saxon Studies in Archaeology and History* 13 (2006): 97–104.

Garde, Judith N. *Old English Poetry in Medieval Christian Perspective: A Doctrinal Approach*. Cambridge: D.S. Brewer, 1991.

Gneuss, Helmut. *Die Battle of Maldon als historisches und literarisches Zeugnis*. Munich: Verlag der Bay, 1976.

Gneuss, Helmut, and Michael Lapidge. *Anglo-Saxon Manuscripts: A Bibliographical Handlist of Manuscripts and Manuscript Fragments Written or Owned in England up to 1100*. Toronto: University of Toronto Press, 2014.

Godden, Malcolm. "Old English Composite Homilies from Winchester." *ASE* 4 (1975): 57–65.

Gould, Graham. *The Desert Fathers on Monastic Community*. Oxford: Clarendon Press, 1993.

Gradon, Pamela. *Form and Style in Early English Literature*. London: Methuen, 1971.

Gretsch, Mechthild. "The Junius Psalter Gloss: Its Historical and Cultural Context." *ASE* 29 (2000): 85–121.

Groschopp, Friedrich. "Das ags Gedicht 'Crist und Satan.'" *Anglia* 6 (1883): 248–76.

Guillet, Jacques et al. "Discernment of Spirits." Translated by Sister Innocentia Richards from *Dictionnaire de Spiritualité*. Collegeville, MN: Liturgical Press, 1970.

Günzel, Beate. *Ælfwine's Prayerbook*. HBS 108. London: Boydell Press, 1993.

Haines, Dorothy. "Unlocking *Exodus* ll: 516–532." *JEGP* 98 (1999): 481–98.

Hall, J.R. "The Old English Epic of Redemption: The Theological Unity of MS Junius 11." *Traditio* 32 (1976): 185–208. Reprinted in *The Poems of MS Junius 11: Basic Readings*, edited by R.M. Liuzza, 20–52, New York: Garland, 2002.

– "Old English *Exodus* and the Sea of Contradiction." *Mediaevalia* 9 (1986 for 1983): 25–44.

– "Old English *sæborg*: *Exodus* 442a, *Andreas* 308a." *Papers on Language and Literature* 25 (1989): 127–34.

– "On the Bibliographic Unity of Bodleian MS Junius 11." *American Notes and Queries* 24 (1986): 104–7.

– "Pauline Influence on Exodus, 523–548." *ELN* 15 (1977): 84–8.

Harsh, Constance D. "*Christ and Satan*: The Measured Power of Christ." *NM* 90 (1989): 243–53.

Hartzell, K.D. *Catalogue of Manuscripts Written or Owned in England up to 1200 Containing Music*. Woodbridge, UK: Boydell Press, 2006.

Head, Pauline. *Representation and Design: Tracing a Hermeneutics of Old English Poetry*. Albany: State University of New York Press, 1997.

Heslop, T.A. "The Production of *De Luxe* Manuscripts and the Patronage of King Cnut and Queen Emma." *ASE* 19 (1990): 151–95.

Higgitt, John. "Glastonbury, Dunstan, Monasticism and Manuscripts." *Art History* 2, no. 3 (1979): 279–90.

Hill, Joyce. "Confronting *Germania Latina*: Changing Responses to Old English Biblical Verse." In *Latin Culture and Medieval Germanic Europe*, edited by Richard North and Tette Hofstra, 71–88. Germania Latina 1. Groningen, The Netherlands: Egbert Forsten, 1992.

Hill, Thomas D. "Apocryphal Cosmography and the 'stream uton sæ': A Note on *Christ and Satan*, Lines 4–12." *Philological Quarterly* 48 (1969): 550–4.

– "The Fall of Satan in the Old English *Christ and Satan*." *JEGP* 76 (1977): 315–25.

– "The Fall of the Angels and Man in the Old English *Genesis B*." In *Anglo-Saxon Poetry: Essays in Appreciation of John C. McGalliard*, edited by Lewis E. Nicholson and Dolores Warwick Frese, 279–90. Notre Dame, IN: University of Notre Dame Press, 1975.

– "The Measure of Hell: *Christ and Satan* 695–722." *Philological Quarterly* 60 (1981): 409–14.

– "Satan's Injured Innocence in *Genesis B*, 360–2, 390–2: A Gregorian Source." *English Studies* 65 (1984): 289–90.

– "Some Remarks on the Site of Lucifer's Throne." *Anglia* 87 (1969): 303–11.

– "The *virga* of Moses and the Old English *Exodus*." In *Old English Literature in Context*, edited by John D. Niles, 57–65. Cambridge: D.S. Brewer, 1980.

Howe, Nicholas. "The Cultural Construction of Reading in Anglo-Saxon England." In *The Ethnography of Reading*, edited by Jonathan Boyarin, 58–79. Berkeley: University of California Press, 1993.

Huppé, Bernard F. *Doctrine and Poetry: Augustine's Influence on Old English Poetry*. New York: State University of New York Press, 1959.

Iser, Wolfgang. *The Act of Reading: A Theory of Aesthetic Response*. Baltimore: Johns Hopkins University Press, 1980.

James, M.R. *The Ancient Libraries of Canterbury and Dover: The Catalogues of the Libraries of Christ Church Priory and St. Augustine's Abbey at Canterbury, and of St. Martin's Priory at Dover*. Cambridge: Cambridge University Press, 1903.

– *A Descriptive Catalogue of the Manuscripts in the Library of Corpus Christi College Cambridge.* Cambridge: Cambridge University Press, 1911.

Johnson, David F. "Divine Justice in Gregory the Great's *Dialogues*." In *Early Medieval Studies in Memory of Patrick Wormald*, edited by Stephen David Baxter, Catherine E. Karkov, Janet L. Nelson, and David Pelteret. Burlington, VT: Ashgate, 2009.

– "The Fall of Lucifer in *Genesis A* and Two Anglo-Latin Royal Charters." *JEGP* 97 (1998): 500–21.

Karkov, Catherine. *Text and Picture in Anglo-Saxon England: Narrative Strategies in the Junius 11 Manuscript.* Cambridge: Cambridge University Press, 2001.

Ker, N.R. *Catalogue of Manuscripts Containing Anglo-Saxon.* Oxford: Oxford University Press, 1957. Reissued 1990.

– *Medieval Libraries of Great Britain: A List of Surviving Books.* 2nd ed. London: Offices of the Royal Historical Society, 1964.

Keynes, Simon, ed. *Anglo-Saxon Manuscripts and Other Items of Related Interest in the Library of Trinity College, Cambridge.* OEN Subsidia 18. Kalamazoo, MI: Medieval Institute Publications, 1992.

– *The Liber Vitae of the New Minster and Hyde Abbey, Winchester: British Library Stowe 944; Together with Leaves from British Library Cotton Vespasian A. VIII and British Library Cotton Titus D. XXVII.* Copenhagen: Rosenkilde and Bagger, 1996.

Kiernan, Kevin. Beowulf *and the* Beowulf-*Manuscript.* Rev. ed. Ann Arbor: University of Michigan Press, 1996.

Korhammer, P.M. "The Origin of the Bosworth Psalter." *ASE* 2 (1973): 173–87.

Lake, Stephen. "Knowledge of the Writings of John Cassian in Early Anglo-Saxon England." *ASE* 32 (2003): 27–41.

Lapidge, Michael. *The Anglo-Saxon Library.* Oxford: Oxford University Press, 2006.

– "Artistic and Literary Patronage in Anglo-Saxon England." In *Anglo-Latin Literature, 600–899*, 37–91. Rio Grande, OH: Hambledon Press, 1996.

– "The Hermeneutic Style in Tenth-Century Anglo-Latin Literature." *ASE* 4 (1975): 67–111. Reprinted in *Anglo-Latin Literature, 600–899*, 105–49, Rio Grande, OH: Hambledon Press, 1996.

– "Hypallage in the Old English *Exodus*." *Leeds Studies in English* 37 (2006): 31–9.

– "Israel the Grammarian in ASE." In *Anglo-Latin Literature, 900–1066*, edited by Michael Lapidge, 87–104. London: Hambledon Press, 1993. First published 1992 in *From Athens to Chartres: Neoplatonism and Medieval Thought*, edited by Haijo J. Westra, Leiden, The Netherlands: Brill.

– "The Origin of the Collectanea." In *Collectanea Pseudo-Bedae*, edited by Martha Bayless and Michael Lapidge et al., 13–24. Scriptores Latini Hiberniae 14. Dublin: Dublin Institute for Advanced Studies, 1998.

– "Three Latin Poems from Æthewold's School at Winchester." *ASE* 1 (1972): 85–138.

Lapidge, Michael, and Bernhard Bischoff. *Biblical Commentaries from the Canterbury School of Theodore and Hadrian*. Cambridge: Cambridge University Press, 1994.

Lapidge, Michael, John Blair, Simon Keynes, and Donald Scragg, eds. *Blackwell Encyclopedia of Anglo-Saxon England*. Malden, MA: Blackwell, 2001.

Law, Vivien. *Wisdom, Authority and Grammar in the Seventh Century: Decoding Virgilius Maro Grammaticus*. Cambridge: Cambridge University Press, 1995.

Lawrence, John. *Chapters on Alliterative Verse*. London: Henry Frowde, 1893.

Lienhard, J.T. "'Discernment of Spirits' in the Early Church." *Studia Patristica* 17, no. 2 (1982): 519–22.

Liuzza, R.M. "Anglo-Saxon Prognostics in Context: A Survey and Handlist of Manuscripts." *ASE* 30 (2001): 181–230.

–, ed. *The Poems of MS Junius 11: Basic Readings*. New York: Routledge, 2002.

– "Who Read the Gospels in Old English?" In *Words and Works: Studies in Medieval English Language and Literature in Honour of Fred C. Robinson*, edited by Peter S. Baker and Nicholas Howe, 3–24. Toronto: University of Toronto Press, 1998.

Lockett, Leslie. "An Integrated Re-examination of the Dating of Oxford, Bodleian Library, Junius 11." *ASE* 31 (2002): 141–73.

Love, Rosalind. "The Library of the Venerable Bede." In *The Cambridge History of the Book in Britain*. Vol. 1, *c.400–1100*, edited by Richard Gameson, 606–32. Cambridge: Cambridge University Press, 2012.

Lucas, Peter J. "MS Junius 11 and Malmesbury." *Scriptorium* 34 (1980): 197–220 and *Scriptorium* 35 (1981): 3–22.

– "On the Incomplete Ending of *Daniel* and the Addition of *Christ and Satan* to MS Junius 11." *Anglia* 97 (1979): 46–59.

Lynch, Clare. "Enigmatic Diction in the Old English *Exodus*." PhD diss, Cambridge University, 2000.

MacEóin, Gearóid. "Observations on *Saltair na Rann*." *Zeitschrift fur Celtische Philologie* 39 (1982): 1–28.

Marsden, Richard. "Wrestling with the Bible: Textual Problems for the Scholar and Student." In *Christian Tradition in Anglo-Saxon England: Approaches to Current Scholarship and Teaching*, edited by Paul Cavill, 69–90. Cambridge: Cambridge University Press, 2004.

Martin, Ellen E. "Allegory and the African Woman in the Old English 'Exodus.'" *JEGP* 81 (1982): 1–15.

Mayr-Harting, Henry. *The Coming of Christianity to Anglo-Saxon England*. University Park: Pennsylvania State University Press, 1972.

McNally, Robert E. "'Christus' in the Pseudo-Isidorian 'Liber de ortu et obitu patriarchum.'" *Traditio* 21 (1965): 167–84.

Menzer, Melinda. "Ælfric's English 'Grammar.'" *JEGP* 103 (2004): 106–24.

Meritt, Herbert Dean. *Old English Glosses*. New York: Modern Language Association, 1945.

Molinari, Alessandra. "A Crease in Gathering 17 of Bodleian MS. Junius 11." *Linguæ & – Revista di lingue e culture moderne* 14 (2015): 55–85.

Morey, James H. *Book and Verse: A Guide to Middle English Biblical Literature*. Urbana: University of Illinois Press, 2000.

Murdoch, Brian O. *The Irish Adam and Eve Story from Saltair na Rann*. Vol 2, *Commentary*. Dublin: Dublin Institute for Advanced Studies, 1976.

Nichols, Stephen G. "An Intellectual Anthropology of Marriage in the Middle Ages." In *The New Medievalism*, edited by Marina S. Brownlee, Kevin Brownlee, and Stephen G. Nichols, 70–95. Baltimore: Johns Hopkins University Press, 1991.

Noel, William. *The Harley Psalter*. Cambridge: Cambridge University Press, 1995.

Novacich, Sarah Elliott. "The Old English *Exodus* and the Read Sea." *Exemplaria* 23 (2011): 50–66.

O'Brien O'Keeffe, Katherine. "Hands and Eyes, Sight and Touch: Appraising the Senses in Anglo-Saxon England." *ASE* 45 (2016): 105–40.

Ohlgren, Thomas H., ed. and comp. *Anglo-Saxon Textual Illustration: Photographs of Sixteen Manuscripts with Descriptions and Index*. Kalamazoo, MI: Medieval Institute Publications, 1992.

– "The Illustrations of the Cædmonian Genesis: Literary Criticism through Art." *Medievalia et Humanistica: Studies in Medieval and Renaissance Culture*, n.s. 3 (1972): 199–212.

– "Some New Light on the Old English *Cædmonian Genesis*." *Studies in Iconography* 1 (1975): 38–73.

– "Visual Language in the Old English Caedmonian Genesis." *Visible Language* 6 (1972): 253–76.

Okasha, Elisabeth. "Old English 'hring' in Riddles 48 and 59." *Medium Ævum* 62 (1993): 61–9.

Orchard, Andy. *The Poetic Art of Aldhelm*. CSASE 8. Cambridge: Cambridge University Press, 1994.

Overing, Gillian R. "On Reading Eve: *Genesis B* and the Readers' Desire." In *Speaking Two Languages: Traditional Disciplines and Contemporary Theory in Medieval Studies*, edited by Allen J. Frantzen, 35–63. Albany: State University of New York Press, 1991.

Page, R.I. "New Work on Old English Scratched Glosses." In *Studies in English Language and Early Literature in Honour of Paul Christophersen*, edited by P.M. Tilling, 105–15. Occasional Papers in Linguistics and Language Teaching 8. Coleraine: New University of Ulster, 1981.

Parkes, M.B. "The Paleography of the Parker Manuscript of the *Chronicle*, Laws, and Sedulius, and Historiography at Winchester in the Late Ninth and Tenth Centuries." *ASE* 5 (1976): 149–71.

– "*Rædan, areccan, smeagan*: How the Anglo-Saxons Read." *ASE* 26 (1997): 1–22.
Pfaff, R.W. "Eadui Basan: Sciptorum Princeps?" In *England in the Eleventh Century: Proceedings of the 1990 Harlaxton Symposium*, edited by Carola Hicks, 267–84. Stamford, UK: Paul Watkins, 1992.
Porck, Thijs. "Treasures in a Sooty Bag? A Note on *Durham Proverb* 7." *Notes and Queries* 62 (2015): 203–6.
Portnoy, Phyllis. *The Remnant: Essays on a Theme in Old English Verse*. London: Runetree, 2005.
– "'Remnant' and Ritual: The Place of *Daniel* and *Christ and Satan* in the Junius Epic." *English Studies* 75 (1994): 408–22.
Powell, Kathryn. "Meditating on Men and Monsters: A Reconsideration of the Thematic Unity of the 'Beowulf' Manuscript." *RES*, n.s. 57 (2006): 1–15.
Pratt, David. "Persuasion and Invention at the Court of King Alfred the Great." In *Court Culture in the Early Middle Ages*, edited by Catherine Cubitt, 189–221. Turnhout, Belgium: Brepols, 2003.
Prescott, Andrew. "'Their Present Miserable State of Cremation': The Restoration of the Cotton Library." In *Sir Robert Cotton as Collector: Essays on an Early Stuart Courtier and His Legacy*, edited by C.J. Wright, 391–454. London: BL, 1997.
Raw, Barbara. *The Art and Background of Old English Poetry*. London: Edward Arnold, 1978.
– "The Construction of Oxford, Bodleian Library, Junius 11." *ASE* 13 (1984): 187–207.
– "The Probable Derivation of Most of the Illustrations in Junius II from an Illustrated Old Saxon Genesis." *ASE* 5 (1976): 133–48.
Reading, Amity. *Reading the Anglo-Saxon Self through the Vercelli Book*. New York: Peter Lang, 2018.
Remley, Paul G. "Aldhelm as English Poet: *Exodus*, Asser, and the *Dicta Ælfredi*." In *Latin Learning and English Lore: Studies in Anglo-Saxon Literature for Michael Lapidge*, vol. 1, edited by Katherine O'Brien O'Keeffe and Andy Orchard, 90–108. 2 vols. Toronto: University of Toronto Press, 2005.
– *Old English Biblical Verse: Studies in Genesis, Exodus and Daniel*. CSASE 16. Cambridge: Cambridge University Press, 1996.
Robinson, P.R. "Self-Contained Units in Composite Manuscripts of the Anglo-Saxon Period." *ASE* 7 (1978): 231–8.
Rowley, Sharon. *The Old English Version of Bede's Historiae Ecclesiastica*. Cambridge: D.S. Brewer, 2012.
Rumble, Alexander R. *Property and Piety in Early Medieval Winchester: Documents Relating to the Topography of the Anglo-Saxon and Norman City and Its Minsters*. Winchester Studies 4, no. 3, The Anglo-Saxon Minsters of Winchester. Oxford: Clarendon Press, 2002.
Rushforth, Rebecca. "The Prodigal Fragment: Cambridge, Gonville and Caius College 734/782a." *ASE* 30 (2001): 137–44.

Salmon, Paul. "Die zehnte Engelchor in deutschen Dichtungen und Predigten des Mittelalters." *Euphorion* 57 (1963): 118–23.

– "The Site of Lucifer's Throne." *Anglia* 81 (1963): 118–23.

Sawyer, Peter. *Anglo-Saxon Charters: An Annotated List and Bibliography.* London: Royal Historical Society, 1968.

Schaller, Dieter, and Ewald Könsgen, with John Tagliabue. *Initia Carminum Latinorum saeculo undecimo Antiquiorum.* Göttingen: Vandenhoeck und Ruprecht, 1977.

Schipper, William. "Style and Layout of Anglo-Saxon Manuscripts." In *Anglo-Saxon Styles,* edited by Catherine E. Karkov and George Hardin Brown, 151–68. Albany: State University of New York Press, 2003.

Schmidt, Gary D. *The Iconography of the Mouth of Hell.* Selinsgrove, PA: Susquehanna University Press, 1995.

Scragg, Donald G. "The Compilation of the Vercelli Book." *ASE* 2 (1973): 189–207.

– "Homilies." In *Blackwell Encyclopedia of Anglo-Saxon England,* edited by Michael Lapidge, John Blair, Simon Keynes, and Donald Scragg, 241–2. Malden, MA: Blackwell, 2001.

Sharma, Manish. "The Economy of the Word in the Old English *Exodus.*" In *Old English Literature and the Old Testament,* edited by Michael Fox and Manish Sharma, 172–94. Toronto: University of Toronto Press, 2012.

Shepherd, Geoffrey. "Scriptural Poetry." In *Continuations and Beginnings,* edited by E.G. Stanley, 1–36. London: Nelson, 1996.

Sisam, Kenneth. "The Order of Ælfric's Early Books." In *Studies in the History of English Literature.* Oxford: Clarendon Press, 1953.

Solo, Harry Jay. "The Twice-Told Tale: A Reconsideration of the Syntax and Style of the Old English *Daniel,* 245–429." *Papers on Language and Literature* (1973): 347–64.

Southern, R.W. *Saint Anselm and His Biographer.* Cambridge: Cambridge University Press, 1966.

Stancliffe, Clare. *St. Martin and His Hagiographer.* Oxford: Clarendon Press, 1983.

Stone, Michael E. *A History of the Literature of Adam and Eve.* Society of Biblical Literature: Early Judaism and Its Literature 3. Atlanta, GA: Scholars Press, 1992.

– "Lists of Revealed Things in the Apocalyptic Literature." In *Magnalia Dei: The Mighty Acts of God; Essays on the Bible and Archaeology in Memory of G. Ernest Wright,* edited by Frank Moore Cross, Werner E. Lemke, and Patrick D. Miller, Jr., 412–52. Garden City, NY: Doubleday, 1976.

Switek, Günther. "'Discretio spirituum': Ein Beitrag zur Geschichte der Spiritualität." *Theologie und Philosophie* 47 (1972): 36–76.

Szarmach, Paul E. "Ælfric's *Judith.*" In *Old English Literature and the Old Testament,* edited by Michael Fox and Manish Sharma, 64–88. Toronto: University of Toronto Press, 2012.

– "Three Versions of the Jonah Story: An Investigation of Narrative Technique in Old English Homilies." *ASE* 1 (1972): 183–92.

ten Brink, Bernhard. *Early English Literature*. Translated by Horace M. Kennedy. New York, 1883.

Thompson, Nancy M. "Hit segð on halgum bocum: The Logic of Composite Old English Homilies." *Philological Quarterly* 81, no. 4 (2002): 383–419.

Thomson, Rodney M. "Identifiable Books from the Pre-Conquest Library of Malmesbury Abbey." *ASE* 10 (1981): 1–19.

– *William of Malmesbury*. Rev. ed. Woodbridge, UK: Boydell Press, 2003.

Thornbury, Emily V. *Becoming a Poet in Anglo-Saxon England*. Cambridge: Cambridge University Press, 2014.

Thornley, G.C. "Accents and Points of MS Junius 11." *Transactions of the Philological Society* (1954): 178–205.

Timofeeva, Olga. "*Of ledenum bocum to engliscum gereorde*: Bilingual Communities of Practice in Anglo-Saxon England." In *Communities of Practice in the History of English*, edited by Joanna Kopaczyk and Andreas H. Jucker, 201–23. Philadelphia, PA: John Benjamins, 2013.

Too, Yun Lee. "The Appeal to the Senses in the Old English 'Phoenix.'" *NM* 91 (1990): 229–42.

Treharne, Elaine. "The Form and Function of the Vercelli Book." In *Studies in Anglo-Saxon Literature and Its Insular Context in Honour of Éamonn Ó Carragáin*, edited by Alastair Minnis and Jane Roberts, 253–66. Turnhout, Belgium: Brepols, 2007.

Trilling, Renée R. *The Aesthetics of Nostalgia: Historical Representation in Old English Verse*. Toronto: University of Toronto Press, 2009.

– "Ruins in the Realm of Thoughts: Reading as Constellation in Anglo-Saxon Poetry." *JEGP* 108 (2009): 141–67.

Tselos, Dimitri. "English Manuscript Illumination." *Art Bulletin* 41 (1959): 137–49.

Utley, Frances Lee. "The Flood Narrative in the Junius Manuscript and in Baltic Literature." In *Studies in Old English Literature in Honor of Arthur G. Brodeur*, edited by Stanley Greenfield, 207–26. Eugene: University of Oregon Books, 1963.

Vickrey, John F. "Adam, Eve, and the *Tacen* in *Genesis B*." *Philological Quarterly* 72 (1993): 1–14.

– "*Selfsceafte* in *Genesis B*." *Anglia* 83 (1965): 153–71.

– "Some Further Remarks on *Selfsceafte*." *Zeitschrift für deutsches Altertum und deutsche Literatur* 110 (1981): 1–14.

Voigts, Linda E. "A New Look at a Manuscript Containing the Old English Translation of the *Herbarium Apulei*." *Manuscripta* 20 (1976): 40–60.

Waite, Greg. *Old English Prose Translations of King Alfred's Reign*. Cambridge: D.S. Brewer, 2000.

Walton, Audrey. "'Gehyre se ðe Wille': The Old English Exodus and the Reader as Exegete." *English Studies* 94 (2013): 1–10.

Webster, Leslie, and Janet Backhouse. *The Making of England: Anglo-Saxon Art and Culture AD 600–900.* Toronto: University of Toronto Press, 1991.

Wehlau, Ruth. "The Power of Knowledge and the Location of the Reader in 'Christ and Satan.'" *JEGP* 97 (1998): 1–14.

Wilcox, Miranda. "*Meotod,* the Meteorologist: Celestial Cosmography in Christ and Satan, Lines 9–12a." *Leeds Studies in English,* n.s. 39 (2008): 17–32.

Withers, Benjamin C. *The Illustrated Old English Hexateuch, Cotton Claudius B.iv: The Frontier of Reading and Seeing.* Toronto: University of Toronto Press, 2007.

– "A 'Secret and Feverish Genesis': The Prefaces of the Old English Hexateuch." *Art Bulletin* 81 (1999): 53–71.

Wolf, Maryanne. *Proust and the Squid: The Story and Science of the Reading Brain.* New York: Harper Collins, 2007.

Woolf, Rosemary. "The Devil in Old English Poetry." *RES,* n.s. 4 (1953): 1–12.

Wormald, Francis. *English Drawings of the Tenth and Eleventh Centuries.* London: Faber and Faber, 1952.

Wright, C.D. "Hiberno-Latin and Irish-Influenced Biblical Commentaries, Florilegia, and Homily Collections." In *Sources of Anglo-Saxon Literary Culture: A Trial Version,* edited by F.M. Biggs, T.D. Hill, and P.E. Szarmach, 87–123. Binghamton, NY: Center for Medieval and Early Renaissance Studies, 1990.

Wright, Michael, and Stephanie Hollis. *Manuscripts of Trinity College, Cambridge.* In *Anglo-Saxon Manuscripts in Microfiche Facsimile,* vol. 12. Tempe, AZ: ACMRS, 2004.

Zacher, Samantha. *Rewriting the Old Testament in Anglo-Saxon Verse: Becoming the Chosen People.* Bloomsbury: New York, 2013.

Index of Manuscripts

General Index

Toronto Anglo-Saxon Series

1 *Preaching the Converted: The Style and Rhetoric of the Vercelli Book Homilies*, Samantha Zacher
2 *Say What I Am Called: The Old English Riddles of the Exeter Book and the Anglo-Latin Riddle Tradition*, Dieter Bitterli
3 *The Aesthetics of Nostalgia: Historical Representation in Old English Verse*, Renée R. Trilling
4 *New Readings in the Vercelli Book*, edited by Samantha Zacher and Andy Orchard
5 *Authors, Audiences, and Old English Verse*, Thomas A. Bredehoft
6 *On the Aesthetics of* Beowulf *and Other Old English Poems*, edited by John M. Hill
7 *Old English Metre: An Introduction*, Jun Terasawa
8 *Anglo-Saxon Psychologies in the Vernacular and Latin Traditions*, Leslie Lockett
9 *The Body Legal in Barbarian Law*, Lisi Oliver
10 *Old English Literature and the Old Testament*, edited by Michael Fox and Manish Sharma
11 *Stealing Obedience: Narratives of Agency and Identity in Later Anglo-Saxon England*, Katherine O'Brien O'Keeffe
12 *Traditional Subjectivities: The Old English Poetics of Mentality*, Britt Mize
13 *Land and Book: Literature and Land Tenure in Anglo-Saxon England*, Scott T. Smith
14 *Writing Women Saints in Anglo-Saxon England*, edited by Paul E. Szarmach
15 *Anglo-Saxon Manuscripts: A Bibliographical Handlist of Manuscripts and Manuscript Fragments Written or Owned in England up to 1100*, Helmut Gneuss and Michael Lapidge

16 *The King's Body: Burial and Succession in Late Anglo-Saxon England,* Nicole Marafioti
17 *From Lawmen to Plowmen: Anglo-Saxon Legal Tradition and the School of Langland,* Stephen Yeager
18 *The Politics of Language: Byrhtferth, Ælfric, and the Multilingual Identity of the Benedictine Reform,* Rebecca Stephenson
19 *Weaving Words and Binding Bodies: The Poetics of Human Experience in Old English Literature,* Megan Cavell
20 *Joinings: Compound Words in Old English Literature,* Jonathan Davis-Secord
21 *Imagining the Jew in Anglo-Saxon Literature and Culture,* edited by Samantha Zacher
22 *Latinity and Identity in Anglo-Saxon Literature,* edited by Rebecca Stephenson and Emily V. Thornbury
23 *Inhabited Spaces: Anglo-Saxon Constructions of Place,* Nicole Guenther Discenza
24 *England in Europe: English Royal Women and Literary Patronage, c.1000–c.1150,* Elizabeth M. Tyler
25 *Undoing Babel: The Tower of Babel in Anglo-Saxon Literature,* Tristan Major
26 *Compelling God: Theories of Prayer in Anglo-Saxon England,* Stephanie Clark
27 *Biblical Epics in Late Antiquity and Anglo-Saxon England:* Divina in Laude Voluntas, Patrick McBrine
28 *Childhood and Adolescence in Anglo-Saxon Literary Culture,* edited by Susan Irvine and Winfried Rudolf
29 *Epistolary Acts: Anglo-Saxon Letters and Early English Media,* Jordan Zweck
30 *Preaching Apocrypha in Anglo-Saxon England,* Brandon W. Hawk
31 *Reading Old English Biblical Poetry: The Book and the Poem in Junius 11,* Janet Schrunk Ericksen

www.ingramcontent.com/pod-product-compliance
Lightning Source LLC
LaVergne TN
LVHW090157080826
844660LV00013B/852/J

* 9 7 8 1 4 8 7 5 0 7 4 6 6 *